Cultivating Moral Citizenship

Cultivating Moral Citizenship

An Ethnography of Young People's Associations, Gender, and Social Adulthood in the Cameroon Grasslands

JUDE D. FOKWANG

Spears Books

Denver, Colorado

Spears Books
An Imprint of Spears Media Press LLC
7830 W. Alameda Ave, Suite 103-247
Denver, CO 80226
United States of America

First Published in the United States of America in 2023 by Spears Books
www.spearsmedia.com
info@spearsmedia.com
Information on this title: www.spearsmedia.com/cultivating-moral-citizenship
© 2023 Jude Fokwang
All rights reserved.

Library of Congress Control Number: 2022947558
ISBN: 9781957296029 (Hardback)
ISBN: 9781957296012 (Paperback)
ISBN: 9781957296036 (eBook)

Designed and typeset by Spears Media Press LLC
Cover designed by Doh Kambem
Cover photo by author

Distributed globally by African Books Collective (ABC)
www.africanbookscollective.com

*For dad, who inspired and guided me
into the world of native ethnography
and
Mom, for nudging me onto higher heights*

Contents

List of Figures

Preface

This book is the culmination of precisely two decades of ethnographic research on young people in Africa. During my graduate studies at the University of Pretoria, South Africa, I was fortunate enough to win a Social Science Research Council (SSRC) fellowship in 2001 titled "African Youth in the Global Age" which provided funding, mentorship and opportunities to workshop with other young scholars interested in studying the socioeconomic and political conditions of young Africans at the turn of the new millennium. Little did I know I would spend the rest of that decade researching African youth subjectivities in all its dimensions – whose end products would be disseminated in film and text. In *Cultivating Moral Citizenship*, I pull together my findings of the past decades to offer readers a theoretically-informed account of one of my case studies – the remarkable story of young people in a run-down community in Bamenda, Anglophone Cameroon's most populous city.

Although drawn principally from my dissertation work, writing this ethnography has taken much longer than I ever would have imagined. It began in 2009 while teaching at the University of Cape Town, South Africa. Back then, I was an elated laureate of the African Humanities Program, sponsored by the American Council of Learned Societies. Regrettably, the fellowship was prematurely rescinded following my resignation from the University of Cape Town due to harrowing personal challenges. I then returned to Toronto, Canada where I spent the next three years teaching at various universities with extremely limited time to write. When I joined Regis University in 2013, I anticipated I would eventually find the time to continue work on the monograph, but it was not until I took my sabbatical in the spring of 2020 (which coincided with the onset of the Covid-19 pandemic) that I made considerable progress. I was convinced the entire manuscript would be ready for the press by the end of my sabbatical in the summer of 2020 but the vicissitudes of the pandemic and the return to virtual teaching with all its challenges threw my plans into disarray. It would take another two years of writing and fine-tuning before I felt confident to submit it for publication, this – six years after the release of a documentary film that captured aspects of this monograph in audio-visual format. That said, I would recommend that the ethnography be read first before watching the documentary film. It is my conviction that the text offers broader context and richer details than could be accomplished in forty-seven minutes of film.

Between the release of the documentary film and the completion of this monograph, I published two articles based on data obtained from my field work, one of which constituted a chapter in my dissertation work. "Fabrics of Identity: Uniforms, Gender and Associations in the Cameroon Grassfields" appeared in the journal, *Africa* in 2015. In that paper, I drew on data from all three associations covered in this study to argue that the uniform, conceived as a special type of *social skin*, has been incorporated by individuals and groups into a complex chain of processes and meanings in the Cameroon Grassfields; I describe this practice as the uniformization of sociocultural life, demonstrating that uniforms, unlike ordinary clothing, are salient precisely because of their unique role as markers of collective identity but also because they embody and simultaneously express the paradox of similarity and difference. In 2016, "Politics at the margins: alternative sites of political involvement among young people in Cameroon" appeared in the *Canadian Journal of African Studies*. In that paper, I analysed young people's political discourses and experiences, highlighting their disillusionment with the postcolonial state. None of these papers are included in this monograph.

However, what I offer in this ethnography is the product of many years of fieldwork in the community of Old Town, which began in 2005 and has continued to this day. As a registered and active member and patron of the Ntambag Brothers and Chosen Sisters respectively, I have never quite left the "field" even when my daily physical engagements in Old Town ended in 2006 with a few weeks' immersion in 2009. The Ntambag Brothers for example have been running a WhatsApp group for over five years, of which I have been a member, which has afforded me first-hand and front-row access to developments in the community. Hence, the ethnography provides insights into the lives of its members since 2005, many of whom have experienced tremendous changes in their personal and professional lives – which interestingly, mirrors mine – having started off as a graduate student and now, a tenured professor. The monograph is thus a privileged account from a *native* ethnographer for whom the *field* is neither remote, nor the subjects *the other*.

The ethnography argues that young people's associations may be understood as vital sites for the formulation of specific subjectivities that in turn are expressed through a variety of practices. Initially positioned as "youth" – a subjectivity I conceptualise as *structural dependency*, these young men and women seek social adult status as an aspect of a highly valued personhood in the Cameroon Grasslands. By cultivating virtuous character, embracing an ethos that emphasises the common good and embarking upon charitable causes, these young people become moral citizens – through practices that validate and affirm their claims to social adulthood – this, in concert with precolonial conceptions that value interdependency, conviviality and the acquisition of *vital substances* from elders and notables. The major themes addressed in the ethnography include personhood, gender, subjectivity, social adulthood and moral citizenship. Its central actors are young people - men and women between the ages of 20 and 50, united by their shared quest to build moral and meaningful lives. Through their everyday practices, I show how these young people in a marginal place have responded to globalising forces and the demise of a nation-state that always felt remote to them.

The ethnography is aimed at introductory or methods courses in anthropology, sociology, and the social sciences generally, aimed at illustrating contemporary processes of sociocultural change in urban contexts as experienced by young people. The book would also be suitable in the subdiscipline of urban anthropology as it provides a micro-account of how young people, differently positioned and with varying gendered subjectivities respond to urban challenges in a postcolonial state facing diminishing legitimacy in a marginalised region of the country and of the global south. Written by an African ethnographer who shares a similar background as the subjects of the ethnography, the book will provoke relevant discussions about the positionality of the ethnographer as well as contemporary discussions on personhood, citizenship and intersubjectivity.

Acknowledgments

My folks in Bali say that the river meanders because it chose to travel alone. I am also reminded of another African proverb which holds that a single hand cannot tie a bundle. These proverbs not only underscore the communitarian worldview in which I was raised but more importantly, of our indebtedness to those that complete and complement our humanity. It is in this sense that I owe the realisation of this monograph to many. I began to research and write about young people's socioeconomic and political conditions in the late 1990s and subsequently benefitted from a generous grant from the Social Science Research Council as well as outstanding mentorship between 2001 and 2003 from Alcinda Honwana, Ron Kassimir, Mamadou Diouf, Filip de Boeck, and Jean and John Comaroff. Amongst my peers from that period, I am particularly grateful to Wale Adebanwi for his friendship over the years and for reading and commenting on sections of this monograph. He was also generous enough to write a glowing commendation for the monograph. Subsequent fellowships with the Council for the Development of Social Science Research in Africa (CODESRIA), summer school at the University of Amsterdam and presentations at Rhodes University and the African Studies Association, USA contributed in sharpening some of the arguments presented in this monograph.

In its original iteration as a dissertation at the University of Toronto, this work benefitted from insightful comments, critiques, and encouragement from Michael Levin. Michael Lambek, Dickson Eyoh, and Todd Sanders provided perceptive comments prior to my departure for the field as well as during the writing process. Miriam Goheen (RIP), a titled subject of Nso and seasoned anthropologist also provided sharp insights and asked critical questions only someone profoundly familiar with the cultural landscape of the Grasslands could ask. Mitzi, as she was fondly called, provided critical intellectual guidance, and made suggestions for improvement. She will always remain an inspiration to me and other ethnographers of the Cameroon Grassfields. Francis Nyamnjoh, Mufor Atanga and Nantang Jua have provided mentorship over the years and this monograph would be incomplete without their encouragement and treasured feedback on my earlier work.

Significant revision for this monograph began during my sabbatical in the spring of 2020, interrupted as it were by the terror of the Covid-19 pandemic. I am nevertheless indebted to my colleagues in the Department of Sociology, Regis College who inspired me to complete this monograph, rooted in the conviction that teaching and scholarship are two sides of the same coin. Eve Passerini, Damla Isik, Jazmin Muro and Damien Thompson provided unparalleled collegiality as I ruminated on the fate of this monograph. My research assistant, Erin Strong provided exceptional help with some of the illustration. Her interest in this project also reminded me to focus the clarity of my writing for an undergraduate readership unfamiliar not only with Africa, but also, the sometimes-opaque jargon of anthropological theorising. Successive generations of students in my ethnographic methods courses have reinforced this conviction and provided comments on drafts of some sections.

Research for this monograph would not have been possible without the initial financial support of Elizabeth Cockburn who helped at a critical moment as I left for the field without external funding and uncertain of my fieldwork's prospects. Liz and her family encouraged and supported me in more ways than I could ever recount. Lynn Cockburn provided vital administrative assistance during my time in the field and lightheartedly appointed herself my 'Toronto Secretary'. She was also instrumental in transporting vital field supplies to me in Bamenda, especially my first video camera which I readily put to good use in documenting the lives of my friends in Old Town. While in the field, I also received timely and generous funding from the International Development and Research Centre (IDRC), and the School of Graduate Studies, University of Toronto. My friends, Wilson Tita and Wency Chapnkem also provided moral and financial assistance during fieldwork.

Providence could not have provided me with a better research team than the vibrant, energetic, and enthusiastic young people I met in Old Town. I will always remain indebted to Emmanuel Forsuh for introducing me to the Ntambag Brothers Association (NBA). The NBA, the Chosen and United Sisters of Old Town all welcomed me so generously into their communities and made my stay most memorable. I am particularly grateful to Ndimbu Polycarp, Eric and Elvis Forcha, Gerald Galabe, Ani Charles (RIP), Goddy Nyinchiah, Marcelline Dubila (RIP), Ani Catherine, Linda Mangwi, Azah Ernestine, Musi

Caroline, Tumi Judith and Zamchang Marie-Diane. Most of these friends appeared in the documentary I made about associational life in Old Town and have continued to keep me informed about the latest developments in Old Town. Patience Lukong (RIP), a dedicated member of the Chosen Sisters who passed away suddenly in September 2007 is also fondly remembered as one of the most dynamic and punctual individuals during my time in the field. Gordon Anyele, Wilson Forbi, Ekese Ateh, Eugene Anyele also participated during the initial stages of my fieldwork and provided fascinating perspectives on the predicament of young people in Bamenda.

Living in Bamenda for 16 months was facilitated by a very close network of friends and family. My siblings - Cynthia, Francis, Raymond, Immaculate, Theo, and Lydia provided immeasurable moral and material assistance. When I was not in the field, I relished every moment spent with my parents, John and Emerentia Fokwang, my other family of orientation in Njimafor, Peter and Mary Sama, and my parents-in-law, Augustine and Helen Ndangam. Their insights on the social construction of youth and personhood in the Grassfields greatly informed my understanding of cultural processes and social change. Emmanuel Ngang, Collins Muluh, Divine Fuh, and Basile Ndjio also contributed perceptively to discussions on what it means to be young in Cameroon. Divine Fuh would go on to conduct fieldwork and to write about our mutual friends in Old Town. I am especially grateful to Divine Fuh, Primus Tazanu, Walter Nkwi and Lori-Anne Theroux-Benoni for reading sections of this monograph and for their invaluable feedback. I remain grateful for their intellectual acuity and friendship. I am also indebted to Martin Jumbam, Collins Muluh and Theodore Fokwang for proofreading sections of this monograph.

Most of the writing and revision of this monograph took place in domestic settings animated by indescribable warmth. My children, Kehmia, Gima and Bidmia continue to inspire as I juggle my cherished roles as father, teacher and writer. My wife, Lilian has witnessed, endured, and propped up this project from its conception to fruition. I am eternally indebted to her companionship and for supporting my scholarly endeavours, especially when its pursuits have unexpectedly entailed restless mobility.

For a monograph that has been in the making for over a decade, I am certainly beholden to more individuals than I could ever exhaust in these pages. To everyone that enriched this monograph in some form or former iteration, I say thank you. I take full responsibility for its imperfections and hope its shortcomings notwithstanding, the monograph will deepen knowledge about the lives of young people in Africa and that a fair account of my observations and interpretations have been rendered. Except for the names of places, public figures and the studied associations, all names in this monograph are pseudonyms to protect the privacy of the persons so represented.

The Predicament of Being Young in Africa

Weather forecasts tend to be defied by the unpredictable rainy season in Bamenda; at least, that is what locals insist. Such was the case on a hot Sunday afternoon in early May 2005, the day chosen by members of the Ntambag Brothers Association (NBA) for a house function that had been planned in honour of one of their members. As we gathered in preparation for the feast, dark clouds also began to pull themselves together. Before long, the dark clouds looked threatening and as the minutes went by, we became certain the rains would interfere with our plans. Locals insist that with the return of the rainy season, residents must plan every social function with the "rain" as an additional item on the agenda. Che, our host, had clearly forgotten to take this into account. His bachelor's room was too small to accommodate all the members and it appeared his father's living room was occupied by members of another association, busy with their weekly reunion. Che had planned for the party to be held on a neighbour's veranda but as soon as the afternoon storm began, everyone sought refuge in the neighbour's living room, which as luck would have it, was modest enough to fit a crowd of about thirty young men.

Che was a committed and founding member of the Ntambag Brothers Association, a voluntary group of young men in the legendary and notorious neighbourhood of Old Town, Bamenda. Unlike many of his peers in the neighbourhood, he had a stable job as a support staff at Our Lady of Lourdes College, a prestigious girls' Catholic boarding school. At 27, he was a proud new father and the day's function was intended to underscore his newly achieved status. Che had invited his friends from the association to celebrate the ritual presentation of his new born son to members of his social circle, popularly known in the Bamenda Grasslands[1] as *born house*.[2] It did not matter that he was unmarried and still lived under his father's roof. At least, he was employed and had a good sense of how his social status had been transformed. He also made it clear to friends and family that he was negotiating a suitable date for his wedding, delivering further proof of his accession to social adulthood.

I had only recently "discovered" this association and at the time, was relatively foreign in the eyes of its members. Although I considered myself a local (see next chapter), I was also keenly aware of my outsider status, on account of my educational standing and socioeconomic status. But as an ethnographer, I did my best to fit in and to be seen as a fellow member, having paid my membership fees as requested by the leadership and contributed to the "born house" as expected of all members. So, the function had hardly begun when the torrential downpour intervened, forcing us to seek refuge in a neighbour's living room. The rains raged on for over forty minutes, punctuated with powerful bursts of wind and lightning which provoked our concerns about the resilience of the corrugated iron roof. Our voices were literally drowned by the deafening noise of the dense rains as they struck the zinc roof. Our involuntary silence was compensated for by watching a supposedly live Dutch soccer division match on our host's 20-inch TV. When the rains became lighter, Che rose from his seat, a side table that had been temporarily converted for that purpose and welcomed everyone for honouring his invitation. Seated on a sofa next to him was Miranda, a young woman with chubby cheeks, probably in her early twenties with the baby wrapped in blue-knitted cloth. Being the only female in our midst, it was obvious that she was Che's girlfriend and now mother of their son. After a few words on the significance of the ceremony, Che introduced Miranda to the gathering who remained seated, her eyes fixed on the sleeping baby. He had hardly finished his introduction when someone, as if moved by a spirit, burst into song and began to sing a popular offertory song in the mainline Christian churches and within a few seconds, everyone was on their feet, in a spontaneous moment of communitas, singing and clapping:

1. A term used to describe the area known today as the North West region including the neighbouring French-speaking Western region of Cameroon. Originally used by German explorers to describe the vast savannah region, this coinage has been adopted by ethnographers. A variant of the term is the 'Grassfields' and shall be used interchangeably in this book.
2. A *born house* is a ritual performed in the Bamenda Grassfields to mark the birth of a new child into a family. Its modernised version is performed by various associations and kin groups to celebrate the birth of a new child. For first time parents, it is marked as a rite of passage characterised by music, food and merriment.

Na the ting wey you give we papa
Na ye dis we di bring am so
Eh papa ye, make you take am with all your heart!

While the singing went on, the baby was passed from hand to hand for members to touch, and bless Che and Miranda's bundle of joy. At the end, the baby was returned to his mother and Che made a few more remarks, exhorting his "brothers" to settle down and take up adult responsibilities as he had done. To this, the young men cheered, prompting a response from Carlson, the group's leader who rose from his seat and congratulated the new parents. "You see, brothers" he continued, "what Che has done is a big challenge to all of us. We are proud to learn today that he and his girlfriend have decided to take the next big step at a date yet to be determined but nevertheless, it is a cause for celebration. They have shown us that difficult as the times may be, none of us is growing younger. Therefore, let us settle down as soon as our conditions permit." Members cheered and a few guests rose and offered brief speeches – all celebratory of the new unmarried parents. After the speeches, the group leader requested two members to bring in two cartons of soap, each containing about twenty-five bars which were ceremoniously handed over to Che and his girlfriend.[3] Food and drinks were served including an assortment of Cameroonian beers.

This book is neither about pre-marital parenthood nor about the rituals of born house. On the contrary, it is an ethnographic description and analysis of the ways in which young people (already de facto adults) facing the predicament of blocked opportunities, "arrested adulthood" (Côté 2000) or what Alcinda Honwana has coined as *waithood* (Honwana 2013)[4], negotiate their livelihoods and transition to social adulthood. The ethnography is preoccupied with how young people gain recognition as social adults and moral citizens in a cultural milieu where these statuses imply not only marriage and procreation but also the redistribution of one's resources within a wide network of kin and

---

3.   Other common gifts at *born house* events include a wash basin, powder detergent, baby napkins and/or an assortment of items needed for the upkeep of a newborn baby. It is also customary to serve porridge plantains to guests with an often-exaggerated quantity of palm oil – all deeply symbolic and open to a variety of interpretive schemes.
4.   *Waithood*, she contends, refers to "a prolonged period of suspension between childhood and adulthood" (Honwana 2013), not necessarily characterised by idleness, but through bricolage – or the art of getting by which involves engaging in a variety of activities to provide for their needs and dependents.

community. In a context where postcolonial elites continue to cling to power, and traditional paths to social adult status are blocked or have diminished, how do young people negotiate the lack of their individual means to attain social adult status? The answer, this book argues, lies in membership in associations, which spearhead high profile social projects, consequently gaining visibility and the moral high ground to police members' moral standing and sensibilities, thus contributing to the production of moral citizens.

I examine the experiences and social projects of three associations of young people in an inner-city community in Bamenda, Cameroon's leading Anglophone city. Seeing themselves as doubly marginalised – first as youths, and secondly as Anglophones in a Francophone-dominated state, these young people seek to by-pass the state by positioning themselves as moral actors through involvement in associations which harness their individual and collective capabilities in the pursuit of prestigious social projects that are individually and collectively rewarding. Thus, I will show that associations are vital cultural resources that are instrumentalised by young people to generate new identities and claim highly valued social statuses. The book argues further that for many young people in Bamenda and the Grasslands in general, the processes of positioning and the production of personhood are largely experienced through involvement in associational life. Examined through the concepts of personhood and subjectivities, the ethnography describes and analyses the central role of associations in negotiating young people's identities and positioning as social adults in contexts where traditional patterns of transition have been eroded. To this end, life in associations facilitates the production of moral citizenship and the attainment of social adulthood.

Marginal Lives in Marginal Places
In the last two or three decades, the world has grown 'younger', probably more than at any time in human history.[5] This claim is particularly true of Africa which ranks as the most 'youthful' continent in the world with young people between 15-24 making up approximately 20% of its population.[6] That

5.   See the annual reports issued by the United Nations, especially the *World Youth Report 2005* and *World Youth Report 2007* in which the authors estimate the global youth population (15-24) to be roughly 1.2 billion (United Nations (200, 2007). This population is expected to increase to 1.3 billion by 2030 (United Nations 2015)
6.   "According to the United Nations, 226 million youth aged 15-24 lived in Africa in 2015 representing nearly 20% of Africa's population, making up one fifth of the world's youth population. If one includes all people aged below 35, this number increases to a staggering

young people constitute the continent's numerical majority reveals the enormous challenge young Africans and state actors face in translating the latter's dreams and aspirations for a fulfilling and meaningful citizenship. This is a major challenge because young Africans live in very perplexing times, characterised by the end of certainties or the disappearance of what Andy Furlong (2000) has termed "old predictabilities", tremendous economic fluctuations, the diminishing capacity of the postcolonial state to control its resources and destiny, the failure of the nation-building project once popular in the early post-independence period, the ravages of AIDS and recently, Covid-19 and large-scale unemployment, just to name a few. Young Africans of the 21st century paradoxically face harder times compared to the generations that came of age in the 1960s and 70s. Unlike their peers today, young people in the 1960s were often perceived as the hope of the emergent African nations – a status that enjoyed tremendous 'cultural prestige' in the words of Mamadou Diouf (2003) on account of their perceived role as the chief agent of the transformation of recently decolonised African societies.

Today, being young in Africa has different meanings compared to the values attached to 'youth' four decades ago. Youth is undergoing significant redefinitions as it assumes new meanings shaped by class, gender and generation (Adebanwi 2005; Bolten 2020; Fuh 2009, 2012; Orock 2013). Structural dependency seems to play a crucial role in defining the position of youth in contemporary Africa. This is evident in the sense that unlike the generations of the 1960s who were concerned with filling society's niches, young people today are busy "navigating perilous waters" and negotiating their way through seas of uncertainty (Evans & Furlong 1997) – socioeconomic uncertainty in particular. In fact, young people's capacity to navigate these perilous waters is often associated with the degree of risk one is capable of or willing to take (cf. France 2000). Young people's positions in the economy determine to a large extent their capacity to provide for themselves and families and to a certain degree, their status as youth. A major challenge facing young people the world over and Africa in particular is the question of unemployment. For instance, in 2016, the International Labour Organization (ILO) reported that global youth unemployment worldwide stood at 13.1% (International Labour Organization 2016) - a figure predicated on its definition of youth as persons between 15

---

three quarters of Africa's population. Moreover, the share of Africa's youth in the world is forecasted to increase to 42% by 2030 and is expected to continue to grow throughout the remainder of the 21st century, more than doubling from current levels by 2055" (UN, 2015).

and 24. Perhaps, if the ILO was flexible enough to accommodate the African Youth Charter's definition which refers to youth as persons between 15 and 35[7] the number of unemployed would well be over 25% or about 150 million people. Perhaps, more than in other parts of the world, youth unemployment is most acute in Africa and not even South Africa that has claimed some level of exceptionalism is spared from this. For instance, some analysts maintain that "South Africa's biggest security threat is the "time-bomb" of social conflict driven by a permanent underclass of educated but unemployed youth who face a bleak future."[8] While this assertion speaks patently of contemporary South Africa, its implications are true of many African countries, and Cameroon in particular where unemployment is relatively high although there are no reliable statistics that measure current rates.[9]

Faced with massive unemployment, many young Africans feel their youth is protracted and accession to social adulthood delayed. This is specifically true for a lot of young people in their 20s and 30s who remain jobless, unmarried and uncertain of their future, yet they are continuously reminded by the leadership to "wait for their turn"[10] or called upon to remember that inevitably, "youth are the leaders of tomorrow". This extended transition or 'arrested adulthood' seems to be the defining experience for a lot of young people who struggle to

7.   The Charter also makes a distinction between youth and minor, where the latter consists of young people between 15 and 17 years. See African Youth Charter (2006).
8.   See "Jobless youth biggest threat to SA security'" by Michael Schmidt in *The Cape Argus*, May 21, 2005 page 4; also see "Unemployment in South Africa is worse than you think" by Dennis Webster, *Mail & Guardian*, 5 Aug 2019, https://mg.co.za/article/2019-08-05-unemployment-in-south-africa-is-worse-than-you-think/ Retrieved, March 27, 2020. Webster's analysis is a rebuttal to the official government statistics which places the unemployment rate at 29%. "By the official count, 6.7-million people are unemployed in South Africa, which is 29% of everybody who could be working. By the expanded definition, more than 10 million people are unemployed, or 38.5% of people who could be working."
9.   The World Bank suggests that formal unemployment for 2019 stood at 5.7%. https://data.worldbank.org/indicator/sl.uem.1524.zs However, this doesn't consider that a significant proportion of the population, especially young people work in the informal section where any reliable statistics are hardly generated.
10.   President Biya's address to the youth on the occasion of the 32nd Youth Day in Cameroon, 10 Feb 1998. In his speech, he reminded young people to wait for their turn, supporting his call for patience as follows: "In reality - and you must have certainly noticed it - this new era for the youth has already begun. The National Assembly has been injected with young blood. So it is with the Government. Why would these young Members of Parliament and young Ministers not stand by you? They who, not long ago, were amongst you? Follow their example. Participate in public life. Make your contribution to the great task of democratisation in your country. *The day will come when you yourselves will hold public office*." (Emphasis mine)

find or give meaning to their lives.

A second problematic concerns the attributes attached to youth in the contemporary era. Unlike the cultural prestige attached to youth in the 1960s, today it is constructed as a 'threat' following the "dramatic irruption" of young people in the public and domestic spheres in the post-1990 era (Diouf 2003) and even more so in the wake of a military insurgency in the Anglophone regions of Cameroon since 2017. According to Diouf, a major concern for adults is young people's "behaviour, their sexuality and their pleasure" (2000:3). They are perceived to be sexually loose and disrespectful of elders compared to previous generations – perceptions that have provoked moral and civic panic among adults. Predictably, this charge appealed to those who saw the AIDS pandemic of the 1980s and 90s as a disease of the young and some even explained the tragic ravages of the disease as an expression of God's wrath on a permissive generation. Thus, perceived and constructed as morally immature, young people are also represented as prone to violence or easily recruited by others towards violent ends – hence, their exclusion and victimisation by state agents (see Abbink & van Kessel 2005; Fokwang 1999, 2003, 2007, 2009; Orock 2013; Samara 2005; Sharp 2002).

Politically, young people feel marginalised. Unlike the generations of the 1960s, they are often exploited and abandoned by those in whom they have entrusted their hope and aspirations. It is no accident then that many feel they are either a 'lost generation' (Cruise O'Brien 1996) or have been 'sacrificed' (cf. Sharp 2002) for reasons that are not always apparent to them. This is particularly true for many young Cameroonians who actively participated in the clamour for democratic reforms in the early 1990s but found themselves excluded from critical conferences aimed at charting a course for the future (cf. Mbaku & Awasom 2004). For many of these young people, political and economic citizenship bear no meaning in their lives as they are forced to look for alternative avenues of political participation and to redefine citizenship in accordance with their experiences and aspirations. In sum, many young Africans who have already reached adult age aspire to social adulthood through effective and meaningful participation in the socioeconomic and political life of their communities but many continue to be trapped in waithood.

This ethnography therefore documents and analyzes how young people respond to these challenges and the kinds of agencies they employ in constructing their moral and sociocultural worlds despite extremely challenging circumstances. It is an attempt at 'studying up' what it means to be young through the eyes and experiences of young people themselves. Although based on 16 months of continuous ethnographic research (2005-2006), this book is actually the product of two decades of prolonged study of young people in the English-speaking regions of Cameroon. During these two decades, I sought to investigate how young people in urban Cameroon perceived and lived out their subjectivities, participated in the political process and made meaningful lives for themselves against a background of socioeconomic crisis, the bankruptcy of the ambitious nation-building project and a stalled democratic transition. Part of this effort culminated in the release of an ethnographic film, *Something New in Old Town* (2016) which focused on the lives of young men and women who strive to change their community as "searchers" of solutions to the manifold problems that beset young people and the urban environment in many African cities. I see this ethnography not only as a complement to the above-named film, but more importantly, as a timely response and fulfilment of Abbink's (2005) call for theoretically informed ethnographic studies that explore and account for the ways in which younger generations of Africans experiencing blocked mobility deal with their predicament on account of postcolonial elites' continuous cling to power and resources.

Cameroon: A Postcolony Steeped in *La Crise*

Cameroon has experienced acute economic crisis since the mid-1980s, which led to the introduction of the Structural Adjustment Programme (SAP) and later, the Highly Indebted Poor Countries Initiative (HIPC) – both programmes of the International Monetary Fund (IMF) and the World Bank (Gordon & Gordon 2013) aimed at addressing the debt crisis as well as the country's continued economic mismanagement. Plagued by economic and political crises, Cameroonians have tended to define their lives as structured by *la crise* – the French term for economic crisis. Irked by the poor economic climate and the excesses of monolithic dictatorship, Cameroonians clamoured for democratic reforms in the early 1990s leading to a return to multiparty democracy. However, soon after the first multiparty presidential election of October 1992, heavily rigged in favour of the incumbent, Paul Biya, Cameroonians realised they had fought for and obtained only a cosmetic democracy, deprived of substance (Mbaku 2002, 2004; Mbaku & Takougang 2004; Mbu 1993; Monga 1994; Nyamnjoh 1999, 2002a; Takougang 2003). But *la crise* conjures even more than simply the spectres of economic and political doom – it also denotes a fundamental moral crisis. *La crise* in Cameroon, Johnson-Hanks (2005) observes, has been elevated "to an inevitable force that accounts for incompetence, graft, sexual infidelity, school failure, and even witchcraft"

(Johnson-Hanks 2005:366). Indeed, almost all aspects of national life are interpreted through the prism of *la crise,* inflected occasionally to convey a sense of *madness* or moral bankruptcy.[11] The pidgin phrase – *kontri don spoil* – (the land has gone bad) captures this dimension of contemporary Cameroon. Corruption in both the public and private sectors has worsened over the years and anti-corruption programmes have yielded little or no progress. The German-based anti-corruption watchdog, Transparency International ranked Cameroon twice in succession as the most corrupt country in the world (1998 and 1999) and since then the country has remained at the bottom of the most corrupt countries. In 2019, Transparency International ranked Cameroon at 153 out of 180 countries.[12]

Cameroon's notoriety as a haven for corruption has spread over the years, thanks in part to the emergence of a new generation of swindlers and conmen popularly known as *feymen* (singular *feyman*), the practice described as *feymania,* (cf. Malaquais 2001; Ndjio 2006) and quite similar in striking ways to the popular Nigerian 419 scam (cf. Apter 1999). Some have observed that the practices of feymania complement corruption in the private and public sectors – processes that have led to the criminalisation of the state in Cameroon (cf. Bayart, Ellis, & Hibou 1999). Commenting on corruption in Cameroon, Nyamnjoh (1999) observes that "to many people in or seeking high office, Cameroon is little more than a farm tended by God but harvested by man.... Everyone is doing it at his own level, from top to bottom - the only difference being that those at the top have more to steal from..." (1999:111-12). It is common practice that young people bribe their way into the *grandes écoles*[13] (government professional schools), and shockingly, even into some public elementary and secondary schools. Bribery is often justified with the popular

---

11.   In this sense, an unusual association is drawn between *la crise* and the English word, craze or craziness. Thus, *la crise* becomes a metaphor for the country's state of folly.

12.   See Transparency International Corruption Perceptions Index 2019, https://www.transparency.org/cpi2019. In another corruption-related news, the U.S. Department of Justice and the UK Serious Fraud Office announced on May 24 that the Anglo-Swiss multinational Glencore pleaded guilty to bribes in several countries, including Cameroon. "In Cameroon, a lawyer defending the company has already admitted the facts, saying that Glencore paid CFA 7 billion to curry favor with the heads of the National Oil and Gas Corporation (SNH) and the National Refining Company (Sonara)." See https://www.businessincameroon.com/public-management/3105-12583-glencore-says-it-bribed-snh-and-sonara-with-cfa7bln accessed on June 1, 2022. Additional information about the guilty plea may be found here: https://www.justice.gov/opa/pr/glencore-entered-guilty-pleas-foreign-bribery-and-market-manipulation-schemes

13.   Some of these schools include the Ecole Normale Supérieure, Ecole Nationale d'Administration et de la Magistrature, the Faculty of Medicine, University of Yaounde I, just to name a few.

expression – "a goat eats where it is tethered" and few are held accountable, except in circumstances that aim at winning political capital. The National Episcopal Conference of the Catholic Church, which has consistently represented itself as the voice of conscience and moral authority in the country has regularly expressed deep concerns about the fact that "corruption bolts every door...wherever you may need a legitimate service."[14] It also composed a prayer against corruption although the heavens are yet to smile favourably on Cameroon. Thus, corruption thrives unabated in very creative ways and some have cynically described it as fundamental to the national character of contemporary Cameroon.[15] Thus, the state in Cameroon has failed its young in more ways than can be catalogued. Increasingly privatised and instrumentalised in favour of the ruling oligarchy, thanks to the support of its international partners, the state in Cameroon enjoys less and less relevance to most of its citizens.

Conditions have worsened since 2017 as a result of an armed conflict between Anglophone separatists defending their self-declared state, Ambazonia, against Cameroon military forces. A strike action initiated by Anglophone teachers and lawyers in November 2016 to protest the francophonisation of the legal and education systems was met with brutal and excessive military reprisals against its leaders. Hundreds of young people were arrested including Bibixy Mancho – who brought his own coffin to the protest, declaring his readiness to die for the cause of the Anglophones.[16] Many of the young people who were arrested were subsequently tried in a military court and given life or extended jail sentences at the maximum security prison in Yaounde. In January 2017, leaders of the Cameroon Anglophone Civil Society Consortium (CACSC) were

14. Letter of the National Episcopal Conference, 1997.
15. Corruption and the raging conflict in the Anglophone regions were blamed for the Confederation of African Football (CAF) decision to strip Cameroon of the hosting rights to the continent's biggest soccer event, the African Nations' Cup (AFCON) originally scheduled for June 2019. Whistleblowers claimed that over $2 billion of Cameroonian public money was misappropriated in contracts that were never open for bidding. See the following news stories for this major scandal: "Is a financial scandal behind Cameroon's Africa Cup of Nations fiasco? - https://www.france24.com/en/20190111-focus-cameroon-stripped-hosting-africa-cup-nations-corruption-allegations-stadium-delays ; Conflicts and corruption in Cameroon drain the economy, https://www.dw.com/en/conflicts-and-corruption-in-cameroon-drain-the-economy/a-47202553 ; Cameroon stripped of right to host 2019 Africa Cup of Nations, https://www.theguardian.com/football/2018/nov/30/cameroon-stripped-right-host-africa-cup-of-nations-2019 all accessed on March 30th, 2020.
16. This became known as the coffin revolution (see Augustine Ndangam's *Ceded at Dawn* (2020) for details about the coffin revolution).

abducted on the night of 17 January 2017 and transported to Yaounde. They were eventually tried for treason and terrorism. These leaders, representing the broad wishes of the peoples of the former West Cameroon, had called for, amongst several other demands, a return to the two-state federation arbitrarily dismantled in 1972 by French Cameroon's founding president, Ahmadou Ahidjo. Anglophone citizens were desperate to see an end to the continued erosion of their legal and educational institutions. These concerns amongst others were unanimously backed by traditional leaders,[17] members of the clergy in the Presbyterian Church in Cameroon (PCC) as well as all the Bishops of the Roman Catholic Church in both the North West and South West regions.[18] Contrary to expectations, Biya proceeded to declare war against groups that had taken up arms in the Anglophone regions to defend themselves against military excesses. Conditions deteriorated following the declaration of indendepence by the Governing Council of the Southern Cameroons/Ambazonian Consortium United Front (SCACUF) on 1st October 2017. Since the conflict erupted, over 10,000 deaths have been recorded, mostly of civilians, and over half a million persons have been internally displaced, including over 50,000 refugees in neighbouring Nigeria.[19] Repeated calls for an inclusive dialogue between the Cameroon government and separatist groups have fallen on deaf ears.

Cameroon therefore provides a unique vantage point from which to examine the predicament of what it means to be young in early 21st century Africa. Despite this general atmosphere of crisis and now full-blown conflict, voluntary associations still play a major role in organising and shaping young people's lives. I aim to show in this ethnography that young people's associations are central to negotiating how they seek respectability, create meaningful lives and generate as well as enforce ideas of what it means to be a moral citizen. These analyses will focus on three associations that were the subject of my extended fieldwork in Bamenda between 2005 and 2006 with follow up fieldwork in 2009; two exclusively female and a male-only club. These associations are the Chosen Sisters, the United Sisters and the Ntambag Brothers Association (NBA).

---

17.   See "Fons to Confront Biya over Anglophone Problem", by Chris Mbunwe in *Cameroon Postline*, Feb 10, 2017, www.cameroonpostline.com/fons-to-confront-biya-over-anglophone-problem/
18.   See the "Memorandum Presented to the Head of State, His Excellency President Paul Biya, By the Bishops of the Ecclesiastical Province of Bamenda on the Current Situation of Unrest in the Northwest and Southwest Regions of Cameroon", 22 December 2016.
19.   See "Human Rights Abuses in the Cameroon Anglophone Crisis: A Submission of Evidence to UK Parliament" Faculty of Law, University of Oxford, 30 October 2019.

Transition, Liminality and the Life Course

Analyses of youth tend to focus on the paradigm of transition as the definitive framework for understanding young people's predicament. In this light, youth is seen as a phase on a journey that ends with the attainment of adulthood. This model has been quite popular with scholarship on youth in the Western world precisely because it tended to assume that transition from school to the job market marked the end of youth and the beginning of adult life.[20] This view is aptly summarised by Wyn and Woodman (2006) who note that "the concept of youth as primarily a process of transition from school to the workplace has held a powerful sway over research and thinking in the field of youth studies" (2006:495). Dissatisfied with this framework for its narrow focus on economistic models (graduation from school to work), Wyn and Woodman propose a shift from "transition" to "generation" because the latter examines "subjectivities that are anchored in the political and material conditions of young people's lives" (2006:500). Other researchers of youth are equally apprehensive of the transition paradigm. Soares (2000) for instance maintains that transition "is often used as an excuse to justify situations of chaos and inequality which favour a small minority, stave off criticisms, and demand sacrifices for the sake of an age where transition will come to an end and peace will again reign over the face of the earth" (2000:209). However, Soares observes that transition makes sense if conceptualised as embodying processes, differences and particularities rather than a linear development (2000:209). Ken Roberts (2007) notes that scholars do not need to part entirely with transition in order to understand young people's predicament. To him, operating within a transition paradigm involves among other things, "charting the routes via which young people from different ports of departure reach different adult destinations" (2007:264). Besides, it is critical to understand that youth is not a homogeneous category (cf. Cruise O'Brien 1996) and that generation "lacks the demographic precision of gender, and, to a lesser extent, ethnicity. Nor do generations appear to always share the same material interests" (Burgess 2005:viii). Thus, a perspective that combines the strengths of transition (as *process*) and generation can illuminate various aspects of young people's lives – informed by the understanding that the experiences and structural

20.   The idea of transition has also been applied to African youth where the educational system is seen as the medium that negotiates the transformation of youth into full adults and citizens. This assumption is highlighted by Aguilar (1998) who, writing about youth in Kenya, observes that "it is through education that children become adults, boys are transformed into Kenyans, and girls into women, and Kenyans as well" (1998:17-18).

positions of young people today are dramatically different from those of their parents who came of age in the 1960s and 70s.

Often associated with the notion of transition is the concept of liminality, drawn from the pioneering work of Arnold van Gennep (1960) on the rites of passage. Arnold van Gennep identified the *rites of passage* as a special category which can be subdivided into "preliminal rites (rites of separation), liminal rites (rites of transition), and postliminal rites (rites of incorporation" (1960:11). According to this perspective, the human life cycle is characterised by several rites of passage that begin with birth and end with death. Various rituals mark out specific phases in one's life which signify the transformation of one's status and role in accordance with the expectations of a given culture. Hence, in the human life cycle, youth is perceived as that transitional or liminal phase which ends with the incorporation of the initiate into the adult world – making him/her a full adult person. Victor Turner later elaborated on the notion of liminality in his classic work, *The Ritual Process* (1969) in which he maintains that the liminal phase in every rite of passage is characterised by ambiguity. According to Turner, "liminal entities are neither here nor there; they are betwixt and between positions assigned and arrayed by law, custom, convention, and ceremonial" (1969:95). Elsewhere, Turner asserts that during the "liminal period, neophytes are alternately forced and encouraged to think about their society, their cosmos, and the powers that generate and sustain them" (Turner 1967:105). He sums this up as "a stage of reflection". Thanks to the works of van Gennep and Turner, anthropologists have long been attentive to the significance of liminal positions and persons and their potential to disconcert or threaten (Hall & Montgomery 2000:13). It is largely against this background that scholarship on youth has tended to associate youth with liminality (see for example Burgess 2005; Comaroff & Comaroff 2005; de Boeck & Honwana 2000; Durham 2004; Fuh 2009, 2012; Hoffman 2003; Johnson-Hanks 2002; Maira & Soep 2004; Moyer 2004; Northcote 2006). While liminality indeed captures and articulates the predicament of many young people, it eludes the lives and experiences of those who straddle the worlds of 'youth' and 'social adulthood' simultaneously – in other words, those who exist 'here and there' without necessarily belonging fully to either. In fact, the notion of liminality is predicated on an understanding of transition as *movement* – that is, rooted in the notion of the life course characterised by predictable stages. However, anthropologists increasingly recognise that "liminal states between stable statuses are rare. Most vital events - such as marriage, motherhood, and migration - are instead negotiable and contested, fraught with uncertainty, innovation, and ambivalence" (Johnson-Hanks 2002:865). I will show in this study that instead of undergoing smooth transitions into adulthood, young people (as individuals and as members of groups) navigate unpredictable paths in their search for stability and meaningful lives. Some of these young people, despite being adults, are positioned and tend to position themselves as 'youth' but ultimately seek and celebrate social adult status. Some of them embody both identities as youth and adult – an embodiment not fully captured by references to liminality. By drawing on the notion of transition as process I hinge my analysis on a *navigational* framework which explores the different biographic trajectories undertaken by young people. This framework acknowledges the multiplicity of identities and the agency inherent in intersubjectivity. It combines ambiguity with predictability, agency and subjection. However, these issues need to be understood against the cultural universe within which ideas of personhood and social adulthood are constructed and deployed.

Personhood and Social Adulthood in the Cameroon Grasslands

Ethnographers of the Western Grasslands of Cameroon have identified the composite nature of personhood, characterised by different rites of initiation and incorporation (discussed in chapter two). Modern personhood in the Grasslands has been shaped and transformed by successive colonial and postcolonial influences. Despite these changes, most chiefdoms in the Grasslands reject the idea of "the autonomous person" (Comaroff & Comaroff 2001) in favour of the intersubjective or interdependent person, epitomised by the proverb "a child is one person's only in the womb" (cf. Nyamnjoh 2002b, 2017) – which means that a person belongs to the community rather than to his/her household or specific lineage. Most ethnic groups in the Grasslands also subscribe to the principle of personhood as a mode of *becoming*, rather than just a mode of *being*. In other words, full personhood is hardly perceived as an end product but characterised by continuous negotiation, flexibility and adaptability. It is in brief, as the Comaroffs describe for the Tswana "a work in progress" (Comaroff & Comaroff 2001). Thus, although personhood is commonly associated with social adulthood, a person is always a child of someone and of the community (cf. Warnier 1993:305).

Thus, youth as a cultural construct cannot be fully understood in isolation from the cultural universe in which it is produced and experienced. Based on the foregoing, youth in the Cameroon Grasslands is currently experienced as a *structural position of dependency* or to make use of Warnier's (1993) metaphor, an empty vessel unable to fill itself. Many young people in the Grasslands in their 20s and 30s aspire to full personhood and social adulthood through employment and marriage. They desire to establish an independent household, provide for themselves and their families and enjoy the symbolic capital of respectability, acquired through the redistribution of one's success. For most of them, this is unattainable, as it is true for many other young Cameroonians. Unlike their African counterparts, many young people in the West do not consider their 'youth' as a status of entrapment or privation. In fact, James Côté observes that whilst the period of youth has become increasingly prolonged in Western countries, certain features of this prolonged youth are increasingly preference based (Côté 2002:117; also see Westberg 2004). These differences validate Burgess' claim that youth "varies widely according to time and place; it tends to emerge out of local idioms and languages, and is lost or gained through the aging process and a variety of personal decisions and life events" (2005:viii). In this light, this study does not assume to explain youth as a universal or transhistorical experience but as a specific kind of experience that defines the way human beings see themselves at a particular point in their lives (cf. Soares 2000:210).

Subjectivity and Young People's Associations

Subjectivity broadly defined, refers to the subjective experience of an individual. In other words, it deals with how actors endowed with agency perceive and relate to a given social structure. In this ethnography, I draw on Holland and Leander's (2004) conceptualisation which explains subjectivities as "actors' thoughts, sentiments, and embodied sensibilities, and, especially, their senses of self and self-world relations" (2004:127). They state further that "subjectivities are created by experiences of *being positioned* and, in turn, contribute to the production of cultural forms that mediate subsequent experiences" (op. cit. 2004:127 my emphasis). According to Bretell and Sargent (2004), individuals or subjects can occupy multiple subject positions, some of which they define for themselves and others which are defined for them. It is in this sense that an individual's subjectivity can be understood as moral, political, economic and otherwise. Thus, "subjectivity involves making choices about identity as well as resisting those identities that are imposed by others and outsiders" (Brettell & Sargent 2006:4). Power relations play a significant role in shaping individuals' sense of self, and identity through acts that categorise, distinguish and treat a person as gendered, classed, raced or other sort of subject (Holland & Leander 2004:127). In this sense, youth and social adulthood may be understood as different kinds of *subjectivities*. As cultural constructs, they are products of power relations and thus experienced differently across time and space. It is specifically within this context that we may understand youth as positioned and as positioning (cf. Christiansen, Utas, & Vigh 2006:11; also see Durham 2004). Furthermore, the notion of positioning "directs attention to how positions are produced in particular historical periods and to the social coordination necessary for successful positioning to be achieved, and it problematizes the subjective consequences of experiences of positioning for those who participate" (Holland & Leander 2004:130). This ethnography focuses on how a group of young people are strategic in positioning themselves as "social adults" distinct from their peers still positioned in what Sunaina Maira and Elisabeth Soep have termed *youthscapes*[21] (2004).

My analysis will also show that the processes of positioning are actualised by the "day-to-day technologies of self-care" which young men and women in Old Town draw upon to cultivate "virtuous characters" (Mattingly 2012:4), self and moral transformation, and ultimately communal change. While these efforts of ethical self-care are individualised, I argue that their fullest expressions are largely experienced through involvement in associational life. The African urban landscape is filled with an assortment of associations – home village associations, voluntary, improvement or welfare associations, cultural, religious and political associations just to name a few. Their members are heavily invested in maintaining productive relations with fellow citizens and despite the enormous difficulties of urban life such as crime and insecurity or the heavy-hand of the state, they still maintain productive lives that require "reciprocities, negotiation, and cooperation…." (Simone 2014:33). Kenneth Little (1965, 1972) traces the emergence and proliferation of voluntary associations to urbanisation during colonial times, as the modern town offered fresh opportunities for young men and women. According to Ottenberg (1955), associations tend to "carry out various economic, educational, political, social, and general improvement activities directly related to changing cultural conditions" (1955:1). Central to these associations is the notion of 'development', by which they mean the socioeconomic and cultural improvement of members and

21.   Sunaina Maira and Elisabeth Soep (2004) suggest that *youthscape* may be understood, not just as a geographic or temporal site, but also as sites suffused with social and political meanings, "bound up with questions of power and materiality" (2014:2). They further submit that the metaphor of youthscapes draws directly from models of globalisation, see Appadurai (2008) and properly analysed, can shed light on the "social and political implications of young people's responses" to globalising forces as well as how local meanings and subjectivities intersect with those from thousands of miles away.

the areas or region they claim to represent (cf. Lentz 1995:395). While welfare and voluntary associations are not novelties in urban Africa, evidenced by the academic interests shown in the study of these urban formations by sociologists and anthropologists (cf. Barkan, McNulty, & Ayeni 1991; d'Almeida-Topor & Goerg 1989; Hooker 1966; Kerr 1978; Simone 2001; Skinner 1978; Soen & Comarmond 1971a, 1971b, 1972; Tostensen, Tvedten, & Vaa 2001; Trager 1998; Wallerstein 1964), less attention has been devoted to the study of young people's associations whose objectives and activities sometimes complement or differ significantly from those of home town and professional associations.

Moral Citizenship

Citizenship has become a contentious issue in both academic and global political debates, thanks in part to democratisation and rapid urbanisation in the late twentieth and early twenty-first centuries (Holston 2009), increased migration (Nyamnjoh 2006) as well as contestations around economic development and belonging (Geschiere 2009; Geschiere & Meyer 1998; Meyer & Geschiere 1999). These contestations have resulted in what Holston has described as the "entanglement of democracy with its counters, in which new kinds of citizens arise to expand democratic citizenship and new forms of violence and exclusion simultaneously erode it" (Holston 2009:1). For many involved in these debates, citizenship remains a matter of juridical rights within the nation-state, that is, a set of legislations that delineate an individual's rights and obligations towards the state. Others conceive it simply as a status that defines a "person as a competent member of society, and which as a consequence shape the flow of resources to persons and social groups" (Turner 1993:2). The idea of citizenship presupposes the equality of all citizens before the law, a claim largely dismissed as 'false' on account of the view that citizenship "is embedded in everyday power relations and particularist ideologies" (Werbner 1998:4) that tend to exclude or marginalise social minorities such as the poor, women, and youth (see Werbner 1999; Williamson 1997; Yuval-Davis 1997). I will argue that conceptualisations of citizenship based mainly on the political or juridical realm are not only limited but also limiting. This is particularly true for people on the margins – whether they are ethnic or sexual minorities, youth, people living with disabilities, the urban poor and so on. Consequently, I draw on conceptualisations of citizenship that transcend the juridical or political connotations – that is as "a social status which specifically acknowledges the ethical, ... non-instrumental, basis of association between persons in a political community, and articulated through a diversity of practices" (Prokhovnik 1998:85). If the city has "been the locus of citizenship's development" (Holston 2009:1), it is important therefore to understand the ways in which marginalised citizens and noncitizens contest their exclusions.

This ethnography examines the emergence and cultivation of a particular kind of citizenship among young people in Bamenda which I refer to as *moral citizenship* - that is, a citizenship that generates specific kinds of moralities and orthodoxies, manages individual and collective conduct thereby legitimating certain subjectivities whilst reproducing prevailing inequalities. Specifically, I understand moral citizenship as the pursuit of ethical actions that draw on the cultivation of virtuous character and self-care in fulfilling one's obligations towards the moral and physical transformation of one's community. Moral citizenship focuses more on one's responsibilities and less on one's entitlement while setting its eyes firmly on the common good. It also entails the range of practices that affirm one's status or claims to social adulthood. This book elaborates the mechanisms through which moral citizenship is cultivated and put into circulation in both public and private realms in the community of Old Town, Bamenda. It offers not so much an account about the contestation of democratic citizenship within the nation-state, but rather, a situated account of the expansion of citizenship practices by marginal groups in their attempt to push back at the frontiers of victimhood, while creating meaningful lives for themselves.

This book argues that young people in Bamenda, in their quest to attain social adulthood, instrumentalise associations to build reciprocal relationships during which, they draw on local and global meanings of personhood to position themselves as moral citizens. The book shows that young people's associations are central although not an exclusive site where they inscribe their agencies on public space and make strategic claims on social adult status by investing in varied practices (e.g., hygiene operations and charitable acts while enforcing moral orthodoxies that ambiguously expand and erode citizenship). By positioning themselves as moral vanguards, they indict society and assert themselves as alternative moral actors upon whom society may count on for regeneration. Consequently, young people position themselves not as Warnier's metaphorical empty vessels unable to fill themselves but rather, as engaged in a diversity of public and private practices whose accomplishments will entitle them to the status and prestige that social adulthood affords. Young people's associations are understood as sites that enable the mediation of local idioms of personhood with global expectations of what it means to be young, modern, successful and morally upright. Through associational life, young people articulate a kind of ambiguous relationship between the fields of youth and social adulthood. However, youth is negated in preference for social adulthood.

By studying the subjectivities of young people as individuals and members of formal and informal associations, the book sheds light on the issues of structure and agency, the global and the local as well as the ways in which citizenship concerns are generated, lived out and contested. Ultimately, the book unravels how young people seek to make meaningful lives in unpredictable and sometimes extraordinary circumstances. It details the hopes and anxieties of those that have resisted yielding to despair, thanks to the conviviality that associational life affords.

The Chapters

This book is organised into eight chapters. The ethnography unpacks the processes through which young people in the inner city of Old Town respond to local and global challenges while positioning themselves as social adults. The major themes addressed in the ethnography include personhood, gender, subjectivity, citizenship, and social adulthood. Its central actors are young people - men and women between the ages of 20 and 50 united by their shared quest to build moral and meaningful lives and to transform their community. While prominence is given to group activities and collective identities, the book also details individual biographic trajectories, showing how identities and personhood in the Grassfields are not only interdependent but always a work in progress. In chapter one "Outsider and Native" I detail the opportunities and ambiguities I experienced as a Cameroonian ethnographer from Bamenda conducting research on young people. As an outsider and native, I reflect on the challenges of doing research in one's home town and the need to adjust one's positionality in the field in relation to research participants. I conclude with a description of my initial encounters with the various associations, and how they were recruited for this study.

Chapter two "Personhood, Social Adulthood and Society in the Grasslands" introduces the reader to the ethnographic context of the Cameroon Grasslands. What does it mean to be a person in this part of the world? How have these meanings changed over time and to what extent do these changes inform our understanding of young people's construction of their subjectivities and responses to the challenges of becoming social adults?

In chapter three, "Cultivating Moral Spaces", I provide a detailed introduction of the three associations that constitute the core of this ethnography, establishing the circumstances under which they were founded and the characteristics of their memberships. I show how and why young people join associations, the transnational nature of these associations as well as the mechanisms by which associations in Old Town became highly gendered spaces. Further detail is provided on the structure and organisation of the associations and their principal role in mediating individual and collective subjectivities.

What roles do associations perform, especially young people's associations? The answer to this question is outlined in chapter four, "Sanitary Activism and Urban Renewal in Old Town". The chapter describes and analyses how young people in Old Town, acting through various associations inscribe their agencies on urban space through the politics of neighbouring (cf. Jerrems 2020) and sanitary activism. It details young people's preoccupation with and discourses on hygiene as well as their strategies and operations that seek to redress urgent health and environmental problems in their community. I show that young people's preoccupation with sanitary matters enables them to mobilise their resources, exercise power, and further their quest for visibility and influence in Old Town.

Young people's sanitary activism mirrors their campaigns against 'social ills' which is the focus of chapter five, "Cultivating Respect, Gendered Spaces and Moral Transformation in Old Town." This chapter describes and analyses the ways in which young people in Old Town position themselves as moral citizens through the construction of a moral community circumscribed by highly gendered notions of respectability, self-care, and charitable action. The moral community forged by these young people is in part driven by their shared desire to root out social ills –perpetrated either by delinquent members or other "youth" in the community – pursuits that affirm their collective will to social adulthood through practices perceived to bring respect and honour.

Chapter six, "Alternate Pathways to Social Adulthood and the Economy of Faux Dossiers" explores the intersections of migration, the faux dossier economy and social adulthood. By means of ethnographic examples, I show that for many young people experiencing "deferred" or semi-citizenship in Cameroon, migration offers them a viable pathway towards the pursuit of their personal dreams and ultimately the attainment of social adulthood.

Finally, the conclusion "Personhood, Moral Action, and Social Adulthood in the Cameroon Grasslands" recaps the meanings of social adulthood and moral citizenship for the young people in Old Town and its implications for understanding young people's lives across the African continent. I revisit the idea that associational life provides a powerful platform within which gendered subjectivities and moral citizenship are cultivated – processes which permit us to see the ways in which citizenship practices can be expanded and eroded simultaneously. I conclude that there is considerable ethnographic and comparative worth in studying the lives of young people in Africa by exploring the tremendous challenges they face as well as the imaginative and ingenuous improvisations they devise to counter waithood and victimhood.

CHAPTER ONE

Outsider and Native: Fieldwork in Old Town, Bamenda

Fieldwork for this monograph was conducted in the neighbourhood of Old Town in Bamenda, a city with a population of about a million souls.[1] Bamenda is the largest urban centre in the North West region of the country. It emerged during the German colonial period as a trading and administrative centre (see chapter two). The choice of Old Town for this study was serendipitous. I had set out to study young people's politicised associations based on my prior engagements studying young people and students' politics (Fokwang 1999, 2003, 2009). Some of these associations included President Biya's Youths (PRESBY) and the Southern Cameroons Youth League (SCYL). However, my plans began to fall apart when I soon discovered that PRESBY no longer commanded a good following and that its activities had declined over the years since its emergence into the Cameroon political landscape in 1996. More perplexing was my discovery that none of the popular youth associations were officially registered with the local administration.[2]

The early period of the fieldwork involved hanging out with youth members of several political associations such as the Southern Cameroons National

---

1. The city's population has declined significantly due to the ongoing conflict between separatist forces and the Cameroon military. Some observers have noted that the city has suffered a decline of about half of its population since 2017 when conflict erupted into a full-scale civil war.
2. Many of these associations were offshoots of the main political parties or nationalist movements. The Socialist Youths, for example, was considered unofficially as the Youth wing of the SDF, although it was less visible than its political rivals like the youth wing of the ruling Cameroon People's Democratic Movement (YCPDM) and the SCNC Youths. The SCNC youths could be distinguished from the Southern Cameroons Youth League (SCYL) that emerged in the mid 1990s as a separate nationalist movement headed by radical youths who advocated a military solution aimed at the restoration of the Southern Cameroons.

Council Youths (SCNC)[3] and PRESBY members in the vicinity of T-junction in Bamenda. A friend had recommended that I should check out a computer shop that also served as a popular hub for young activists. I was initially introduced to Bill whose brother, Donald owned the shop. Donald was an entrepreneur and member of the provincial executive of PRESBY. Soon after we were introduced to each other, he granted me permission to pitch my research "tent" in his shop where I would continue to explore and refine my research questions.

The shop was located at the intersection of Cathedral Street and the Commercial Avenue. The latter was the city's busiest street with limited parking, bereft of any functional traffic lights. Opposite the shop, on the north side of the street, a group of women sold fresh fruits daily except on Sundays. One of them sold roasted plantains, corn, peanuts and avocadoes. Others sold oranges, sugar cane and bananas. Towering over the women was a huge billboard that advertised Guinness Smooth, a new brand of Guinness beer that had just been introduced to the market. On the billboard was an inscription in bold: *Découvrez la vraie douceur* (Discover real smoothness – my translation) with no English equivalent despite Bamenda being an English-speaking city.

Donald's shop competed for popularity with two adjacent *off-licences*.[4] His shop provided a range of services such as typing, printing, photocopying, the sale and repair of cell phones, as well as both mobile and landline telephone call services. It was staffed by two female secretaries, each with a desktop computer wherein they typed documents and watched Nigerian movies when conditions permitted. The shop also ran a movie rental service from its large collection of Nigerian and pirated Hollywood movies.

It was here that many unemployed young men in their twenties came to hang out. The shop provided an initial site for my observations while I interacted with several young men on a daily basis. This would not last because it became evident that the political associations I had intended to

---

3. Members of the SCNC youth are different from the SCYL which operates as a movement independent of the SCNC. SCNC youths were made up predominantly of young men who organised themselves as informal neighbourhood associations to learn more about and to sensitise their peers about the objectives of the SCNC. Some of them attended the regular meetings of the SCNC at Cow Street, Bamenda.
4. In Bamenda and throughout the English-speaking regions of Cameroon, an off-licence is a bar or pub where drinks are bought and consumed on site, contrary to its original British meaning. In its proper sense, an off-license is a store where alcoholic beverages are sold for consumption elsewhere. In other words, the store has the license to sell alcoholic drinks which must be consumed off the property.

study commanded less and less influence.[5] It would be prudent for me to explore other young people's associations. One of Donald's contacts, Manu, recommended that I visit an association of which he was a member. Manu's invitation proved decisive.

On Sunday, 1st May 2005, Manu led me to the Ntambag Brothers Association (NBA) in Old Town, a relatively new association in the neighbourhood that had recently won popular acclaim on account of their donation of trash cans to the Bamenda Urban Council (BUC). The NBA met every Sunday at noon although actual business often commenced a few minutes or so later. Upon our arrival, Manu introduced me to several members who stood outside the meeting venue, as a friend researching young people in Bamenda. When the introductory rituals were completed, one of the young men, Carlson, who I soon learnt was the group's president, pulled me aside and assured me that I had come to the 'right' place. He promptly stated that they were a friendly association and would gladly work with anyone interested in their activities. While we waited for the latecomers, he brought out the association's photo album and we flipped through photos of recently accomplished projects.[6] In the meantime, more members had arrived by now and someone beckoned us to come in.

The building was visibly old and in a state of dilapidation. The paint on the walls had faded beyond recognition and the room was cold and damp. The gaped ceiling betrayed the possibility of a regular leakage when it rained. Several benches were arranged against the walls of the three-by-four-metre-room and directly opposite the door were two chairs and a table reserved for the chairman and the secretary.

The meeting began with a prayer followed by the reading of an agenda. At this point, my presence was acknowledged, and the chairman suggested I would be given an opportunity to address the association towards the end of the meeting. When my turn came, I rose from my seat and explained that the purpose of my visit to Bamenda was to investigate the socioeconomic and political conditions of young people. I then expressed my wish to attend their

5.   Most of those who identified as members of PRESBY stated that they had joined the association to access government jobs or seek admission into government-run professional schools where they hoped to be recruited as civil servants upon graduation. The failure of such dreams to materialise had occasioned their disillusionment with PRESBY.
6.   Prior to the advent of smart phones, a common welcome ritual for guests in Cameroonian homes was the showing of a photo album. Besides serving as entertainment, it also enabled the 'stranger' to be socialised about one's kin network and friends.

meetings and to interact with them as individuals and as a group. Many nodded
their heads, probably out of curiosity or perhaps outright doubt. The chairman
then rose and thanked me for honouring them with a visit. He expressed the
association's readiness to work with me, and as president of the association,
granted me official permission to observe, and at my will, participate in their
meetings and other association-related activities. As a "professional intruder",
I was reassured of their willingness when after the meeting, several members
approached me and we exchanged phone numbers.

Thus, began my immersion in Old Town. However, I was not contented
with researching just young men. Upon further enquiry, I learnt of the existence
of two female-only associations in the neighbourhood: the Chosen Sisters and
the United Sisters. I was even more thrilled to learn that the Chosen Sisters
had existed for much longer than the Ntambag Brothers.[7]

Unlike the NBA, the Chosen Sisters met every Wednesday in the living
room of one of the matriarchs in the neighbourhood. This schedule had been
chosen to suit many of its members who worked during the day or had other
meetings to attend on Sundays. The Chosen Sisters was made up of 35 registered young women between the ages of 25 and 38. The membership included
young women from different ethnic groups and educational levels. On my
first visit to the association, I was accompanied by the NBA president who
offered to introduce me to the ladies as a fellow NBA brother. Remarkably, he
had informed the leadership of the association of our intended visit. When
we eventually showed up, Sirri, the Chosen Sisters' president welcomed us
at the entrance and ushered us into a poorly lit living room. I was pleasantly
surprised to recognise the president, whom I had known as a fellow student
at the University of Buea, Cameroon's only English-speaking university in the
mid-1990s. She had read law and minored in sociology. Due to a power outage,
the room was lit by several candles and the lone torch of a member who sat in
a remote corner chatting with her friends. The ladies were dressed beautifully
in what appeared to be uniformed fabric.[8] At the centre of the room were a
table and chair, most likely reserved for the secretary or president. I was offered
a seat next to a gentleman who looked like someone in his thirties. I would

7.   Contrary to popular opinion, particularly among young men that their female counterparts
     could not run and maintain an association, the female associations had existed for at least
     four years, whereas one of the male associations in the neighbourhood, the Able Brothers
     (AB) had disbanded less than six months after its creation.
8.   In "Fabrics of Identity" (2015), I analyse the symbolism of uniformed clothing in the
     Cameroon Grassfields and beyond.

later learn he was a patron of the association. Before the meeting commenced, Sirri rose from her seat and introduced me, after apologising for the lack of electricity in the room. She explained to the association that I was an ethnographer interested in investigating young people's associations and activities in the community of Old Town. She then gave me permission to address the association. I thanked them for permitting me to visit and proceeded to explain the nature of my research, emphasising my role as someone who had come to learn from them. Sirri then thanked me for coming and exhorted the sisters to assist me in whatever way they could.

Between May and July 2005, I focused my activities on the Chosen Sisters and Ntambag Brothers but soon decided to widen my population of study to include the second female-only association. The United Sisters consisted of a cohort of younger women between the ages of 20 and 28. By the time I sought to include the United Sisters, I had already earned the confidence and friendship of many NBA members and was often seen hanging out with young men in the neighbourhood. One of them was a patron of the United Sisters who readily offered to introduce me to the association. The meeting venue turned out to be the same room used by the Chosen Sisters. When we arrived at the venue, my companion first consulted with a young lady on her way into the venue who confirmed that the meeting had effectively started. When we entered the living room, I noted that the attendance was surprisingly poor. It consisted of just seven young women. One of the ladies was busy cleaning a wooden bench while another was addressing the sparse assembly. We then sat on the dusted bench where I observed the proceedings in silence as the young women went about their business. Two members who sat on a sofa opposite the door attracted the rebuke of the others on account of their noisy banter. A lady who occupied a seat near the door warned the suspects to discontinue their chit-chat, otherwise she would write their names for rowdiness – a threat that seemed to have punitive consequences. When there was sufficient calm in the room, the meeting continued without further interruption. "Matters arising", said the lady at the desk with an open exercise book. She must be the secretary, I speculated. Silence ensued as everyone stared at each other for a while. Eventually, a lady in blue dress sought permission to speak and just before she rose from her seat, Claude, my companion whispered to me that she was the president of the association. "I disagree with those who take excuses on Sundays on the grounds that they have to do their hair" she began. "I think I could also choose to do my hair on Sundays, and consequently stay away from the meeting but because we love this association, we decided to attend despite our other commitments. I don't know about you, but we should henceforth consider such excuses as invalid" she stated firmly. It seemed her suggestion was in response to a series of written excuses that had been submitted by members to explain their absence from the meeting. No one reacted to her suggestion. Now seated, she then asked again if members agreed with her view, whereupon a few voices spoke up and agreed that henceforth, permission shall not be granted to members who excused themselves from the Sunday reunion on the grounds that they had to do their hair. An uneasy silence fell upon the house again. "We're still on matters arising," the lady at the desk reminded the small assembly. Again, the lady in blue raised her right hand. "I think we should do something about those who did not show up for work."[9] Immediately, a lady who sat about three feet me from sprung from her seat and began to speak. "Yes, many of us came back with blisters" she screamed, showing her palms to the members. "We need to give heavy fines to those who did not show up because the usual fine is nothing compared to the amount of labour we put in." To my astonishment, Claude also rose from his seat and supported the last speaker's suggestion while showing his blistered palms to the assembly. When he sat down, he turned to a latecomer who had just arrived and had occupied a seat next to him. I overheard him accusing her of not having showed up for "work".

Another awkward wave of silence fell on the house. Then the lady in blue finally spoke. "Now that no one has anything to say, I see that brother Claude has brought a stranger. We'll like to know what his mission is and if he has anything to tell us, he is welcome to do so now." Claude then stood up and introduced me as an ethnographer working with youth associations in the community. He stated that I had expressed interest in learning about the United Sisters and if given the opportunity, I would explain the purpose of my visit even better. The president then got up, welcomed me and asked me to introduce myself. I reiterated Claude's statement, explaining that I was researching young people's associations in Old Town. I stated that I had come to seek their permission to observe and participate in their activities. The president quizzed me on what I would do with the knowledge gathered from my interactions in the community. I clarified that I would write a book about the experiences of young people as they transition into full adult status. I then regained my seat and waited for further questions but none were forthcoming. Claude then recommended to the assembly that I should be granted permission to

9.   Work, in this context refers to a clean-up or sanitary operation carried out by the association.

attend several meetings so they could know me better and the purpose of my research. He added that even though I had been attending NBA meetings for a couple of months, I had not interviewed most people because I too needed time to build rapport with members and the community. "Yes, I think it will be difficult to have a good interview with someone you don't know, and maybe people will give you wrong information due to the lack of trust" the president added. "Maybe if you asked someone if she's married, the person might say no, whereas the contrary is true. How do you intend to make sure that people speak the truth?" she quizzed. Before I could respond, Claude was already up to respond on my behalf. He explained that once they became acquainted with me, they would find it difficult to give me wrong information especially as I would be around for a long time. "Ok, when more members arrive, we will discuss the issue and communicate our decision next Sunday. I am speaking on behalf of the group, but I think individuals will make their personal decisions if they are interested." I was subsequently granted permission to participate in their activities and several months later, was co-opted as one of the patrons of the association, validating my accession to insider status.

Researcher's Positionality and Fieldwork

As shown above, research participants were recruited gradually. Over time, I gained what I would consider an insider status which permitted me to participate in the activities of individual associations and a few events that brought all the associations together. Besides attending weekly meetings and developing my field notes, I accompanied members of the various associations to activities such as anniversary celebrations, excursions, hospital visits, funerals, "death celebrations", football matches, seminars, prize award ceremonies, and many other events. During these activities, I harnessed the full merits of participant observation (DeWalt & DeWalt 2011), mindful of the fact that I was not quite an outsider in the strict sense of the term.

I was born and spent my early childhood in Bali, just 16km outside the city of Bamenda. I attended a prestigious Catholic boys' secondary and high school in Bamenda and visited family in Old Town during my school days. Consequently, I did not fit the archetype of the classic anthropologist who abandons the comfort of home to venture into a tropical faraway place, armed with the singular quest to understand native life.

There is a longstanding debate in the anthropological literature on the positionality of the field researcher, which needs to be addressed briefly with respect to my fieldwork experience. At issue is the question of the researcher's

power in negotiating access to the field and his/her interaction with participants in the research process. Some have questioned the extent to which one's
race, gender, or sexual orientation can determine or influence the quality of
data obtained (see Berreman 2007; DeWalt & DeWalt 2011:34). For instance,
questions have been raised if white people can gain as much insight about
black people's experiences or women, men's (Marks 2001:9-11; Merriam et al.
2001) compared to 'insiders' who share the same identities as their researched
subjects or participants. In my case, the question could be asked if established
adults can gain insight into the lives of young people? Early discussions in
anthropology contended that the field researcher was always an outsider who
sought temporary insider status (risking the danger of going native) – a binary
distinction that has little relevance to contemporary debates especially as more
"natives" have become anthropologists and the discipline itself is undergoing
calls for further decolonisation (cf. Asad 1990; Bank & Bank 2013; Narayan
1993). There is consensus that one needs to continuously reconstruct one's
insider/outsider status in terms of one's positionality as concerns race, class,
gender, ethnicity among other factors (Merriam et al. 2001:405).

In my case, I initially approached fieldwork as an insider, given my native
status to Bamenda. As a young man with historical ties to the city, I assumed
that accessing the field would be easy for me. I was concerned less about my
gender than with my social status, given that I had just returned from abroad
and could be conflated with a typical *bushfaller*.[10] The fact that I was from
abroad, particularly from North America, could potentially shape participants'
expectations and perceptions of me (for more on Cameroonian bushfallers,
see Wanki & Lietaert 2019; Nyamnjoh 2011; Tazanu 2012). Generally, Cameroonians are ambiguous about their own 'people' researching their lives
given the long-standing notion which associates research with 'whiteness' and
financial endowment (see Nyamnjoh & Page 2002). Although I introduced
myself as a graduate student (which I was at the time), research participants
generally perceived and expected me to provide financial support to them
or their associations, an expectation I frequently met as part of building and
maintaining rapport. Even after I completed my dissertation research and
gained employment as a university lecturer, these expectations continued. I
remain a patron of the Chosen Sisters and have retained my membership in

---

10.   Bushfaller is the popular term used in the English-speaking regions of Cameroon to refer
      to young people that have ventured to foreign lands (especially Europe and North America)
      and are noted for their conspicuous consumption and sartorial distinction.

the Ntambag Brothers' association over the years, contributing towards school projects, funerals and more recently the purchase of hospital equipment.

It is in the above sense that I was both an insider and outsider. I was an insider insofar as I drew upon my historical ties to Bamenda in negotiating new friendships. However, coming from abroad, I was seen as an outsider irrespective of my status as a young man with ties to Bamenda. To most, if not all participants, I was seen as far more privileged than they were and as such could not claim to share their challenges or daily struggles. Similarly, I could not claim as much *insider* status in certain female spaces compared to young men's. Whereas I could hang out freely with young men in their bedrooms, in palm wine bars and pubs, the same was not true for the most part with young women. It was generally seen as inappropriate to hang out with young women in private spaces such as in their bedrooms without the suspicion that something beyond "fieldwork" was at play. This meant that most interviews with young women took place in their living rooms, job sites and other public places. This notwithstanding, I enjoyed insider status at their weekly meetings given that I gradually slipped into "invisibility" by refusing to be drawn into their discussions despite initial attempts by the leadership of the associations to do so. Once both female associations understood my preference for *observation* during meetings, regular deliberations went on as if a male "intruder" was not present. This became evident in some of the issues that were addressed during their meetings, issues that were considered exclusively girl-talk. My insider status was also confirmed at public functions when for example, the Chosen Sisters introduced me as the only Chosen "brother" or when I accepted the status of 'patron' in the United Sisters. These experiences drove home to me the gendered nature of fieldwork and that my identity as a male ethnographer inevitably shaped the nature of my field experience (Bell 1993:2; DeWalt & DeWalt 2011:99).

As with many anthropological experiences, familiarity and rapport with participants were established over several months. Understandably, some individuals were more willing to open up than others. Sometimes, a fieldworker is fortunate to witness a spectacular encounter, reminiscent of Geertz's Balinese experience that serves as a turning point in the field (cf. Geertz 2005). A less exotic but significant event occurred a few weeks after I began attending the NBA's Sunday meetings. The occasion was a *born house* ceremony previously detailed in the introduction. Cramped into a neighbour's living room on account of a torrential downpour that had disrupted our initial plans, individuals who had hardly uttered a word to me now felt the urge to do so given the inescapable confinement. A young man who sat opposite me sought to know why I had chosen a soft drink instead of a beer. "That's uncameroonian" he blurted, echoing the widely held opinion that Cameroon is a nation united by their proclivity for drinking. He then went on to qualify that although he had severed his friendship with alcohol, he now suffered from a different addiction – women. The young men around me laughed enthusiastically. Someone next to me wanted to know how long I intended to spend in the neighbourhood and another sought to know if I could assist him in procuring documents to travel abroad.

Interviewing

Data collection entailed participating in the activities of the three associations and hanging out with individual members where and when it was deemed safe and appropriate. In order to map out a general idea of my target population, I collected biographic data by administering a short questionnaire aimed at eliciting information on a range of issues such as voting attitudes, age, educational level and religious affiliation. I also organised a series of structured and unstructured interviews with individual members of the respective associations during which I obtained life histories and attitudes or opinions on a range of issues.

In general, interviews sought to elicit information on family background, educational level, employment status, political and religious affiliation, ethnic origin and attitudes towards the socioeconomic and political conditions in the country. Where I was unable to hang out with participants, perhaps due to their schedule, I would arrange a formal interview and collect information on their life histories and experiences. In this respect, I sought information on issues such as their marital status, subsistence sources and strategies, household size (number of siblings or children etc). Evidence for educational level included participants' educational attainment (number of years spent in formal schooling), schools attended (public or private) and parents' educational level. I also sought to identify individuals' ethnic affiliation by establishing their parents' village (ancestral home) of origin and membership in ethnic-related associations. Given the pre-eminence of ethnic associations in Cameroon as a whole (cf. Geschiere & Nyamnjoh 2000; Mercer, Page, & Evans 2008; Orock 2015) and specifically in Bamenda, I saw it fit to assess their significance in the lives of young people. Most urban-based ethnic associations are known to play important roles in citizenship formation, the socialisation of the younger generation and in negotiating socioeconomic opportunities for its members.

During my fieldwork, I also sought to identify participants' economic activities or subsistence strategies. Most young people were involved in economic activities of some sort and tended to combine several opportunities to meet basic needs. Persons known to juggle economic activities in this manner were often referred to as *débrouillards* – a French term for resourceful persons that has gained currency in Cameroon Pidgin English (CPE), the country's lingua franca.

Furthermore, I explored individuals' level of political literacy on a range of current and past issues, voting history and the perception of their role or impact in formal and informal socio-political processes. As stated earlier, I had set out to investigate the citizenship experiences of politicised youth groups in Bamenda but redefined my focus upon realising that these associations had become moribund or lost legitimacy. Nevertheless, I was still interested in how young people understood and defined what they considered political. Inspired by this conceptual approach, I uncovered young people's voting habits, opinions on local political leaders and their perception of socio-political processes in the country and Bamenda in particular (see Fokwang 2016).

Participant observation and interviews facilitated the collection of life histories. The latter enables the researcher to contrast between persons of different gender, social class, age and stage in the life cycle. For instance, young people in their 20s had different perceptions and experiences from those in their 30s, even though they all defined themselves or were categorised as youth – experiences that underscored the claim that youth is a differentiated category, rather than a homogenous entity. Life histories provided cases from which different sub-categories were compared with those obtained from the general population. In this light, I expanded my sample population to include a few elderly men and women to obtain generational perceptions on the predicament of youth. The elders were recruited from the families of young people already involved in the study.

Finally, secondary sources from the Bamenda provincial archives provided an understanding of the origin of some of the socio-political debates surrounding the category of youth in Cameroon[11] as well as colonial ethnographers' scant attention to this category. Secondary data revealed that the problem of youth emerged during the late colonial period on account of the destabilisation of old structures that had hitherto provided predictable transitional pathways

11. "Origins of The National Youth Day in Cameroon" by Jude Fokwang, *The Post Online*; http://www.postnewsline.com/2009/02/from-plebiscite-to-youth-day.htm Accessed Feb 17, 2009

for young people into adult roles.

Mobile Ethnography in the Age of Social Media

Although I left the "field" upon completion of my "traditional" fieldwork in April 2006, I never quite left. I returned in September 2007 to catch up on the latest developments in Old Town and again in September 2009 to complete the shooting of a documentary film project I had initiated in 2005 and again in the summer of 2014 to update myself on what had changed in the intervening years. Meanwhile, the Ntambag Brothers had created a Facebook group for the association in February 2010, enabling me to follow developments in Old Town and within the association specifically. In February 2016, the "field" came knocking again when the Ntambag Brothers, (now transformed into a Common Initiative Group[12]) created a WhatsApp group and invited me to join. Launched in 2009, WhatsApp is a text and voice messaging app with billions of users. It is arguably, the world's most popular messaging application given its free availability on both desktop and mobile devices. Users are able to take advantage of Wi-Fi and mobile phone data to place audio or video calls using the application. Both the Ntambag Brothers' Facebook group and their WhatsApp forum afforded me the opportunity to carry out a mixture of online observations, interviews and content analysis of photographic and video data for about a decade.

While the Facebook group has over 500 members, the WhatsApp forum has just over a hundred members, most of them based in Old Town and a handful dispersed across the world. Both platforms and especially WhatsApp, enable members to stay abreast of news from Sunday meetings, deaths within the association or community, and on-going projects etc. Diaspora members are expected to maintain their membership and to contribute towards all projects as decided by members in Old Town.

This study is consequently the product of a multi-sited fieldwork (a sort of mobile ethnography) in the sense that it has sought to understand the "circulation of cultural meanings … and identities in diffuse time-space" (Marcus 1995:96). More importantly, it has combined both traditional and virtual/online platforms to understand how the young people I initially encountered over a decade ago have continued to make sense of their lives and identities through

12.   A Common Initiative Group (CIG) per the Cameroon government's classification is an
       association or organisation that seeks to promote the economic and social development of
       its members (who are considered volunteers) as underscored by their common interests
       and collective projects.

the life cycle. As cultural products, online platforms or communities provide new and not-so new scope for the investigation of everyday life (Dalsgaard 2016; Sade-Beck 2004; Wilson & Leighton 2002). In this monograph, I treat them as extensions of the "real" world, whereby communicative practices such as norms, mores and regulations fashioned and adhered to in the physical world are equally enforced in mobile-mediated spaces.

Conclusion

Anthropological fieldwork is undeniably shaped by a researcher's identity and positionality. As both insider and outsider, participant observation enabled me to understand my friends' introspective meanings, their non-verbal cues and overt communication while reflecting on my positionality as a foreign-based male ethnographer with historical ties to the identities and predicament of my research participants. Immersion in the activities of the associations online and offline permitted me to gain access to the circulating ideas and discourses on the predicament of youth, from young people themselves and to weave an ethnography that bears and articulates the multiple perspectives of their voices and experiences. Hence, I make no authoritative claims to the objectivity of my positionality because to acknowledge particular and personal locations is to admit the limits of one's domain from these positions and "because from particular locations all understanding becomes subjectively based and forged through interactions within fields of power relations" (Narayan 1993:679). This monograph is consequently the outcome of an intersubjective process that spans over a decade between myself as ethnographer and my friends in Old Town and around the world.

CHAPTER TWO

Personhood, Social Adulthood and Society in the Grasslands

The Grassfields in the Anthropological Imagination

Approaching the Bamenda station especially in the rainy season, one is una-voidably struck by the rolling hills and greenery of the landscape. With peaks over 5200 ft, Bamenda is well-known for its crisp and cooler climate compared to the humid coastal and forest zones of Cameroon. Located about 366km northwest of Yaounde, the country's capital, Bamenda is well connected by road and air to major commercial cities such as Douala and Bafoussam. As one descends the Bamenda station hills, a panoramic view of the city gradu-ally emerges, particularly the high-rise buildings on the Commercial Avenue, Bamenda's main business district. Besides the storey buildings, other con-spicuous landmarks in the city include the gigantic church buildings of the main Christian denominations, namely the Catholic Cathedral just beneath the station escarpment, the Presbyterian Church in Ntamulung, strategically located on a knoll and the Baptist Church in Nkwen.

The Grasslands (also Grassfields) derives its name from the German colo-nial period, due in part to the predominance of savannah vegetation throughout its territories. Over time, the region came to be classified in the anthropological literature as a "culture area" on account of the prevalence of centralised and hierarchical kingdoms and chiefdoms, in contrast to the so-called acephalous or decentralised polities of the forest zones of south-east and coastal Cameroon (cf. Fokwang 2008; Geschiere 1993; Nkwi & Warnier 1982). Anthropologists and historians have further contrasted between the Eastern Grassfields (now the Francophone Western Region of Cameroon) and the Western Grassfields (now the Anglophone North West region of the country). Our focus in this eth-nography is on the Western Grassfields, composed of dozens of ethnic groups and languages. Its principal ethnic groups include the Tikar, Ngemba, Meta, and the Chamba. Although archaeological findings show that this region has been inhabited for millennia (Warnier 2012), some anthropologists contend that most Grassfields communities "are recent, irrespective of how long they have been around" (Fowler & Zeitlyn 1996:xviii). This is because, as Fowler and Zeitlyn argue, "identity in the Grassfields has been constantly reworked across a range of groups of quite different orders and magnitude" (1996:xviii) but also because oral historical sources support claims to recent settlement of some of the areas during the 18th and 19th centuries.

This notwithstanding, there is consensus in the literature that most Western Grassfields kingdoms share similar socioeconomic, linguistic, religious and political organisation. Anthropologists and historians have recorded a long history of trading, intermarrying and sustained diplomatic relationships amongst Grassfields polities (Nkwi & Warnier 1982). These cultural similarities are particularly evident in their beliefs and worldviews as well as in the shared conception of personhood and social adulthood.

Personhood and Social Adulthood in the Grassfields

The study of the person has long been an area of scholarly interest for anthropologists and sociologists since the founding of both disciplines in the 19th century (Carrithers, Collins, & Lukes 1985). Contrary to the assumption, at least in contemporary western societies, that the person or individual is an autonomous rights-bearing human being irrespective of age, sex, creed, social race or national origin, anthropologists have noted that societies differ significantly in how persons are conceived. In addition, anthropologists have observed that societies' conceptions of people as individuals (of what constitutes a person) can be linked to its "forms of social institution, of how society works" (Carrithers 2010:532). In other words, how a given society conceives of the individual can be tied to what roles are available for him/her and consequently how socioeconomic, political and religious life are organised. In some societies, full personhood can only be achieved by certain categories of people and only over a certain period of time, whilst others are excluded from attaining such a highly coveted status. Other societies emphasise the significance of "social relations and the fulfilment of social obligations specific to each role, e.g., mother and wife, father and husband, dutiful son or daughter" (Carrithers 2010:533) in their conceptions of personhood.

In the Western Grassfields of Cameroon, precolonial conceptions of personhood generally emphasised the principle of *becoming* rather than a mode of *being*. By this, it means that personhood was conceived as "a work in progress" characterised by continuous negotiation, flexibility and adaptability through different rites of initiation and incorporation. A human being gradually attained personhood, marked by important rites of passage from infancy, childhood, youth (adolescence), social adulthood, and ancestorship (cf. Mbunwe-Samba, Mzeka, Niba, & Wirmum 1993). Paul Mzeka for example, maintains that amongst the Nso, one of the most populous kingdoms in the Grasslands, society differentiated between; *wan* (infancy), *wanle* (childhood)[1], *wanle nsum/ nggon* (youth or adolescence), *lumen/wiy* (manhood, womanhood or maturity stage) and *tata/yaya* (old age). Although these distinctions were predicated on biological age, transition from one stage to the other was often marked by elaborate rites of passage and depended on a range of negotiated factors. This was particularly true of the transition from youth to adulthood (determined more by the acquisition of vital substances necessary for social reproduction) than simply on biological maturity. This notwithstanding, young men and women in the Grassfields generally belonged to the category of a *muted group*, that is, persons "reduced to silence"[2] or with limited capacity for *speech*, ostensibly subordinate to those of titled men and chiefs (Warnier 1996:116).

Jean-Pierre Warnier identifies two categories of adult status in traditional Grasslands society, which pertain especially to men – "first, unmarried cadets perceived as children irrespective of their age … seen as void of transmissible life essence, as symbolically impotent. Second, married men who are coopted into the line of descent of a notable, and who can engender by transmitting the life essence received from the latter" (1993:305). According to Warnier, unmarried men and young women generally constituted what he refers to as *social cadets*. Drawing on the metaphor of the container, Warnier contends that Grassfields societies conceived the social cadet as "an empty vessel lacking the means to fill itself" (1996:121) and as such remained in a position of

---

1. There is evidence that Europe was not alone in marking out "childhood" (cf. Ariès 1962; Postman 1994) and "youth" as phases in the human life cycle. According to Neil Postman, "the printing press created a new definition of adulthood *based on reading competence,* and, correspondingly, a new conception of childhood *based on reading incompetence*" (Postman 1994:18, italics original). Many age-based societies in Africa marked out "youth" as a distinct stage and often tapped their "liminal force…for the collective good" (Comaroff & Comaroff 2005:22). In precolonial East Africa, youths were often mobilised into warrior groups and charged with protecting the boundaries of the village or kingdom (cf. Comaroff & Comaroff 2005:22).

2. Young people were also reduced to silence in the sense that colonial ethnography paid scant attention to their voices or concerns.

dependency and subjection. According to this ideology, marriage could boost one's status but not eliminate one's social cadetness. However, reproduction after marriage played a crucial role in enhancing one's status in a hierarchical world dominated by titled men and lineage heads. This was because reproduction, to draw on the metaphor of containers, entailed the transmission of life essence whereby such containers had acquired the capacity to be filled. Besides biological reproduction, social reproduction also played an important role in conceptions of maturity and adulthood even though men and women experienced these processes differently (Waller 2006). For young women, adulthood was recognised by the attainment of reproductive maturity and eventually, marriage, while for young men, becoming a household head as well as overcoming one's "symbolic impotence" through procreative reproduction was emphasised. Compared to women, young men generally experienced a protracted youth, marked by a series of initiations of which marriage was but one stage (see Hansen 2005 for similarities in Zambia).

The attainment of social adulthood did not entail full personhood. Full personhood was generally understood as a work in progress, structurally determined and sometimes, contested (see Goheen 1996). In Grassfields societies, full personhood was not open to all individuals but reserved for certain categories of persons: the *fon* or king, titled men and lineage heads, individuals who were believed to be destined for ancestorship (cf. Jindra 2005). However, Christian ideologies have significantly altered notions of death, the afterlife, ancestors, and ultimately, hierarchy and personhood in the Grassfields (cf. Jindra 2005, 2011) leading to the democratisation of ancestorship. By this, I mean that the Christian emphasis on the uniqueness of each human being (created in the image of God) conveys the view that every individual (both men and women) has the potential to become an ancestor "a status attained previously mainly by titled men" (Jindra 2005:357).

Besides new religious ideologies, colonialism, modern education and greater exposure to western influences have led to major shifts in the conception of personhood (cf. Rowlands 1994, 1996) and the various phases that constitute it. For instance, colonialism radically altered the economic and sociocultural basis on which "youth" as a life-phase was defined and experienced. This was achieved by the imposition of new models of organisation and behaviour,[3] which discounted the "past" as a symbolic source of author-

---

3.   New ideals of responsible behaviour were introduced such as the view of productive masculinity, which was achieved through employment in the colonial service, proper citizenship

ity. In this vein, colonialism altered the boundaries and erased the erstwhile markers of youth, leading to dramatic redefinitions on the status of young men and women. Thus, *when* and *how* boys became men and girls women was gravely transformed (Waller 2006:81) and of course, with consequences that are evident to date.[4] One of the accomplices of the *mission civilisatrice*, the mission church, contributed significantly in undermining precolonial society by reshaping maturity for both young men and women. For young men, adulthood was reshaped by colonial expectations of law and order and through education and the labour process[5] (Waller 2006:81-82). In certain parts of Africa, warrior bands, militias and initiation groups, "important spaces for the socialization and self-determination of young men and the proving of manhood, were disbanded or severely curtailed…" (Waller 2006:82; see also Aguilar 1998; Ly 1988;). This had major consequences for many African societies because through their employment, the young acquired financial power which encouraged their defiance of the old order. Armed with "literacy" and dressed in western "fashion", young African men provoked and threatened elders who, despite all, still controlled the resources of the land and traditional labour (Argenti 2005, 2007). For example, in 1901, armed young men who had broken away from authority (variously known in the region as Kamenda boys, Tapenta boys or Free boys) held the region to ransom. Some of these young men had been recruited into the German colonial *Schutztruppe* to undertake punitive expeditions into Mankon and Bafut – kingdoms that were perceived as resisting German colonial rule (cf. Fardon 2006; O'neil 1996). A missionary who witnessed the activities of these young men wrote the following account:

The youths in particular who form the tail of the troop, are the bane of

and marriage (Waller 2006:78).

4.   Colonialism marked a new beginning for youth. It did not create youth, it simply altered the socioeconomic conditions in which youth was defined and understood. Starting from the colonial period, the formal educational system constituted the modern arena for the transition of young men and women. By going through the formal educational system, boys became men and girls women. But this was limited to those who enrolled in schools, and even then, it did not guarantee a smooth transition from school to the job market.

5.   The colonial economy encouraged young people to leave their homes to work in various sectors of the economy. In Southern Africa, migrant labour became a principal source of income in many households as men travelled to the mines in Kimberley and Johannesburg to seek employment. Migration also became a rite of passage in consequence, a trend that has become entrenched in some cultures to date. Upon their return from the urban areas or the mines, young men were recognised and granted adult status and rights (see for example Schapera 1970).

the country. Corrupted by the magic of the Whites, they attack men,
women and children like wild beast. They steal anything that isn't nailed
down – fowls, goats and foodstuff. Their organisation has ramifications
everywhere. When they are checked, they cry: Lef mi, mi big boy, mi be
Tapenta boy (cited in Warnier 1996:117).

Evidently, colonialism and its legacies have shifted conceptions not only
of personhood but also how social adulthood is experienced and negotiated.
Social cadets who in the past were subordinates of titled men or served as a
source of surplus value to paraphrase Comaroff and Comaroff (2005), can
potentially aspire to full personhood by drawing on a combination of traditional, Christian and modern logics of identity and success. Whereas in
the past, only certain titled men and nobles could attain full personhood by
becoming ancestors, today, everyone, men and women in principle can attain
full personhood. The attainment of social adulthood is a major milestone in the
journey towards full personhood. Unlike in precolonial society, its definitions
have been broadened to incorporate new meanings and experiences, especially
what it means to be a successful person. In the contemporary Grasslands,
social adulthood denotes a status of relative success based on an assortment
of factors – marriage, parenthood (procreative reproduction), employment
(labour), the ability to establish an independent household where the head
provides for his/her needs and one's kin. Success that is not redistributed is
regarded with suspicion, if not outright hostility. According to Rowlands
(1994), individualised success in the Cameroon Grasslands is often believed
to have been achieved at the expense of others. He further notes that "personal
success is essentially destructive unless seen to be acting for the good of all
and this ensures that such achievements should be accompanied by egalitarian
redistributory mechanisms" (Rowlands 1994:17). Thus, social adulthood is
tied to an individual's ability to redistribute one's success or achievements –
success that could only have been achieved through the recognition of one's
incompleteness – or rather, that we are what we are through and in relation
with others. This ideology of personhood is articulated in the Grassfields with
the popular proverb, "a child is one person's only in the womb" or its now
globalised African equivalent - "it takes a village to raise a child." Back to the
Grasslands, ideas of personhood and success are now intertwined as suggested
by the view that "achievement is devoid of meaning if not pursued within, as
part of, and on behalf of a group of people who recognise and endorse that
achievement" (Nyamnjoh 2002:115). Contrary to the view of the autonomous

rights-bearing individual whose achievements are erroneously attributed to him/herself, anthropologist Francis Nyamnjoh draws on Grassfields ideologies of personhood and morality to emphasise the importance of domesticated agency which provides for "the freedom to pursue individual or group goals… within a socially predetermined framework that emphasises conviviality with collective interests while simultaneously allowing for individual creativity and self-fulfilment" (Nyamnjoh 2017:201). I show in this study that the constitution of personhood and the production of social adulthood are processes that are manifest in collective as well as individual agencies. Whilst anthropological studies of personhood have tended to focus on the relationship between the individual and his/her culture, this study pushes the boundaries by exploring how young people's associations in the community of Old Town draw on existing conceptions of personhood and social adulthood to engender what I refer to as moral citizenship.

Bamenda: The Social and Economic Life of a Restless City

Unlike some rapidly urbanising cities in Africa, Bamenda has no slums and homelessness is not yet an issue. This is partly because the city is bordered by rural villages, linked by modest road networks that provide a buffer to potential urban problems such as overcrowding. With a population of almost a million, Bamenda doubles as the capital of the Mezam Division and the North West Region. The North West Region has an urban growth rate of 7.95% (compared to the national average of 5.6%). Since the last census in 2005, the North West Region has grown from 1.2 million in the mid 1980s to about 1.9 million inhabitants in 2015[6]. With a population density of 99 per square kilometre, the region is by far, one of the most densely populated areas in Cameroon, compared with the national average of 22.6 people per square kilometre.

Bamenda itself is comparably a young city in Cameroon. Its story begins with the arrival of the Germans. In 1902, the Germans established a military station in Mendankwe, the area from which Bamenda derives its modern name.[7] Although German colonial rule had been established in the coastal town

6.   https://www.citypopulation.de/en/cameroon/cities/ accessed on Oct 1, 2020.
7.   During the early colonial period, the entire territory known today as the North West Region was often referred to as the Bamenda Grasslands. Bamenda eventually became an administrative division during the British colonial period including the subdivisions of Mbengwi, Ndop, and Batibo. Today, Bamenda refers specifically to the urban area including the surrounding chiefdoms of Mbatu, Mankon, Nkwen, Mendankwe, Banja and Nsongwa (Fombe 1983:8). Bamenda is also used in a generic sense by people from the North West

of Douala in July 1884, it was not until 1889 that the first Germans arrived the Grasslands, determined to expand German conquest in the hinterlands. Upon their arrival in the Grasslands, the Germans, led by the explorer Dr Eugen Zintgraff, signed a pact of friendship with the powerful king of Bali, Galega I and eventually established a German station in Bali (Chilver 1966). It was from here that the Germans waged a fierce campaign against the other major kingdoms in the region, notably the Mankon and Bafut in 1891 (Chilver 1966; Zintgraff 1895). The German station was eventually transferred to the hills of Mendankwe (Bamenda) in 1902, about 25km northeast of Bali, probably for strategic reasons. It is believed that the highlands of Mendankwe provided greater military advantage to the Germans besides being a relatively cooler area than the plains (Awambeng 1991:4).

The first decade of the 1900s also recorded increased immigration of Hausa-Fulani groups into the Bamenda plateau and sub-regions. These immigrants, especially the Hausa, had maintained a trade route between the Bamenda Grasslands and northern Nigeria for many decades (Nkwi & Warnier 1982). In due course, these migrants established a small encampment near a stream in Mendankwe where their numbers gradually grew. In April 1915, the Germans were forced to flee in the face of impending defeat at the hands of the British from neighbouring Nigeria. The British installed themselves in the former German quarters and once settled, evicted the Hausas out of their settlement. The administrative centre became known as "the station". Allegedly, the early morning call for prayers by the predominantly Muslim Hausa settlers disrupted the peace of the British (Soh 1983:22). The Hausa families then descended to the Bamenda plains and founded another settlement in the Mankon territory of Ntambag which became the nucleus of modern Bamenda. This new settlement was variously known as Hausa village, Abakpa (also called Abakwa), Abakpa-Mankon stranger's Town, Stranger Settlement of Abakpa etc., (Awambeng 1991:5).

Thus, modern Bamenda owes its origins to foreign settlements in the Ntambag area whose initial inhabitants were Hausa immigrants. Trade activities between the Hausa "settlers" and other ethnic groups soon prompted the latter to establish their own settlements beside the Hausa traders. Here, they sold local commodities such as palm oil and kola nuts to the Hausa in return for foreign items such as cattle, brass work and jewellery. It is estimated

---

Region as a marker of their identity, distinct from other populations or persons from different provinces of Cameroon.

that between 1921 and 1923, this settlement had grown to a population of 753, excluding the British settlement at the Bamenda station. The settlement gradually increased with the influx of migrants from Bali, Meta, Wum, Oku, Kom and other chiefdoms from the Grasslands. There is also evidence that soldiers returning from the war and newly converted Christians from the coastal areas preferred to settle in the emerging urban environment rather than return to their villages. However, the decade between 1921 and 1931 witnessed a relatively stable population because the popular migration route was still directed towards the coastal plantations (cf. Ardener 1996; Ardener, Ardener, & Warmington 1960).[8] This period also witnessed a slight decrease in the Hausa population in Abakwa because of the founding of new Hausa settlements in Bamessi, Bamunka and Bamessing – areas now located in the present Ngoketunjia Division, about 45km east of Bamenda.[9]

Nevertheless, Abakwa continued to grow and became a popular centre of commercial activity. By 1934, the population was estimated at about 1300. Abakwa's reputation as an emerging commercial centre continued to spread far and wide, attracting even more migrants from Nigeria (particularly the Igbo, renowned for their entrepreneurial skills). By 1953, the population of the town had grown to over 14,000 and although new neighbourhoods or quarters had emerged, (such as Ntamulung, established in the late 1920s), the majority of the population lived in Abakwa town. By the 1950s, prominent companies such as the United African Company (UAC),[10] the Emmens Textile International, Hollando etc., had established themselves as key commercial actors in Abakwa. The Barclays Bank International also opened its branch in Abakwa in 1955 although its operation was short-lived. None of the above-named companies can be found in Bamenda today, most of them having closed down following the Southern Cameroons' decision to join with French Cameroon to create a federated state in 1961. Nonetheless, the arrival of these prominent commercial actors underscored Bamenda's status as an emerging market in the 1950s and early 1960s (Fombe 1983:19-20).

8. The Germans had set up massive agro-industrial plantations in the coastal territories for the production of raw materials.
9. The influx of people from neighbouring chiefdoms such as Bafut, Bali, Mbatu, Kom, Oku, Nkwen and as far as French Cameroon gradually overwhelmed the initial dominant Hausa population. See Bamenda Provincial Archives, *Hausa town: Bamenda*, File NW/Re/a/1921/1.
10. For a history of the United African Company, see http://en.wikipedia.org/wiki/UAC_Nigeria

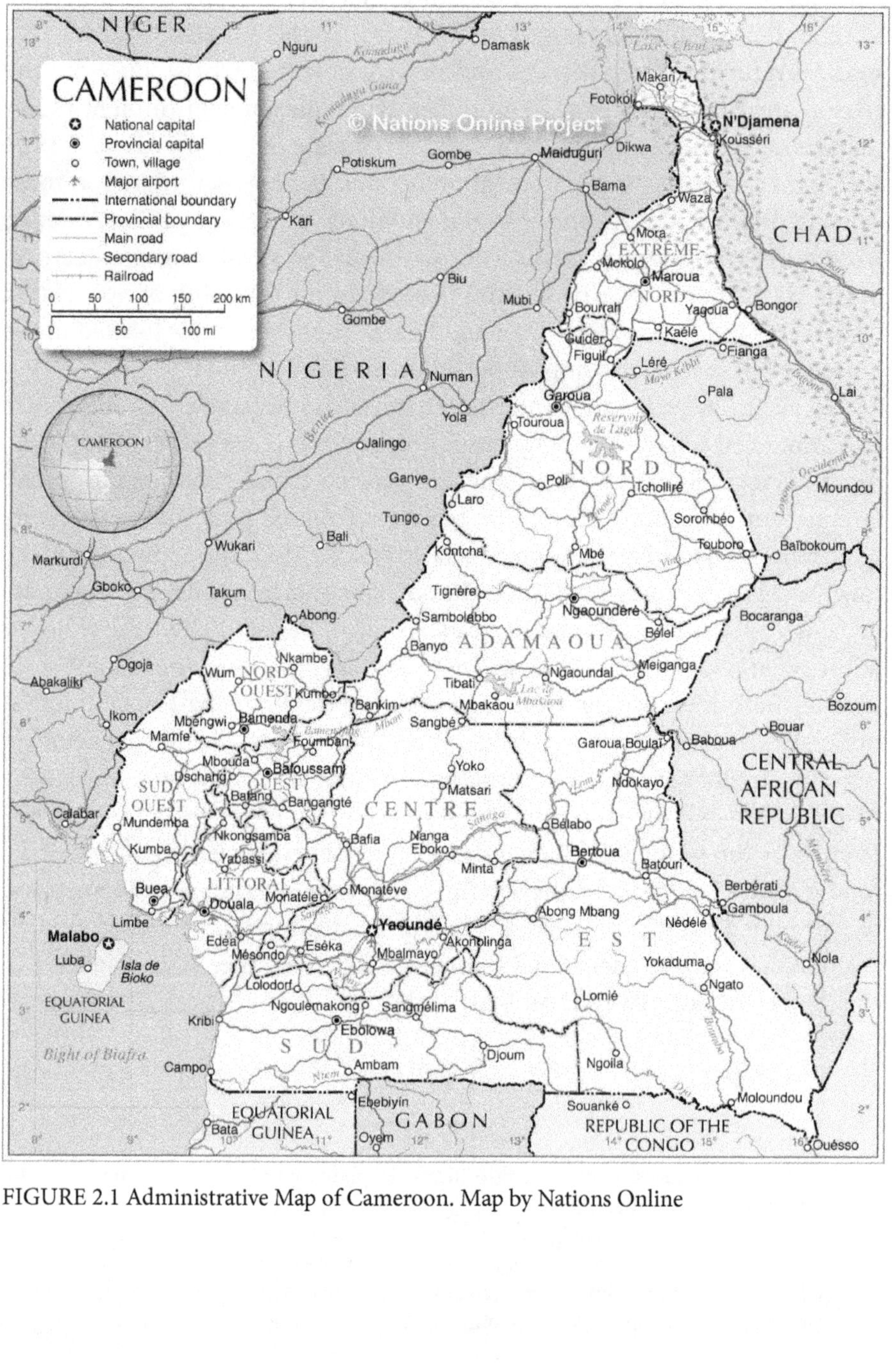

FIGURE 2.1 Administrative Map of Cameroon. Map by Nations Online

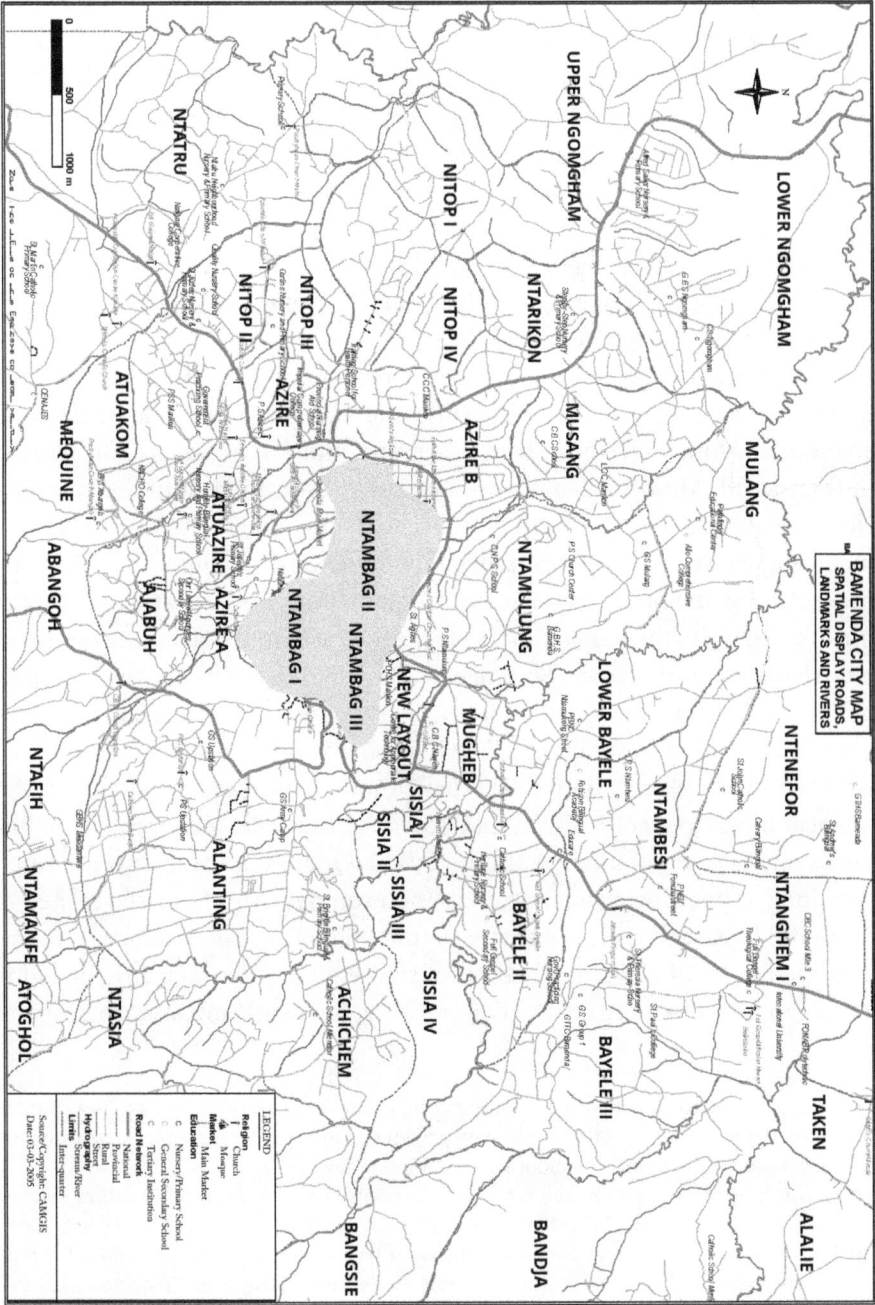

FIGURE 2.2 City of Bamenda showing Ntambag in shaded area.

Today, Ntambag is just one of over 40 neighbourhoods in Bamenda, indic-
ative of how vast the city has grown over the years.[11] The emergence of new
neighbourhoods prompted the renaming of Abakwa to "Old Town" even
though government and local municipal records retain the use of Ntambag.
Old Town therefore is simply the popular name for Abakwa or Ntambag, and
specifically "old" in relation to the newer neighbourhoods that have cropped up
over the past fifty years. Located in the heart of Bamenda, Old Town (Ntambag) is now divided into three municipal wards, namely Ntambag I, II and III
and still remains the densest residential quarter in Bamenda with about 112
people per square kilometre, slightly above the average population density in
the North West Region (see figure 2.2).

Because of its age, Old Town is easily recognisable from its ancient stone
buildings and rusted zinc roofs. While a few buildings are dilapidated and
abandoned, some have been torn down and modern buildings constructed
in their stead. Most households in Old Town, as in the rest of the city have
electricity. About 77.1% of urban households in Cameroon have electricity,
including those obtained from illegal connections. Despite the availability
of electricity, Bamenda experiences frequent cuts, and dissatisfied citizens
nicknamed AES, the American utility company that managed the country's
electricity as *Always Expect Shortage*.[12] Compared to electricity, fewer households in Old Town and Bamenda in general have pipe borne water in their
homes. The national average of urban households with tap water is only 15.3%
while about 34.6% rely on public taps.[13] These public taps are often paid for
by local municipal councils. In Old Town for example, there are five public
taps serving a population of about 15,000. Queues at these taps are often
very long, especially in the mornings and evenings. Another issue related to
household characteristics is access to toilet facilities. The absence of toilets
in some households was the subject of tremendous advocacy among young
people in Old Town during the course of my fieldwork and as such deserves

11.   Prior to the conflict that is currently raging in the Anglophone regions of the country,
       the city of Bamenda was estimated to have grown to about a million people. Most estimates
       today place the population at about half a million or less.
12.   This has worsened over the years with blackouts lasting days and sometimes even up
       to a week. AES-SONEL (2001-2014) was eventually replaced by ENEO in 2014 and serves
       as the country's lone energy supply company. https://www.eneocameroon.cm/index.php/
       en/l-entreprise-notre-notre-historique-en/l-entreprise-notre-notre-historique-histori-
       que-de-l-electricite-au-cameroun-en
13.   These statistics are obtained from a 2004 survey conducted by the National Statistic
       Institute in Yaounde (Government of Cameroon 2005).

to be mentioned. In Cameroon, only 14.1% of urban households have indoor toilets while 42.1% use latrines (pit toilets). The poor maintenance or lack of pit toilets can be at the root cause of communal crisis, particularly in densely populated neighbourhoods where urban planning is either absent or hardly monitored. Such was the case in Old Town when young people carried out toilet inspection campaigns on behalf of the city council (see chapter four).

The average household in Old Town consists of six persons. Most households include parents and their offspring, cousins or other extended relatives. A majority of the young people I encountered were born and raised in Old Town and so were their parents. Even young women who had married and moved out of Old Town still maintained close ties with their families and held membership in voluntary associations in the area. Most households had at least primary level education, although worsening poverty in the community had forced some families to withdraw their children from primary schools.

While other administrative regions in Cameroon have borne the yoke of over three decades of economic crisis, most citizens in the North West Region insist on having suffered disproportionately and have blamed successive Francophone-dominated regimes for their economic and political marginalisation. These claims are not completely unfounded. The Anglophone minority population in Cameroon are conscious that although the former Southern Cameroons was a much smaller economy when they joined the Republic of Cameroon, their predicament was aggravated by the systematic dismantling of West Cameroonian economic infrastructure by the Ahidjo regime. This has been documented extensively by scholars and Anglophone activists (Atanga 1994; Chiabi 1997; Konings & Nyamnjoh 1997, 2003, 2004; Mukong 1990) and consequently, does not deserve an elaborate discussion here. What needs further attention is to highlight how the prolonged economic crisis has been experienced in the North West Region and its implications for young people's identities and coping strategies.

Although the economic crisis began in the mid-1980s, many economists hold that the economy inherited from Ahidjo by the Biya regime was far from healthy (Mbaku 2004). With the introduction of the infamous Structural Adjustment Programme (SAP), economic conditions only worsened, orchestrated by the closure of state-owned enterprises, a few of which were located in the North West Province such as the Wum Area Development Authority (WADA). This translated into the retrenchment of public workers which contributed to growing unemployment that was already a severe problem particularly as government continued to serve as the dominant employer partly due to the absence of a viable indigenous entrepreneurial class (Mbaku 2004:405).[14] Economic conditions were aggravated by about 60% cut in civil servants' salaries, the non-payment of salaries for about three months and finally, a 50% devaluation of the currency in January 1994. These developments affected every aspect of life in the country, particularly healthcare and higher education, which for the first time since independence saw the introduction of fees. Prior to this, the state had provided monthly stipends to university students and many families in rural areas depended on these stipends to supplement their meagre incomes. The abolition of stipends and the introduction of tuition were thus perceived as a double blow to university students and their families who depended on them.

With an economy based predominantly on agriculture, these developments only added misery to a general atmosphere of disillusionment. In fact, over 95% of rural households in the North West Region depend on subsistence agriculture. The economic crisis compelled even civil servants, both urban and rural to resort to subsistence agriculture to supplement their household needs. Popular crops grown in the region include rice, cultivated mainly in the Ndop plain and Menchum valley. Other staple crops consist of maize, plantains, cocoyams, beans, cassava and sweet potatoes.

Industry represents only a puny fraction of economic life in terms of the number of people employed and the quantity of goods produced. Two soap-manufacturing industries are located in Bamenda and dairy manufacturing also counts for a small proportion. A few others are involved in agricultural processing. Other small-scale industrial activities in the region include wood carving, pottery and weaving, and those involved in these activities often supplement their household needs with subsistence agriculture. This notwithstanding, unemployment is rife in both rural and urban areas, but for apparent reasons, unemployment is more conspicuous in urban areas and its consequences more dire, which in turn, has contributed to the growth of the informal sector. According to estimates of the National Statistics Institute in Yaounde, the informal economy in Bamenda registered a slight decline from

---

14.   By the mid-1980s, the public sector had over 250,000 employees with about 80,000 of them working in state-owned enterprises (see Mbaku 2004:405). In the past couple of years, the government has uncovered over 40,000 ghost workers in its payroll. Ghost workers apparently have matriculation numbers but are either dead or resident abroad while monthly salaries are paid into their bank accounts. See BBC News, *Cameroon tracks 'ghost workers'*, http://news. bbc.co.uk/go/pr/fr/-/2/hi/africa/4785721.stm, accessed June 28 2007. Also see - *Cameroon "Ghost" Workers*, Africa Research Bulletin vol. 43, no. 8 2006, p. 17074.

90% in 1996 to about 88.1% in 2001. By every indication, an overwhelming proportion of the economy remains in the hands of informal actors represented largely by young people.

During my fieldwork, Cameroon was frequently caught in the grip of price hikes for fuel, government services[15] and basic commodities, a trend that threw many citizens into deeper despair. The government repeatedly appealed for more sacrifice in anticipation of greater economic benefits in future. Government officials made desperate attempts to explain that the economic difficulties were externally driven because the country had signed a series of multi-lateral agreements with international financial institutions aimed at reaching the completion point of the IMF/World Bank-sponsored programme known as the Highly Indebted Poor Countries (HIPC) initiative. According to the IMF, the HIPC is a debt relief programme intended for countries overburdened with huge external debts.[16] Countries that subscribe to this programme are expected to undertake certain macro-economic policies recommended by the IMF such as the privatisation of state-owned enterprises and in return, enjoy the reduction of their external debt. Such macro-economic policies in the case of Cameroon entailed the need to increase revenue from the non-oil sector which ironically constituted a driving force behind the continuous hike in commodity prices and the introduction of new taxes. Increases in the price of fuel in particular provoked a series of labour strikes across the country which lasted for a week in Bamenda. Fuel hikes also prompted increases in taxi fares, interurban transportation, construction materials, food products and beer.[17]

15.   For example, the cost of fiscal stamps increased by 100% and passports by over 40%. This has only worsened over the years with most citizens unable to procure a passport through a standard application process. Citizens are not only expected to bribe for these services but also have to wait five to seven months before their passports are issued.

16.   "The HIPC Initiative was first launched in 1996 by the IMF and World Bank, with the aim of ensuring that no poor country faces a debt burden it cannot manage. The Initiative entails coordinated action by the international financial community, including multilateral organizations and governments, to reduce to sustainable levels the external debt burdens of the most heavily indebted poor countries. Following a comprehensive review in 1999, a number of modifications were approved to provide faster, deeper, and broader debt relief and to strengthen the links between debt relief, poverty reduction, and social policies. In 2005, to help accelerate progress toward the United Nations Millennium Development Goals (MDGs), the HIPC Initiative was supplemented by the Multilateral Debt Relief Initiative (MDRI). The MDRI allows for 100 percent relief on eligible debts by three multilateral institutions—the IMF, the International Development Association (IDA) of the World Bank, and the African Development Fund (AfDF)—for countries completing the HIPC Initiative process" (see IMF 2006).

17.   See *The Post* No. 0682, Friday, July 8, 2005, p. 9 'Will Cameroonians Accept another Fuel

The strikes yielded little gain and the appeal for a raise in civil servants' salaries met with government intransigence.

However, in May 2006, news spread rapidly that Cameroon had finally reached the completion point of the HIPC programme. For many years, Cameroonians had become versed with the term, HIPC although few knew what it meant or how it worked. Because Biya had repeatedly promised that the economy will improve substantially upon completion of the HIPC programme, Cameroonians therefore received the news with tremendous jubilation. Citizens expected that this would translate into employment opportunities for youths and the reduction of prices for basic commodities. Paul Biya fuelled even greater enthusiasm by delivering a televised speech in which he stated that:

> ...Cameroon will henceforth benefit from substantial external debt relief and cancellation measures. Some of these measures will have an immediate effect. In general, the debt service which was constraining our development will be considerably reduced.... Reaching the completion point is definitely a decisive step towards our economic revival and recovery. This unquestionably creates very bright prospects for the economy.[18]

A few months later, a presidential decree recommended the reduction of import tariffs on rice and fish products but nothing more ensued. The decree was received with disappointment by many citizens, who had expected an elaborate plan from government aimed at alleviating poverty and unemployment. Proof that the completion of the HIPC programme was of little consequence to most Cameroonians was Prime Minister Ephraim Inoni's speech at the National Assembly in November 2006 in which he appealed to young graduates to return to rural areas and to take up farming. Predictably, this increased young people's sense of betrayal and hostility towards the Biya regime.

Precarity and Being Young in Bamenda
To most citizens who grew up in other neighbourhoods in Bamenda, the name "Old Town" evokes very profound negative perceptions about its

Price Increase?' by Bouddih Adams. Also see "Dark Days in Cameroon" by Francis Wache & Azore Opio, a very detailed documentation of the nation-wide strike that rocked the country in February 2008. Postnewsline, March 3, 2008.

18.   The Post, "HIPC Completion Point: President Biya's Address to the Nation" Online article posted on 15 May 2006 and accessed from http://allafrica.com/stories/printable/200605150985. html on 24 May 2006.

residents and the neighbourhood in general. In the popular imagination, Old Town is defined by its knife-carrying youths (often associated with young Hausa men), marijuana smokers, armed bandits, prostitutes and people bereft of any sense of moral composure. When I told a friend that I was conducting research in Old Town, he looked shocked, then laughed out loud and wondered if anything good could come out of Old Town. My friend's opinion echoes the reactions of many other residents of Bamenda, whose negative opinions have fed and continue to reinforce the view that Old Town is a crime-ridden neighbourhood, trapped in a vicious cycle of crime and poverty and poses a permanent danger to polite society.

Indeed, Old Town has had its share of history of social pathology, poverty and crime. There was a time when the community was notorious for its sex workers, bandits and drug addicts. The area in Old Town known as Seven Doors is a stark reminder of this odious past. Nevertheless, the perception remains that young women from Old Town are ostensibly sex workers, sexually available, unreliable and consequently unmarriageable. Its young men on the other hand are believed to be school dropouts, bandits, gangsters and users of banned substances. This sordid image, I contend, served as the unifying force behind young people's activism on a range of issues including hygiene, moral transformation and healthcare interventions.

Bamenda: Politics and Social Life in a Defiant City

Since the mid-1980s, Bamenda has been at the centre of intense political activity. The current ruling party, the Cameroon People's Democratic Movement (CPDM) was not only founded in Bamenda in March 1985, but it was also the cradle of the first opposition party, the Social Democratic Front (SDF) in May 1990. Since then, Bamenda has been known to Cameroonians as the headquarters of opposition politics in the country, for which its citizens take tremendous pride. Since 1990, Bamenda has experienced a series of socio-political turmoil, which began with the launch of the SDF, followed by the ghost town campaigns and subsequently the imposition of a state of emergency in the entire province. These tensions have brought into sharp focus the popular claim that Bamenda citizens are not only conscious of their rights but are also ready and determined to protect them in the face of government oppression. There is a strong basis for this claim. Nowhere else in Cameroon is opposition to the ruling party and government more evident than in the North West Region and Bamenda in particular.[19] Between 1996 and 2016, the SDF dominated the region as the only game in town despite its dwindling popularity in other provinces of the country. For instance, during the 2002 parliamentary and local council elections, the SDF won 20 of the 21 seats allocated to the North West Region. In 2008, it had a total of 22 seats in the national assembly, down from the 48 it held between 1996 and 2002. Its fortunes further declined from 18 seats in 2013 to just 5, following the February 2020 legislative elections.[20] The SDF now remains a shadow of the party that forced the Biya government to introduce democratic reforms in the early 1990s, in part due to the party's desperate attempt to hold on to its status as a national party, rather than be perceived as an Anglophone party, tasked with advancing the Anglophone cause in a Francophone-dominated country.

For over three decades now, Bamenda has been a popular site of Anglophone nationalism, particularly by the Southern Cameroons National Council (SCNC), one of the leading Anglophone nationalist groups that seeks a separate statehood for the Anglophone populations. In general, Anglophone activism is characterised by demands for the rearrangement of state power from the centralised and Francophone-dominated state, which according to the Anglophones, has militated against their interests and aspirations as a distinct political constituency following their decision to join Francophone Cameroon in October 1961.[21]

19.   During the 1992 presidential election, over 85% of the North West Province voted for John Fru Ndi of the SDF whose victory is widely believed to have been stolen.
20.   See the Commonwealth Parliamentary Association http://www.cpahq.org/cpahq/core/parliamentInfo.aspx?Committee=CAMEROON accessed October 19, 2020. Also see "Cameroon holds elections in a time of crisis" https://reliefweb.int/report/cameroon/cameroon-holds-elections-time-crisis accessed 7 Feb 2020.
21.   This position is best summed up by John Ngu Foncha's letter to the UN Secretary General, Boutrous Boutrous Ghali of 4 July 1996 in which he states inter alia: "I was a signatory to the PETITION AGAINST THE ANNEXATION OF THE SOUTHERN CAMEROONS BY LA REPUBLIQUE DU CAMEROUN. I was also on the 9-man delegation from the Southern Cameroons which filed this petition at Your Excellency's High Office in New York. Having served as Prime Minister of the Southern Cameroons and as Vice President of the Federal Republic of Cameroon, I was on that Southern Cameroons Delegation as the leading personality in the process of the unification of the Southern Cameroons and La Republique du Cameroun. As such it is incumbent upon me to facilitate any work by the UN to reach a just and lasting solution to the problem of the annexation of one UN Trust Territory by another. My present submission therefore, is intended to facilitate such an exercise and enable the UN Secretariat to exploit relevant UN documents which clearly show where things went wrong. Of course and naturally, my secondary purpose is to buttress the case by the Southern Cameroons National Council (SCNC) for a separate independence based

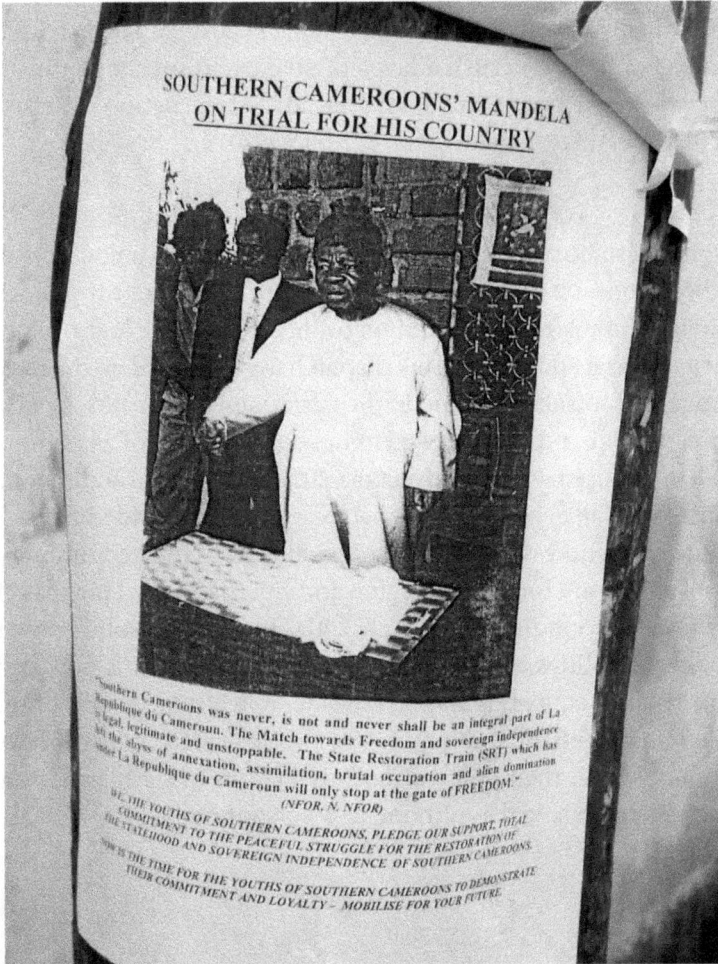

FIGURE 2.3 SCNC Campaign poster on an electric pole on the streets of Bamenda, November 2005. The photographed individual, Nfor Ngala Nfor has been imprisoned in Yaounde since 2017 following his abduction in Nigeria along with 8 other Southern Cameroonian activists/leaders. Photo by author.

While popular demand for the reconfiguration of the state remains widespread in Cameroon, it has a particular trajectory among the Anglophone populations who feel discriminated against and relegated to a second-class citizenship. Government responses to these demands have fluctuated between outright hostility (arrests, torture and imprisonment) and the tendency towards

---

on the UN Charter (Article 76)".

denial. This finally escalated into armed conflict in 2017 following government's repeated use of force to crush a lawyers' strike and subsequently, peaceful demonstration by citizens in September 2017 (International Crisis Group 2019; Willis, McAulay, Ndeunyema, & Angove 2019).

Conclusion

Despite its sociocultural diversity, the Grassfields is a composite region that has been conceived and treated as a "culture area" by anthropologists and government administrators. Common to this region are conceptions of personhood and social adulthood. This chapter has expounded on the meaning of personhood and social adulthood in the Cameroon Grassfields, by explaining how a precolonial and highly patriarchal construction of personhood has become democratised with the advent of Christianity. Social adulthood, a stage in the journey to full personhood is now closely tied to an individual's ability to redistribute one's success or achievements with one's kin or community. These cultural meanings are rooted in a region and city (Bamenda) that has changed radically since its founding in the early 20th century with solid credentials in the domains of politics and business. Although Bamenda is now embroiled in an armed-conflict, its population considerably displaced and diminished, its people remain defiant and hopeful for the day when they will have better control not only over their political destiny, but also, the terms and conditions of their accession to social adulthood and personhood.

CHAPTER THREE

Cultivating Moral Spaces: Rules, Routines and the Constitution of Everyday Life in Young People's Associations

For about sixteen months, my daily routine included planned and spontaneous interaction with young people in Old Town. While Sundays and Wednesdays were devoted to formal meetings, many activities also occurred outside of these formal forums. In this chapter, I show how young people organised their social worlds through participation in voluntary associations. I describe how young people imagined and positioned their subjectivities within their associations and how they gradually transformed them into spaces they defined as "moral". I introduce readers to several associations such as the St Benedict's Youth Association, Ntambag II Youths and Solidarity Youth Movement - which preceded the emergence of the three principal associations that are the focus of this monograph. I detail their memberships, showing how gender as an organising principle became central to the expression of subjectivity and personhood within the Chosen Sisters, Ntambag Brothers and United Sisters. I also discuss what motivated young people to join these associations, the structure and organisation of the associations and their roles in negotiating members' aspirations for personhood and social adult status in the community.

Motivations for Involvement in Youth Associations

The three associations included in this study had a combined membership of about 95 with an average of 25. Membership generally fluctuated because individuals were free to leave at will or could be expelled for unsatisfactory conduct. It is noteworthy that not every registered member was equally active in their association. A member's good standing was measured by the frequency of their attendance at meetings as well as participation in non-meeting activities. So, the question remains – why did some young people seek membership in these associations and how did they negotiate these processes? Two interrelated patterns of gaining admission were identified: recruitment by founders and admission by means of a formal application. In principle, every potential member of each association ought to make a formal application as a condition for admission. While this was necessary, it was not a sufficient cause for admission because other factors were considered. In the Ntambag Brothers Association for instance, there was a preference for young men willing and able to commit to the idea of 'development'. The Chosen Sisters and United Sisters on the other hand, spoke vaguely of their preference for morally upright members; they were interested in members who would not bring the association into disrepute either through gossip or wanton conduct. How an individual attained membership had little or no bearing on his/her potential to hold an elected office in the association.[1]

Motivations for involvement in these associations were diverse. In the pages that follow, I introduce some of the key actors or participants in the study, using their stories to illustrate the motivations for joining and maintaining membership in their respective voluntary associations. Evidently, the founders in all three associations shared a vision and desire to create associations that catered to the needs of young people in Old Town. Founders tended to express motivations rooted in a moralistic desire to engage young people in the community and to change their behavioural patterns. This positioning by the founders resonates strongly with other researchers' findings who have identified young people as an emerging influence or as critical agents for change in African societies (cf. Argenti 2002; de Boeck & Honwana 2000). The founding members were not homogeneous in thought or action but, despite their varying motives, they were all determined to set themselves apart and to chart a new course for young people in their community.

Manka, 22, for instance, was a founding member of the United Sisters, established in 2001. Born and raised in Old Town, she dropped out of secondary school in Form Five,[2] after failing the General Certificate of Education

---

1.   However, there was a perception in the Chosen Sisters that persons who were not born and raised in Old Town were not treated equally as their counterparts. This was difficult to determine beyond mere 'opinion' because one of the complainants was herself an office-holder.

2.   The post-elementary educational system in Anglophone Cameroon is structured into two phases: form one to five makes up the first cycle, where upon completion, students write the General Certificate of Education (GCE) Ordinary Level. Should they succeed, they may proceed to the second cycle (high school) for an additional two years where they write the GCE Advanced level. Success at the advanced level qualifies a student for university education.

(GCE) Ordinary Level in 1998. After leaving school, she enrolled to train as a hairdresser in a local salon, but it remained uncertain if she completed the course. However, during my fieldwork, she had plans to enrol in a nursing programme, which at the time had become a popular career option for many young women in Bamenda, particularly because it was believed to offer an assured path to migration and steady employment abroad in the healthcare sector. Manka had never worked in the formal economy and did not seem particularly concerned about finding a job. As the youngest in a family of five, she benefited from the financial support of her father and older siblings. Despite their generosity, Manka's parents were concerned by her perceived lack of focus. Thus, it was in part, due to her parents' admonition and to the Chosen Sisters' trailblazing presence in the community that Manka and four friends founded the United Sisters in 2001.

> Before I became a member of this association, my parents complained a lot about my behaviour. When I had nothing to do at home, I'll hang out with my friends and sometimes, we found ourselves walking aimlessly in the neighbourhood. I'm proud to tell you that with advice from our elder sisters in the quarter and from fellow friends in our meeting, many young girls have stopped such behaviour.

Susan, 21, another founding member of the United Sisters suggested that "it was deemed improper for young girls to live in the quarter without an association of their own. It was like having chicks without mother hen." According to Susan, they were motivated by the quest to fight against social ills in their community, some of which were committed by their peers: "we needed to enlighten ourselves on the dangers of bad behaviour, we had to come together to educate ourselves on AIDS, STDs and other issues."

Once the associations had become operational, its founders then embarked upon a recruitment campaign in their neighbourhood, seeking individuals whom they perceived as suitable or in accord with the vision of their respective associations. This was often an idiosyncratic and selective process, occasionally based on the preferences of particular founding individuals. The trend was to invite persons from one's circle of friends. Ambe, 24, for instance falls in the category of individuals recruited by founders. Born and raised in Limbe, a coastal town in the South West Region of Cameroon, Ambe arrived Bamenda in 2004. He worked at a local hotel in Old Town until he was laid off with five others without pay. Ambe eventually join the NBA by invitation from Aaron, a founding member of the association:

> You know, we boys were so disorganised in the quarter. Aaron came to me
> one day and talked to me about Ntambag Brothers and asked if I would
> like to join. I accepted without any hesitation. He told me it was not good
> to be by oneself. I thought that was a smart idea because I didn't have
> a lot of friends, especially as I was new to the area. I thought to myself,
> what if some misfortune befalls me, what would I do, where would I seek
> help? So when Aaron spoke to me, I saw the importance of being part
> of a group of young men. Upon fresh reflections, I think someone like
> myself who came from afar definitely needed to be part of a group and
> I'm glad the opportunity came up.

Dolly, 22, joined the United Sisters soon after it was founded. Although she
lived in Ntamulung, a neighbouring quarter, she had strong ties to Old Town
where she had lived as a child. Dolly was recruited by Manka, her childhood
friend and neighbour:

> Manka told me they had just formed a group in the quarter. She said it
> was a good idea to belong to a quarter group. I think the association was
> not up to a month old. She said the group's objective was to combat some
> of the immoral lifestyles among young girls. Hmm, she said the group
> wanted to fight against things like abortion, sexual promiscuity and many
> other things. At that time, Charlotte's elder sister who's now in Germany
> used to advise us. Even me, my life has changed a lot since I joined the
> group. Every Sunday, we used to roam about in town and if someone
> invited us to have a drink, we'd stay. Since I became a member, I've tried
> to change. Besides, the only place I go on Sundays is to church and then
> to our meeting in the afternoon. There's no time to roam around town.

A second category of members included those who sought admission on
their own accord. Musa, 30, the lone Muslim in the NBA at the time, joined the
association because of his desire to participate in development initiatives. He
was convinced that the young men who made up the NBA were determined
to bring 'development' to Old Town. Musa was not new to associational life;
he had been the leader of the defunct Muslim Youth Association (MYA) in
Old Town, a group that aimed to mobilise young Muslims to take part in
community activities. As a strong proponent of development, Musa was keen

to see his ideas embraced in the NBA.

Like Musa, Jessica, 24, was not new to associations. She was an active member of Mother Care, an association of traders based in Meta Quarters, Bamenda. She joined the United Sisters because of what she described as their 'cooperation' and demonstration of maturity:

> I decided to become a member because of the cooperation that exists among the sisters. They are united and I really admired that. I decided to join after learning about some of the activities carried out by the group and although I already had another association, I decided to apply to become a member.

Jessica's situation was somewhat unique. Her younger sister had been a member of the association until her untimely death in 2004. Her loss brought severe grief to her family and the United Sisters of which she had been an active member. A year after her death, the sisters organised a memorial in her honour which included the laying of flowers at her grave at the St Joseph's Cathedral cemetery and a visit to her parents' home, gestures that her family found profoundly comforting. Jessica was deeply moved by this demonstration of solidarity and although she did not admit it, these events likely played a role in her decision to join the association.

Chantal, 34, on the other hand, joined the Chosen Sisters because she did not want to "alienate" herself from her peers in the community. After completing her first degree from the University of Dschang and having lived in the South West Region for several years, she returned home to Old Town and felt a huge gulf had grown between herself and her less educated friends:

> I think they looked at me differently or that's how I felt. I had been away for many years and knew it was going to be a bit difficult to relate with my peers as I did before I left for university. I was not happy about the situation and when I learnt about the Chosen Sisters, I decided to join. In fact, I felt obliged to join because this was a quarter issue and if I didn't join, I would be alienating myself further from my less educated friends.

Although the above cases reveal only a fraction of the reasons why young people were motivated to join voluntary associations, these motivations depended on individuals' socioeconomic circumstances and aspirations. While certain individuals were motivated by the idealistic notion of pursuing a crusade against youth immorality, others simply desired the companionship of their peers. Major reasons advanced included the fear of alienation, the desire to participate in community development and of course, others desired the socioeconomic and emotional support that comes with membership in such associations. These motivations can only make further sense if one understands the nature, structure and activities of these voluntary associations and why the newer associations eventually enjoyed more legitimacy than their defunct predecessors. To achieve this, we will first take a cursory journey into the origins of youth associations in Old Town, Bamenda.

The Origins of Youth Associations in Old Town

Before 1990, religious youth associations were the most popular youth clubs besides the youth wings of hometown associations. Religious associations were unique in the sense that unlike ethnic associations, they mobilised persons of different ethnic backgrounds, class and gender. An example of such a group was the St Benedict's Youth Association (SBYA), a Catholic youth club affiliated with the St Joseph's Cathedral parish. The SBYA was considered the pioneer of youth associations in Old Town, partly because many young people involved in the voluntary associations today were members of the SBYA until its disbandment in 1999. The SBYA consisted of young women and men between 15 and 35 tasked with evangelising fellow youths and to mobilise young people's labour for the mission. Members of this group were often called upon to clean the mission premises, including the cemetery. They also animated at church functions where their singing and artistic talents were highly cherished. Simon, 32, a former president of the SBYA and founding member of the NBA recalled his days in the SBYA:

> There was mutual understanding amongst us.... When we had manual work at the mission, everybody showed up and our activities were carried out efficiently. St Benedict also promoted evangelisation in the neighbourhoods and we even succeeded to attract some Muslim youths to worship with us.

The SBYA held its meetings at Mami Lucia's house, a highly respected senior lady in the neighbourhood who opened her doors to the Chosen Sisters and United Sisters associations after the SBYA disbanded in 1999.[3]

---

3.   The SBYA, along with other associations were dissolved by the Catholic youth chaplain

If we recall that individuals or subjects can occupy multiple subject positions, some of which they define for themselves and others which are defined for them, then the SBYA epitomises an example of the sort of subject position defined for its members. Young people in Old Town on the other hand defined their subjectivities as "youth" outside the circles of religious supervision by creating and setting their own agenda. The community of Old Town had at least two popular clubs, including a notoriously informal group of young men in their twenties and thirties whose primary activity consisted in organising grand annual parties to which they invited their girlfriends. The other popular youth associations were the Ntambag II Youths (N2Y) and the Solidarity Youth Movement (SYM). These clubs may be understood as constituting Old Town's youthscapes in the sense that it was within these spaces that young people constructed and performed their subjectivities as "youth" in contrast to the subjectivities they now advance. Both the N2Y and SYM aimed to promote solidarity and conviviality among young people in the community. N2Y's membership consisted of young people in their twenties and thirties and drew its membership from the southern quarter of Old Town whilst SYM included teenagers, attracting members principally from the northern side of Old Town, especially around the Hausa quarter. Although SYM still exists today, it is more or less nominal, whilst N2Y disbanded in 1999. The collapse of the N2Y created a vacuum in the southern neighbourhood of Old Town, which was subsequently filled by the emergence of the Chosen Sisters in the summer of 1999.

During its existence, the N2Y's membership consisted of both young men and women and its activities were specifically defined as *social*[4] to complement the religious focus of the SBYA of which most of them were also members. Although the N2Y existed for less than two years, its demise was allegedly precipitated by the excesses of the young men who ran the affairs of the association. According to Sirri, a former member of the club:

> The boys who ran the group were irresponsible and embezzled the association's monies. You know, every Sunday, each member contributed 100

of the St Joseph's Cathedral parish in favour of a single youth association now known as the St Joseph's Youth Association.

4. The concept of social groups as employed in Bamenda refers to voluntary associations that combine a range of activities such as rotating and savings schemes (popularly known as *njangi*), with the primary motive of providing an environment in which people can socialise and extend their social capital.

francs into a *sinking fund*, that is, a fund from which we could withdraw money in the event of some ill-fortune. But we realised with time that the executive members, most of whom were young men, used the association's money to buy beer at a popular off-licence. In fact, we discovered that after each Sunday meeting, the boys headed off to a certain off-licence and drank themselves out but we didn't know they were using our money until much later. Members were enraged when they realised this and immediately called the executive to account. In order to stem further embezzlement, the association opened an account at the Bamenda Police Credit Union based here in Old Town. No one knows what happened to the account after the association was dissolved. But I'm saddened to tell you that the only female executive member who was the social secretary also escaped with the association's finances. During a party we organised to celebrate the first anniversary of the association, she was responsible for collecting money raised from "cutting of the cake". She allegedly ran away with some of the money on the grounds that she was protecting it from the greedy male executive members. This angered so many innocent members of the association and this contributed to its collapse.

Although the embezzlement of funds precipitated the demise of N2Y, the association suffered from poor attendance at its weekly meetings. According to Sirri, it seemed the association was doomed to fail because at its inception, they encountered difficulties finding a suitable venue for their meetings:

We had a problem finding a good venue because the landlord whose house we used for free suddenly wanted us to start paying rents which we couldn't afford. The fact that the venue was changed discouraged a lot of members and some people began to withdraw. A kind woman permitted us to use her living room for our meetings. Two of her daughters were members of the association but most of the time, they failed to attend, preferring to sit outside and pretending to be uninterested in our activities. This snobbish attitude angered a lot of members, some of whom withdrew specifically because of their conduct. They could not understand why the girls behaved the way they did despite their mother's support of the association.

Meanwhile, an informal group of young men, most of whom also doubled as members of N2Y also ran a parallel group whose activities were largely seasonal. Known as the Yorkaaz, the young men became famous for their extravagant end-of year parties. Aaron, 31, recalled the arbitrary origins of the name: "we chose that name because we wanted to be like New Yorkers, you know, but with a difference, with an Old Town touch. That's why we spelled Yorkaaz the way we did." Aaron and five former members agreed that amongst the names that were proposed, Yorkaaz was overwhelmingly adopted because it was considered trendy to associate with the city of New York. The Yorkaaz placed premium on expensive clothes, shoes and fine haircuts. Remarkably, their obsession with fashion and emphasis on the public display of expensive clothing as a sign of achievement is reminiscent of Charles Didier Gondola's (1999) depiction of the *Sapeurs* in Congo. Yorkaaz desperately sought recognition and visibility and seemed to enjoy being in the spotlight in Old Town. Carlson, 30, a former Yorkaaz and now one of the executive members of NBA spoke of the *palmaresse*[5] or prestige they gained by throwing lavish parties:

> We simply wanted to win prestige and we felt at the time that indulging in such activities was a sign of maturity. We wanted to be the envy of our community and to distinguish ourselves from other young men who could not meet our standards. We also wanted to raise our prestige among the ladies.

Members of this group were encouraged to adopt trendy nicknames by which they were known and introduced at their events. "I remember we had some interesting nicknames like Bao, Turbo, L'ambassadeur and many more," Carlson said excitedly. When the first party was organised in 1995, most of the Yorkaaz were in their early twenties and some were university students. Aaron confessed that he tricked his family into giving him money to contribute towards Yorkaaz parties: "it was easy to get money in those days. I was still a student at the University of Yaoundé, so it was easy to visit a relative and tell them I didn't have tuition and they would give me about 50,000FCFA (about US$100) which I used to pay my dues for the party. As for the remainder, I would buy a new pair of shoes and designer shirts." When the first party was organised in 1995, members of the group contributed 5000FCFA (US$10) each and held the event at the Babadju Cultural Hall near Mami Lucia's house.

---

5.   A domesticated version of the French word, *palmaresse*. In its original version, the word refers to an award or prize list but in the English-speaking regions of Cameroon, it refers to prestige acquired through the demonstration of one's prowess in sports, music and participation in popular culture.

Carlson recounted the details of the inaugural party a decade later during one of our afternoon chats:

> Those were good days. But to tell you the truth, the party created problems for some of our friends. You know, we wanted to raise our *palmaresse* in the eyes of our girls so we decided not to invite ladies from Old Town. Everyone was shocked, yeah but we did it. Everyone had to 'import' and that was an issue because some of our friends had chicks in the neighbourhood. I still remember the MC announcing that there were no girls from Old Town present in the hall but guess what; Simon's girlfriend was outside, and he had a child with that lady. She was outside yelling, struggling to get in but the bouncers prevented her. I think she heard that Simon had 'imported' another woman from somewhere. It became a huge problem afterwards because even the MC knew Simon's girlfriend. Those were crazy days.

The perceived success of the first party inspired the Yorkaaz to dream even bigger as they sought to host the next extravaganza at Ayaba Hotel, a leading three-star hotel in Old Town. The following year, the Yorkaaz increased their contributions to 25,000FCFA (US$50) per member and staged and even more ostentatious party.

Lavish parties were not unique to the Yorkaaz in the 1990s. Remarkably, the organising of extravagant parties had gradually established itself as a coming of age ritual among young people, particularly students who had written the GCE Ordinary and Advanced levels. Each high school in the Bamenda metropolis distinguished itself by adopting aristocratic names such as, Barons, Dukes, Ambassadors and Masters in their competition for prestige and visibility. Evidently, the Yorkaaz were simply partaking in what had become a popular cultural trend which eventually faded when parents lodged protests with civil authorities. Ironically, this trend emerged at the peak of Cameroon's economic crisis, exacerbated by the devaluation of the local currency by 50% (World Bank 2012). Predictably, the worsening economic crisis had implications for young people's subjectivities as they sought to establish themselves as social adults.

The associations that made up the "youthscape" of Old Town in the late 1990s and early 2000s embodied subjectivities its members defined as *youthful*. The study of youthscapes, Maira and Soep (2004) remind us, can shed light on the social and political implications of young people's responses to globalising forces. This is evident in young men's domestication of foreign names (New

York for instance), titles (barons and dukes) and competing for visibility and prestige as a mode of acquiring cultural capital (cf. Fuh 2020). A decade later, many of the young men who had proudly positioned themselves as trendy Yorkaaz recalled with amusement how far they had come as they re-positioned themselves as development actors and morally upright citizens. Thus, the above narrative not only has deepened our understanding of the origins of young people's clubs in Old Town, but more importantly, established the background for why the associations that eventually emerged in the 2000s became such highly valued platforms for the negotiation of individual and collective social adulthood and the construction of new subjectivities and personhood. While continuities may be observed in the contemporary associations, it is note-worthy that the Chosen Sisters, United Sisters and Ntambag Brothers exhibit significant ruptures from the associations of old. As will become evident, besides their internal structures, these associations emphasised the variables of gender and seniority as key organising principles in the conduct of their affairs. To understand these issues better, I introduce each of the associations in their historical order while exploring the factors that led to their founding, objectives, rules, routines and internal processes.

The Chosen Sisters

The Chosen Sisters association was founded in 1999 by a group of 16 young women, some of whom had been members of SBYA and the defunct N2Y. Although the birth of the association was the collective effort of many impassioned young women, Sirri was the brain behind their efforts. Born and raised in Old Town where she spent most of her life, she left at the age of 20 to study at the Universities of Buea and Dschang respectively between 1995 and 2000, graduating with a postgraduate diploma in environmental sciences. Sirri was by far, one of the most educated members of the Chosen Sisters and through the years became an inspiration to many young women in the community. Evidence of this was her selection by the United Sisters as a patroness of the association. Although she was single and had no children of her own, she had the responsibility of looking after her niece, a task she found extremely challenging on account of her limited income. Having searched in vain for a job commensurate with her qualifications, Sirri eventually settled in 2003 for a position as an administrative assistant in a small NGO with irregular funding, a factor that undermined her ability to provide for herself and little niece. If not for the support of her mother, who ran a make-shift restaurant, things would have been a lot worse.

Despite her limited income, Sirri rented her own room in a compound about half a kilometre from her mother's house. By renting her own space, she communicated not only her independence, but also her ability to provide for her own needs, qualities that underscored her determination to achieve social adulthood. Her studio apartment lived up to its definition in every sense and more; it was her bedroom, living room, kitchen and study. The floor was covered with an old plastic carpet and a queen size bed that took up about two-thirds of the room, leaving just a small passage for movement. On the wall opposite the door was a collection of her handbags and below, about 10 pairs of shoes, lined out symmetrically. Beside her bed was a 15-inch statue of the Virgin Mary with an inscription at the feet - Queen of Peace. Hanging from the statue was a rosary and scapular, obvious symbols of her attachment to the Catholic Church and devotion to Mary in particular. She was also an active choir member at the St. Joseph's Cathedral parish. Evidently, it would be an understatement to say that Sirri was simply a founding member of the Chosen Sisters; she provided the ideological support needed to spur the association into life. By Sirri's account, the immediate push that led to the formation of the association came from witnessing the activities of the Women's Day[6] in March 1999:

> Some of us had gone to the Commercial Avenue to observe the Women's Day celebration. The event was a huge success, especially the march-past. Everyone was moved by what they saw and we started talking about the possibility of creating our own association in order to participate at future celebrations.

In March 1999, Sirri rallied a few friends to a preliminary meeting during which they brainstormed about the future association. They decided to call it, Chosen Sisters:

> Not everyone present at that meeting eventually became a member. We agreed that membership should not be open to anyone below 20. We didn't see ourselves mixing with teenagers. Most of our members are in their mid-twenties and thirties. We didn't place an upper limit for

6.   The International Women's Day is celebrated every 8 March. In Cameroon, the event is marked by elaborate activities throughout the country. Because of the pomp and pageantry with which the event is celebrated, it is almost unofficially, a public holiday in Cameroon (See Pommerolle & Ngaméni 2015; Röschenthaler 2015).

membership even though we don't have any persons above 40. […] You know, you can't choose your biological sisters. They are born into your family. You have no choice or control over this and whether you like it or not, they remain your sisters. But we wanted to choose people we could deal with. We wanted people who we could trust and work with, people who were passionate about similar concerns. These issues made us call our association Chosen Sisters because we finally could exercise the right to choose our social sisters.

In August 1999, the association was officially registered with the civil authorities as a social group, with the following stated objectives:
- To help disabled children in and around our quarter.
- To fight against prostitution and sexual promiscuity.
- To fight against unwanted pregnancies and abortion.
- To guide and help each other when need be.
- To improve on our lifestyles and standards.
- To carry out manual activities in and around our quarter at least twice a year.
- To patronize members in business.
- To enhance and promote the spirit of love and solidarity amongst our members.[7]

Elaborating on these objectives, Sirri recalled:

We wanted to fight against such evils as abortion, promiscuity among youths and to help the underprivileged. You know Old Town has a bad image. Once you tell someone you live in Old Town, they just have this terrible impression about you. We wanted to change that impression and that's what we're struggling to achieve.

The Chosen Sisters scored their first major success in 2000 when they won the first prize at the Women's Day parade. The news was received with much fanfare amongst community members because the award validated the sisters' claim that something good had finally come out of Old Town. Although the association's fame led to a surge in membership, the numbers fluctuated between 28 and 35.

---

7.   Constitution of the Chosen Sisters, Old Town.

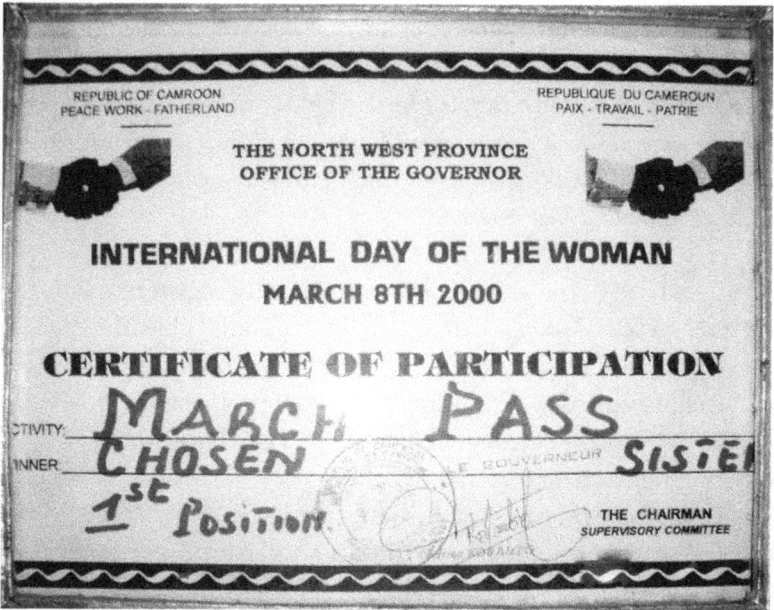

FIGURE 3.1 A plaque, awarded to the Chosen Sisters of Old Town for emerging first at the Women's Day parade in Bamenda. Photo by author.

FIGURE 3.2 A cross section of the Chosen Sisters of Old Town at the Women's Day parade in Bamenda, March 8, 2005. Photo by author

In 2020, its membership stood at 24 with an age range between 35 and 54. A few of its members participate remotely in the affairs of the association – two from Limbe and Dschang and two members are now resident in the USA. Unlike in the 2000s when they met weekly at a fixed venue, the Chosen Sisters now meet bi-weekly, rotating between members' homes. Most of them are now mothers, preoccupied with raising their children, meeting obligations to kin, friends and most importantly to the association.

The United Sisters

The United Sisters was a younger variant of the Chosen Sisters. In many respects, the latter served as a model for the United Sisters and its emergence was inevitable, in part because the Chosen Sisters admitted only members older than 20. In practice, the Chosen Sisters recruited members in their mid-20s and older. The United Sisters officially came into existence in November 2002 with a founding membership of 25 with an average age of 23. Sirri's 22-year-old niece, Angela, was one of the founding members. Unlike her aunt, Angela had dropped out of secondary school and unexpectedly became a mother in her teenage years. She expressed the objectives of the United Sisters as follows:

> We saw what our elder sisters were doing and felt that it was irresponsi-
> ble not to form our own association. In our community, young girls are
> ignorant about a lot of things and we realised that some of us can learn
> from each other. The group helps to sensitize members about AIDS,
> fights against prostitution, abortion and other social ills. This is why we
> created the group, so that we can address these issues amongst ourselves.

Manka, a school dropout and Angela's friend equally felt the need for an association that catered to the specific needs of their age group:

> Even though we admired the Chosen Sisters, not everyone felt they could
> be admitted to the association or would feel free, because you know, they're
> our big sisters. But we felt that we have to follow their examples because
> they had already led the way and all we needed to do was to follow.

The association met every Sunday and flourished for many years, defying the predictions of their male peers in the neighbourhood who were convinced the association would not survive a month. "The boys said we could not run a meeting. Some said we were wasting our time and I remember they also said similar things about the Chosen Sisters but see where they are now. Despite our difficulties, we are succeeding but some people criticise us for preaching what we don't practise."

FIGURE 3.3 Members of the United Sisters with the author in front of their meeting venue after a regular Sunday meeting. April 2006. Photo by author.

In 2010, the United Sisters split due to internal disagreements. All but one of the founding members left and created a new association - the Humble Sisters of Old Town. The new association retains the objectives, social norms and practices as the mother association with a stable membership of about 20. Most of them are now in their mid and late 30s.

The Ntambag Brothers' Association (NBA)

Unlike the previous two groups, the NBA was a male-exclusive association and historically, the youngest of the three. However, it had the largest membership (42) of all three associations. Furthermore, the NBA positioned itself as the leading association tasked with "developing" the community of Old Town. This vision and version of who they are stands in stark contrast to the objectives of the association at its founding. According to Aaron, one of the leading members, it started off as a social group, similar to the women's associations:

> We were attending the wake-keeping (sic) of Simon's mother. You know, it is the custom in our quarter to make financial contributions when a member of the quarter dies. Each household or family contributes something and we keep an exercise book that contains a list of names and their respective contributions. The money is donated to the bereaved family to help with funeral expenses. So, while contributions were going on, someone suggested that if we had our own association, it would be easier for us to organise activities to support our bereaved friend.

In the western Grasslands of Cameroon, bereavement is a communally shared experience and constitutes one of the many practices that highlight cultural conceptions of personhood and interdependence. Simply stated, although funerals are public spectacles, they also privately measure one's social capital. Aaron and his friends claimed they felt compelled to create their own association, after appreciating the unique role associations could play at such events. They admired in particular, the moral and material support Manka, Simon's younger sister had benefited from the United Sisters of which she was a prominent member.

A few weeks after the funeral, Aaron and his friends scheduled a meeting at Capo's Relaxing Club, an off-licence owned by one of their friends where discussions ensued about their vision for a new men's association:

> I think 15 people or so attended the first meeting. The first few months were difficult. Some people were not consistent at all. They would show up this Sunday and only resurface two or three Sundays later although everyone knew we had scheduled our meetings for Sundays. We wanted to limit our members to 40 because we knew that once we opened our doors, many people would like to become members. We also discussed the need to limit or prevent certain individuals from becoming members, especially certain Hausa boys who are notorious for their violent behaviour.

In many towns and villages of the Grasslands, the ethnic term, Hausa tends to be used synonymously with Muslim, mainly because most Hausa practice Islam. Hausa quarters throughout the Grasslands are generally perceived by non-Hausa populations as violent and dangerous, perceptions that have

influenced relations between the two communities. Although the NBA originally sought to exclude certain identified ethnic Hausa men, the association
eventually opened its doors to several Hausa/Muslim residents who remain
active members to date.

The nascent association had hardly existed for a couple of weeks when
Aaron and his friends realised they needed a bigger and quieter venue. Alfred,
a fellow member promptly came to the rescue. He invited them to use Subi
Hall, a then-ramshackle building his family owned which also served as the
exclusive venue for the rehearsals of the famous Subi Dance Group. The next
phase entailed clarifying the objectives of the association. Apparently, most of
the founders had envisaged a "social group" akin to the women's associations
but Carlson proposed the inclusion of "development" as a central objective of
the association. Eventually, the constitution sounded similar to the Chosen
Sisters' in its moralizing tone and spirit:

> The association in question whose objective is to bring together boys to
> fight against social ills in our society; like bribery and corruption, ban-
> ditry and to sensitize the youths about the ramifications of HIV/AIDS.
> The association is aimed at sharing both in times of joy and sorrow of its
> members. Human investment is also one of its major objectives.[8]

The last line about "human investment" expressed its vision for an association where members embraced the development of the community as a
primary responsibility of the "boys". The members also emphasised the fact
that the association was "apolitique (sic) or non-political", concerned that
divergent political views would derail the developmental aspirations of the
nascent association. In one of my discussions with Carlson, he reflected on
the objectives of the association, providing further insights on why moral
issues ranked supreme:

> We wanted to be involved in the development of our community. To
> me, development is anything that brings positive change to the face of
> Old Town. As you know, people are prejudiced against Old Town as a
> neighbourhood of thieves, prostitutes and social failures. In my opinion,
> a group of youths devoted to development can shake things around here,
> we can contribute towards a moral transformation of the community and

8.   Constitution of the Ntambag Brothers Association, Old Town, 2004.

mobilise other young people to care about the things we consider dear
to us, changing public opinion about Old Town.

FIGURE 3.4 Members of the Ntambag Brothers pose with ethnographer, Divine Fuh in front
of their meeting venue. April 2007. Photo by Divine Fuh

Evidently, the NBA's objectives were not radically different from those of
their female peers. What eventually differentiated them from the latter was
the NBA's insistence on using the term "development" as a marker of distinction. However, if we understand the term "development" to mean concerted
efforts aimed at improving the human condition, then the female associations
were equally doing "development" but they did not express their activities
in such language. Both female associations emphasised choral music and
invested in the purchase of musical equipment (e.g., drums) to enhance their
choral singing. Within the context of the gendering of sociocultural life in
Old Town, the female associations' musical ventures were perceived by their
male counterparts as an expression of their femininity. The NBA on the other
hand, distinguished themselves by imposing a compulsory sport regime on its
members (football every Saturday morning at the premises of the St Joseph's

Cathedral). According to this logic, drums were to the female associations what football jerseys were to the NBA.

In 2018, the Ntambag Brothers finally achieved their long-standing vision of transforming their association from a regular "social group" to a development-oriented organisation. On November 25, 2018 its members voted a new constitution that rebranded not only the association's name – Ntambag Brothers Integrated Development Common Initiative Group (CIG) but also refined its objectives to include "Love, Unity, Peace and Development".[9]

The brothers also affirmed and elaborated on three categories of membership – emphasising in particular the global dimensions of its activities by including a category for "diaspora members". Since the late 2000s, over a dozen of its founding members have migrated to Europe, North America and the Middle East. Despite their physical distance from "home", diaspora members are expected to meet their financial obligations to the association. Now composed of 126 paid members with 76 of these based in Old Town, the NBA has not only grown exponentially compared to the female associations, but it has also taken on even grander projects (see next chapter). The association also takes pride in its transnational status in a city that has been globalising for decades.

Structure and Organisation of Young People's Associations

Besides the similarities of their objectives and activities, all three associations shared a similar structure. Gender differentiation and seniority were two salient organising principles. There existed a distinction not only between male and female associations, but also, between junior and senior associations. While this applied wholly to the female associations, the same could not be said of the male associations because the Able Brothers that would have counted as juniors to the Ntambag Brothers, had disbanded prior to my arrival in the community. In this section, I elaborate on how the associations were internally organised, how they financed their activities, and what a regular meeting looked like.

Besides the key markers of gender and seniority, the associations shared similar organisational structures. An elected executive of six or nine persons steered the affairs of each association. Executive offices included the president, vice-president, secretary, treasurer, financial secretary, organising or social

---

9.   Constitution of the Ntambag Brothers Integrated Development CIG, adopted in November 2018.

secretary and a chief whip. In the female associations, a choir coordinator was charged with teaching new songs and coordinating singing during private or public functions. The NBA had a four-man disciplinary committee to which exceptional cases of indiscipline were referred. In addition, the NBA had a sports coordinator with an assistant whose functions were to oversee football activities every Saturday morning. Because of its frequent involvement in manual labour and sport, the NBA also kept a first-aid box, contributed by its members, whose discharge was the prerogative of a health coordinator.

Each association had at least three patrons or patronesses. The United Sisters for example had three patrons and three patronesses and in November 2005, the association co-opted me as a patron. The NBA on the other hand enjoyed the patronage of two men and a female health worker. Patrons and patronesses served as advisers and were consulted on important matters affecting the association. They were also expected to attend meetings at their convenience and to contribute financially or materially towards the well-being of the associations. The selection of patrons was subject to debate and approved by the general assembly. This principle seemed to have been compromised when leading members of the United Sisters conspired to co-opt a patron who was overwhelmingly resented by most members. At issue was the appointment of Barnabas, a member of the NBA who was believed to be of questionable moral standards. He had allegedly been at the centre of a nasty love triangle between two members of the association. The matter was resolved when the members overwhelmingly voted to relieve Barnabas of his position. The NBA also grappled with the unexpected demands of one of their patrons, a businessman in his 60s who reportedly preferred to join the association as an ordinary member rather than as a "patron". His application was rejected on the grounds that he was no longer a "youth".

Among the Chosen and United Sisters, membership was formally acquired upon the complete payment of an annual fee of 1500FCFA and 2000FCFA for returning and new members respectively. The NBA charged a slightly higher amount –2500FCFA and 3000FCFA for returning and new members respectively. Upon admission, members were expected to learn the association's anthem by rote (in the female associations) and for the NBA to make the following pledge:

I pledge to Ntambag Brothers my Association
To always be faithful, loyal and honest,
To always serve Ntambag Brothers with all my strength
To defend and protect her unity

And to always uphold her honour and glory where ever the need may arise.
To abide by all the rules and regulations guiding Ntambag Brothers
To always be present and on time in any activities of Ntambag brothers
Upon my honour I stand by this pledge
So help me God.[10]

An individual could lose his/her membership by withdrawing from the association or by dismissal. Whereas a handful of dismissals were carried out by the sisters, the NBA had lost only a couple of members who opted to withdraw on their own accord.

Besides the Chosen Sisters which met on Wednesday evenings (6-8 p.m.), both the NBA and United Sisters held their meetings on Sundays from 12-2 p.m. and 2-4 p.m. respectively. Latecomers were often fined a fee of 50FCFA and punctuality was always an issue of ferocious debate in all three associations. Members who failed to show up for communal activities also faced the possibility of a fine or public rebuke.

During the early stages of my fieldwork with the Ntambag Brothers, I was struck by a practice which afforded each member an opportunity to chair a meeting. This operated in a rotational fashion, permitting every member to chair a meeting until each person had had their turn.[11] I was appointed to chair a session just after my fourth visit which I politely declined on the grounds that I was still new and still familiarising myself with the group's culture.

In all the associations, each meeting began and concluded with a prayer. Anyone could be invited to offer a prayer, Muslim or Christian. I was invited at least once in each of the associations to offer an introductory or closing prayer. Once the introductory prayer was over and members had taken their seats, the chief whip would place a bowl or plate at the threshold of the door. Members who arrived after this were considered late.

Sometimes, the president of the association or his/her vice delivered a brief welcome address and then invited the chairperson of the day to disclose the agenda. The chairperson then read out the meeting's agenda and invited the secretary to read the minutes of the last meeting. If there were no concerns,

---

10.   Pledge of the Ntambag Brothers Association, Old Town.
11.   This model seemed to be a modest but scathing indictment of Biya's tenure in Cameroon. Unlike Biya who has monopolised power for over four decades, the Ntambag Brothers' rotational scheme of power-sharing represents young people's imaginaries of an alternative politics where every citizen is given a fair chance to exercise their citizenship to the best of their abilities.

the minutes were adopted or modified as needed and deliberations proceeded. Except for minor variations, all the associations shared a similar pattern at their weekly meetings. The following excerpt from my fieldnotes captures what an ordinary Sunday meeting with the United Sisters looked like in August 2005:

When I got to Mami Lucia's house, only five United Sisters were present. It had rained heavily in the morning and now it was simply drizzling, punctuated with frequent bursts of thunder and bright flashes of lightning. Bamenda is well-known for its heavy summer rains and this day was no exception. Given the poor weather, I had anticipated a low turn out. While waiting for the meeting to begin, I joined the sisters who were discussing the rise of new Pentecostal churches in Bamenda. The subject had emerged when Hilda, one of the executive members joked about her membership in a new prosperity gospel church founded by a man named Benson Eni....

By the time the meeting began, there were about 15 members in attendance. I was called upon to offer a prayer after which the minutes of the previous session were read out. Once the minutes were adopted, the secretary announced the next item on the agenda – matters arising. In response, someone raised the question of unpaid fines. At issue was the concern that several individuals still owed fines for various violations. A resolution was passed urging defaulters to pay all outstanding debts to the association. A deadline was set and defaulters were threatened with additional fines. Next on the agenda was "other matters". Camilla, who sat next to me then sought permission to speak by raising her right hand. It was considered disrespectful to raise one's left hand when seeking permission to speak. The chairlady nodded and Camilla rose from her chair, cleared her throat and began to speak. "Before I came to this meeting, I met the seamstress who sewed some of our uniforms for the last Women's Day. She asked me to tell those who owe her to pay their debts before she takes a drastic measure. It is more than six months since we celebrated Women's Day. Those who still owe her should be ashamed of themselves. In all truth, she wanted to accompany me to the meeting today to disgrace the debtors but I begged her to calm down and promised that we'll discuss the issue. Debtors, please, you know yourselves. Do something about it before the matter gets worse." The assembly was quiet for a while, possibly overwhelmed by guilt or shock.

Someone had concerns about visitations to sick members. It is the association's

*policy to visit and donate money to sick members – a healthcare scheme
intended to assist fellow sisters with the cost of drugs. Debbie expressed
her displeasure with the sisters for failing to visit her last month when she
was sick. "I heard some members said the association resolved not to visit
anyone who lives with a boy. When was such a resolution taken? If such a
thing was discussed, then I think it is completely unfair and I deserve an
apology from the house" she said. A couple of sisters took turns to speak,
conceding their failure to visit her, not because she was allegedly living with
a young man but because they could not establish her exact whereabouts. It
seemed she was not resident in Old Town at the time of the supposed illness.*

*Yvette, one of the few married members sought permission from the general
assembly for future absences. "From November, I'll have to start attending
our home village meetings on Sundays and unfortunately, the time overlaps
with the meeting here. Because of this, I'll have to skip some Sundays. The
elders in our village meeting have urged me to be more regular because they
claim they would like to know me better." As Yvette sat down, her friends
started joking about her request. "Since you've started mingling with the
elders, no one should be surprised to learn that you've become an old woman
before your time" Charlotte joked. "You'll be drinking palm wine and eating
kola nut with the old people. And don't forget to dress in your wrapper"
added Hilda, as the assembly burst into laughter....*

In both female associations, the last Sunday of each month had a slight
but significant addition to the customary agenda – a common meal. This day
enjoyed special status because the sisters would dress in one of their fancy
uniforms, generally reserved for special occasions. Evidently, the United Sisters
modelled their event after the Chosen Sisters', albeit with minor adjustments.
Common meals were organised in a fairly simple manner; each member
contributed 500FCFA and the entire sum was given to a pair of pre-assigned
members who took turns to prepare the meals. Among the Chosen Sisters,
it was customary to be paired with one's *friend-in-meeting*, a concept unique
to them. A *friend-in-meeting* was the person with whom a new member was
paired upon admission to the association. Once paired, each member was
expected to exchange visits with her *friend-in-meeting* and to be mindful of
each other's welfare. If a member's *friend* was not present at a meeting, she
was expected to explain the reason for her absence. This arrangement did not
only facilitate the organisation of common meals, but also sought to enhance

in principle, friendship and accountability amongst members.

Attempts to introduce common meals in the NBA were strongly resisted by a few members who expressed concerns that such a venture would divert the association's focus from development, potentially conveying the impression that they were an ordinary social group. Despite the resistance, its proponents never gave up. In December 2005, David raised the issue again:

> I have proposed in this house several times that we should look into the matter of adopting common meals but there are certain individuals here who oppose without concrete reasons. I wish to propose again that if we don't have enough money to contribute on a monthly basis, we could do so once every three months.

David was expressing a view widely shared by members. But this did not deter Carlson from opposing it as he had done on past occasions:

> If we adopt this idea, some members will attend meetings only when they know food is available. Our focus is development, not feeding ourselves. But don't get me wrong, I do not oppose the idea entirely. I am of the view that if such a thing should happen, it should be spontaneous because if we make a plan for it, some people will stay away from meetings and only show up on the day food is served.

Isaac, a leading member and business owner did not find Carlson's response convincing. "Is it a bad thing for us to eat our own money?" he asked, his voice quivering. "We've made countless contributions in this house; we've donated gifts to people, cleaned up the quarter, done so many things for other people, why can't we do something for ourselves?" Isaac's concerns did little to change Carlson's opinion as well as the other executive members who opposed the idea. The matter was never put to a vote. When I spoke to Isaac after the meeting, he was deeply disappointed with the leadership of the association. He accused the leadership of intimidating members from speaking honestly about certain issues such as the common meal. "When you speak to people outside the meeting, they seem to be in favour of the idea but when it's inside the meeting, everyone goes mum." Isaac held that the executive members were to blame for the association's failure to adopt common meals, which in his opinion, played a vital function in building and sustaining conviviality. "Look at the young girls in this quarter. They've been around for much longer than us and they're doing fine. Why can't we learn something from them?"

Sociability and Contested Solidarity in Young People's Associations

Evidently, associations have a long history in the Grasslands that pre-date the modern state of Cameroon (Chilver & Kaberry 1967). However, the proliferation and importance of young people's associations in the post-1990 era is tied in part to the rapid growth of young people as a demographic but also in part to the liberalisation of public space following the collapse of monolithic rule in the early 1990s. Clubs or associations made up of people with a shared occupational, ethnic or gender background tend to serve functions of sociability as well as psychological and socio-political roles. In Old Town, the associations I researched emphasised their sociability and solidarity. Although their activities will be described and analysed in subsequent chapters, it is important to highlight some of the essential functions served by associations. These have been classified into three but overlapping categories: financial, social and moral/psychological. By carrying out these activities, all three associations positioned themselves as modern equivalents of the sodalities that customarily marked social adulthood in the Grasslands (Ndangam 2014; Nkwi & Warnier 1982).

As is legendary with self-help, hometown associations and sodalities, socioeconomic support amongst members remains the most enduring and unifying factor. At their inception, all three associations operated on very meagre resources partly because most members were either underemployed or unemployed. Membership fees provided the essential funds for running the associations. In the women's associations, about two-thirds of a member's registration fee was deposited into a *sinking* or *trouble fund*, that is, a reserve account from which they could withdraw in times of crisis, such as a death or extreme financial need. Amongst the Ntambag Brothers, this was originally referred to as *development fund* but in recent years, a quarter of the membership fees are channelled to the Schools Committee, a subgroup tasked with raising funds for the sponsorship of underprivileged children in the community. Besides the membership fees, other minor financial sources included fines paid by latecomers at weekly meetings, absences from associational activities such as communal labour or other public functions and fines accruing from persons sanctioned for acts of indiscipline during meetings (e.g., being noisy or repeated breach of associational protocol). In recent years, the Ntambag Brothers have been most successful in raising funds from goodwill donors that include Cameroon government officials and individuals with historical ties to Old Town but now resident in Europe and North America.

Despite their relatively limited finances the women's associations directed their funds to two prominent activities: healthcare and a rotating savings and credit association (ROSCA) scheme commonly referred to as *njangi*. The United Sisters, for instance had a policy to pay out 2000FCFA to every sick member. Such a donation would lessen the burden that a member would otherwise have borne. To replenish the disbursed amount, each member contributed 100FCFA during each fundraising round and any excess was deposited into the *sinking account*. In November 2005, Ruth, one of the leading members urged the association to increase the contribution from 100FCFA to 200FCFA to adjust for inflation and the increased cost of healthcare:

> Although some people say that the 2000FCFA we contribute is little, I think there are people here who can testify that it has helped them. But if we really wish to help each other, then we need to increase the amount to 4000FCFA because as you will all agree with me, the cost of almost everything has gone up.

This proposal came up against a background of massive price hikes for essential commodities, fuel and medicines. Ruth's suggestion was appreciated despite major concerns that some members who qualified for such benefits had not obtained them. At the meeting where Ruth submitted her recommendation, a debate erupted when a member complained that the association had failed to honour its policy on the visitation of sick members. Brenda, the complainant, submitted that the association had failed to visit her during her illness. Six other members also complained they had received only part of the 2000FCFA due to them. "Discrimination is the last thing we want to be known for in this association" declared Ruth. "Please, let me beg this house to come together and contribute all outstanding dues so that we don't have a similar problem in future." Just as she returned to her sit, someone alleged that a couple of members had abused the policy by lying about illnesses that never took place. For instance, Brenda's claims that she had been ill were repeatedly dismissed by a selection of members, although the association voted overwhelmingly to disburse 2000FCFA to her. Manka, a leading member of the United Sisters then suggested that safeguards should be taken to prevent future abuse. "We won't tolerate those who have minor stomach cramps and claim to be ill. We all know these are minor issues. Next time, we will have to visit the concerned either at her home or in the hospital before making the contribution" she declared, conveying the point that this was a decision rather than a suggestion.

A second channel of financial activity consisted of a savings scheme popularly known in Cameroon as *njangi*. This is a rotating savings scheme whereby each contributor to a savings pool takes the turn to *chop* or withdraw the sum total of members' contributions until the cycle had been completed. Funds from such savings tend to be invested in business ventures or to meet urgent family expenses. In fact, *njangi* schemes and formal credit unions gradually emerged as more credible channels for financial transaction due partly to the near collapse of the banking sector in the early 1990s. Most voluntary associations in the Grasslands, both urban and rural, carry out some sort of *njangi*; schemes that have grown in complexity and size since the early colonial times (cf. DeLancey 1977, 1987). Amongst the Chosen Sisters, two kinds of *njangi* schemes were carried out: *kitchen* and *soap njangi*. As implied by its name, the kitchen *njangi* enabled beneficiaries to purchase essential kitchen equipment such as chinaware, utensils, pots, blenders etc. Sometimes, the *njangi* was insufficient to meet the cost of a particular item. Where this obtained, the beneficiary would top up the amount. It was alleged that in the past some individuals had failed to use their *njangi* fund for its designated purpose which resulted in the introduction of safeguards intended to curb such practices. To this end, the association began to appoint someone to accompany the beneficiary to the market who reported back to the association. The idea of a kitchen *njangi* failed to gain approval amongst the United Sisters. I was present at one of the meetings when the issue came up and Charlotte vehemently objected to it:

> I don't have a kitchen and I don't need modern kitchen equipment. What is wrong with our ordinary plastic plates? I grew up eating from those plates. What is this noise about kitchen *njangi*? Those who want their kitchen *njangi* should go ahead and organise it but I'm not there.

Charlotte fancied portraying herself as a rustic young woman which her fellow 'sisters' seemed to enjoy. She did not only take pleasure in projecting a rustic persona but also insisted on the supremacy of her opinion. So, it came as no surprise when her objections to the kitchen *njangi* brought the discussion to a premature end.

During a subsequent session, someone submitted a motion for the introduction of a compulsory monthly *njangi* scheme in the United Sisters. If this proposal prevailed, each member would save 2000FCFA on a monthly basis. Its proponents contended that it was a mechanism to teach young women how to save. The motion was opposed by most members on the grounds that they could not afford the sum while others rejected it simply because it was unusual, indeed unheard of to compel persons to be part of a *njangi* scheme. According to the opponents, the idea of a compulsory *njangi* was contrary to the spirit of *njangi* since it was customarily voluntary. Asked about her opinion on the issue after the meeting, Manka alleged that the idea was crafted by a few married members: "They can get money from their husbands, but where do they expect us to get money from? 2000FCFA is a lot of money. Sometimes, a month goes by without some of us seeing that amount of money, not to talk of saving it. Those who brought up these ideas don't have an idea how difficult things are for some of us." She then added that most members were in favour of a soap *njangi* because it was much cheaper and not compulsory.

Unlike the female associations, the NBA consistently rejected calls by some of its members for the introduction of a *njangi* scheme. Each time the idea was proposed, Carlson and his supporters would reject it. During one of their Sunday meetings in November 2005, Achiri, a lanky fellow who had a history of irregular attendance sought permission to convince the association concerning the need to introduce a *njangi* scheme in the association. He began his speech by qualifying what attracted him to the association: "This meeting [association] was created to change the quarter and also to change ourselves. I think many people here have stressed the importance of knowing each other and knowing each other means knowing each other's problems in order to enable the association to help solve some of these problems." Everyone listened keenly. And then finally, he landed: "this is why I am for the idea that it is good to help people, but let's not focus only on others. Let's also look at ways of helping ourselves and upon reflection, the best option is to introduce *njangi* so that people can benefit from it and solve their problems."

A wave of silence swept through the room and everyone stayed still. Carlson looked uneasy and I anticipated he would say something. He rose suddenly from his seat and without hesitation, expressed his disagreement with Achiri's suggestions. "You are in the wrong place if you have that kind of idea" he declared. "This association was created particularly for the purpose of developing the community. When we develop the community, we are also developing ourselves and each other." Although Carlson was a strong opponent of the *njangi* idea, some of his concerns were shared by most of the brothers who feared that introducing *njangi* to the association might lead to internal financial disputes and could potentially precipitate the demise of the association.

Ntambag Brothers is not a social group and I don't think we should divert
from the objectives of our association. I know people have personal problems, some which can be solved by the association and some which can be
handled by your families. While I think we can work out a way through
which to assist members financially, I do not think njangi is the best way
to go about this issue.

He then stated his preference for a mechanism through which the association could lend money to members to start a business or solve a personal
or family crisis.

I have contemplated this issue before but was reluctant to voice it in
the house. It is a serious issue but we must be very careful if we have to
introduce it. If we give our money to someone to start a business, however
small it is, we should be sure that that person will return our money.

It appears many brothers had reservations about contributing seed money
to fellow brothers, particularly bachelors. It was a common perception that
bachelors were irresponsible and tended to spend their money on women.
Carlson concluded his speech by arguing that the association would work out
a mechanism through which they could assist each other financially and be
assured that funds borrowed from the association would be repaid.

The financial issues elaborated above were inextricably entangled with
elements that were broadly referred to as "social". Social activities included
anniversary parties, born house ceremonies, common meals, funerals/death
celebrations etc. It would be appropriate to state that these social affairs constituted the crux of sociocultural life in the community. Financial exactions
simply powered the commitments that gave meaning to what it meant to belong
to an association. Like every other group activity, members were expected to
show commitment by paying their dues when such events occurred. Although
the contributions to each activity depended on the scale or importance of
the occasion, certain fees were standard and clearly stipulated in the statutes,
such as contributions for the death of a family member. Fees for occasional
activities were often debated and adopted by the association and a deadline
established. In the next paragraphs, I illustrate the dynamics of social life in
Old Town with details from two events that involved the Chosen Sisters and
Ntambag Brothers respectively.

In November 2005, Helen, a Chosen Sister lost her brother. As custom demanded, each sister contributed 500FCFA to support their bereaved friend. During its meeting of Wednesday, 9 November 2005, news of the loss dominated the meeting's agenda, despite plans that were already in motion for a forthcoming born house ceremony. The sisters agreed to congregate at Mami Lucia's house the next day at 7 p.m., from where they would depart for the wake. They also agreed on the uniform to be worn and shoes to match. It was customary to wear one of their three uniforms to such occasions.

On Thursday, 10 November 2005, we assembled at Mami Lucia's house and waited for more sisters to arrive. This was my first public outing with the Chosen Sisters and I was excited to accompany them to the event. Some members had brought the association's musical instruments: two stout African drums and a hollow-mouthed aluminium pot which produced a bass pitch when struck with a spongy pad. The instruments were safely guarded by specific members appointed by the association and were only brought out at singing rehearsals or functions where the association was expected to animate with song and dance. The sisters were all dressed uniformly – a long gown popularly known as *kaba*. Most had sweaters beneath their *kabas* and others wore socks which seemed appropriate for the chilly night. The socks ought to protect them from the dry season dust which stubbornly still found its way through their sandals, leaving their feet brownish and dry. Clara, one of the sisters, remarked that she had named her sandals *wake-keeping shoes* because she wore them only to wake ceremonies. When it became apparent that we had a crowd of over 15, we took off for Meta Quarters where the wake venue was located, a twenty minutes' walk from Mami Lucia's house. We arrived at our destination just before 8 p.m. and were directed to a house which, as we later learnt, belonged to Helen's neighbour. A DJ hired for the occasion was busy mixing popular Nigerian gospel music from a make-shift tent on an elevated veranda. Giant speakers were erected at either ends of the veranda and a third across the compound. Opposite the house were three massive canopies with well arranged chairs and benches. Apparently, neighbours had offered their living rooms for the night in view of the fact that a single compound could not contain the growing number of mourners. By my estimates, there were about 500 people at the time of our arrival.

Once in the neighbour's living room, we were offered seats by five strangers who had arrived earlier. Chairs and benches had been arranged on all four corners of the room and as we entered, the strangers directed us to the right section of the room. It took a while for the sisters to settle down and before long, one of them tuned a song and everyone joined. Then the drums followed and the room vibrated with frenzied animation. Most of the songs were widely known which made it easy for the strangers to sing along. Others clapped their hands or tapped their feet in rhythm. After singing for about 15 minutes, the sisters took a break and chatted amongst themselves. The bereaved sister, Helen, came in from one of the side-doors that led into the living room, greeted her fellow sisters and expressed gratitude for their moral support. This was followed by the sharing of snacks and soft drinks. Twenty minutes later, the singing resumed and this time, a circle was formed with the drummers in the middle while everyone danced to the rhythm of the music. As time went by, the numbers grew and the circle expanded. The singing was only punctuated by brief moments of respite and prayers as the numbers gradually reduced with time.

FIGURE 3.5 Members of the Chosen Sisters attend a "death celebration" in Old Town in honour of the parents of one of their members. March 2006. Photo by author

Singing and dancing were staples at wakes and death celebrations. Throughout my fieldwork, the Chosen Sisters participated in three 'death celebrations', a wake and two born house ceremonies. The NBA on the other hand participated in a born house, three wakes and two death celebrations. The United Sisters on their part organised a memorial service in honour of a member who died in 2004. Unlike death celebrations or wake ceremonies, parties were entirely different in structure and content. Parties were meant to be fun and constituted the ultimate opportunity to socialise with one's brothers and sisters.

Each association held at least one party during my 16 months' stay with them. In November 2005, the United Sisters organised a party to celebrate its fourth anniversary and held another on Women's Day in March 2006. The Chosen Sisters on the other hand organised a Christmas cocktail in December 2005 and a party on Women's Day. In October 2005, the NBA organised a massive party to celebrate its first anniversary despite the controversy that surrounded the initiative. At issue was the extravagance, criticised by a couple of members for its similarity to those organised by the defunct Yorkaaz. Unlike the female associations that often set their party fee at only 1500FCFA per member, the NBA agreed on the sum of 10,000FCFA per member, a heavy sum for a largely unemployed population. Claude, a fellow member felt this was completely outrageous: "if this association is for development as it claims, then why is there no plan to use part of the fee for a development project?" Claude was not the lone critic. Pierre, one of the few employed members thought the amount was extremely high: "I have noticed that when brothers are called upon to contribute 1000FCFA or 2000FCFA for development projects in the community or to contribute small sums so that we can sponsor a child in primary school, people are generally reluctant. I find it strange that the sum of 10,000FCFA was adopted by the association and no one has raised their voice against it."

Pierre took his criticism to one of the Sunday meetings held to assess preparations for the party: "I have something to say which I overheard someone saying. I will not reveal his name, but I think what he said was sensible" he began. "Spare us the details and go straight to the point" the day's chairman blurted. "My question is this; can the fee for this party be reduced from 10,000FCFA to 1,000FCFA?" he asked. "No" answered the chairman. "How can we say we're a development association? I don't see how this association will bring development to this community by inviting each member to spend 10,000FCFA in one night and yet people drag their feet when Ntambag Brothers are called upon to contribute 1,000FCFA for development projects. Does this make sense to us?" Pierre questioned. There was no immediate response to his query. A handful of members felt he was arrogant and thought of himself as the one-eyed in the kingdom of the blind. When no one responded to him, the chairman decided to break the silence: "this is not a time or place to discuss that issue Mr Pierre" he said, seemingly oblivious to the irony. "The house already made a decision that each person shall contribute 10,000FCFA and it stays that way" he declared. After the chairman had spoken, Carlson sought permission to challenge Pierre's criticism:

> I just wish to correct Mr Pierre's point. Although we're calling this a party, it's not really so. This is a function to celebrate our first anniversary as an association. We have many things to celebrate because in just one year, we have accomplished a lot of things, perhaps more than other associations that have existed for more than two years. I'm sure you know very well that all work without play makes Jack a dull boy. I should also add that we'll use the function to raise funds for future development projects, and I think we all agree that we need funds for the underprivileged children in the neighbourhood.

After Carlson's 'clarification' the matter was closed to further discussion. Eventually, just about two-thirds paid the requested amount and the party was held at the Babadju Cultural Hall; the same venue where the Yorkaaz had organised their first party in the mid-1990s. Contrary to claims that the function would be used to raise funds for development, funds obtained from the sale of tickets and donations of invited guests were re-channelled for more beer. Claude, who did not contribute and predictably skipped the party, expressed his outrage at the association's failure to raise 'development' funds as previously planned: "how could the brothers spend all that money on food and drinks without thinking of the sick, prisoners and the poor in our community? At least, part of the money should have been used to assist needy or desperate persons in our community." Contrary to Claude's insistence on the moral obligation of the NBA towards the development of Old Town, most members of the association felt, like Carlson, that all work without play made Jack a dull boy. An extravagant party such as the anniversary event was a rare celebration of their triumph against victimhood and the harrowing forces of poverty. The party was perceived as an occasion to make merriment and to enjoy the company of friends, punctuated with an abundance of food, drinks and music.

A third and final function served by the associations was labelled by members as moral. What community members meant by "moral" could be understood in two senses: first, they were united in both their discourse and quest to mount a moral crusade against social ills in the neighbourhood; second, moral pursuits also entailed the "cultivation of virtue and the moral transformation of self" (Mattingly 2012:4), dispositions that enabled them to discharge their duties to community and to position themselves as social adults. These moral pursuits were carried out on two fronts: through the sponsorship of charitable activities in and out of Old Town and members' participation in moral formation discussions at weekly meetings. With respect to the latter, all three associations had slots during regular meetings differently labelled but similar in content and objective. Known as *Something Useful* and *Formation Time* in both female associations and the NBA respectively, this slot attracted spontaneous or pre-scheduled discussions by members on issues such as dating, HIV/AIDS and sex, respect for self and others, marriage and relationships, as well as tips on how to get a job. The associations also organised seminars on relevant themes to which other groups in the neighbourhood were invited. Seminars provided the only forum at which all three associations congregated on a formal platform.

Conclusion

This chapter aimed to chart the routes through which young people from different ports of departure envision a common destination (cf. Ken Roberts 2007, 264) – social adulthood and full personhood. From the youthscapes that characterised life in the 1990s through the formal associations they created and sustained in the early 2000s, I have shown how young people in Old Town gradually positioned themselves and staked a claim for social adult status over the years. If liminality is rightly characterised as "a stage of reflection" (Turner 1967:105), then, the above account shows precisely how young people in Old Town experienced the liminality of youth and ultimately made the transition to social adulthood – transitions that remain fraught with ambivalence, unpredictability and waithood (cf. Honwana 2013).

I have also elaborated on the factors that drove young people in Old Town to join associations. These include the search for socioeconomic support, to build solidarity with friends and their fictive kin, that is, their social 'siblings' with whom they could re-imagine a new social and moral world aimed at accelerating their transition to full social adulthood. Founders of all three associations, individually and collectively, emphasised that a primary objective of their associations was to 'develop' their community through moral projects and to galvanise the community of Old Town in pursuit of this lofty objective. In this respect, members of these associations tended to position and present themselves as moral vanguards whose actions would inspire the emergence of a new moral order in Old Town. This notwithstanding, this chapter shows that the quest for socioeconomic solidarity was a vital impetus across all the associations, particularly amongst the female associations. Such solidarity, far from being characterised by affect and empathy was also ridden with ambivalence (see Bähre 2007 for similarities in Cape Town).

We see ambivalence in the disputes that characterised the basic healthcare scheme and *njangi* aspirations amongst the United Sisters. The fact that some of their members alleged they had not received their "sick benefits" and invoked the language of discrimination underscores the view that solidarity in group relations is not always a seamless experience. We also see ambivalence in Claude's reservations about the NBA's extravagant anniversary party which purported to raise funds for development but ended up serving as a justification for why "Jack" should not always be bugged by the unbridled cares of development.

What also begins to emerge in this chapter are the contours of a gendered landscape forged around different ideas of what it means to be a good woman or a responsible man in Old Town. Inspired by Catholic moral orthodoxy, we see the collective quest by all associations to eschew sexual immorality and to police members' behaviours in their quest to forge a new moral citizenship that would redefine the image of Old Town. Whilst the United Sisters and Chosen Sisters elaborated on their femininity through food, music, uniforms and restrained sexuality, the Ntambag Brothers on the other hand performed their masculinity through sport, extravagance, competition (cf. Fuh 2009, 2012) and the tenacious quest to be seen as productive men (see chapter four).

Furthermore, I demonstrate as previously stated that the constitution of personhood and the production of social adulthood are processes that are manifest in collective and individual agencies. This chapter reveals that associations are the channels through which members position themselves as social adults. Young people's associations are not only structured in similar ways to those of well-established hometown associations in Old Town but their activities also draw on local idioms of domesticated success – namely that one's success (however defined) must be redistributed. By providing for their personal needs, families, fictive kin (sisters or brothers), and to pursue goals on behalf of the community, young people in these associations assume and enact adult roles similar to those of their parents' generations.

Finally, we see that over time, these associations have assumed transnational proportions, echoing migration trends that have affected not only the community of Old Town but the city of Bamenda and beyond. The Ntambag Brothers for example count amongst their membership, over a dozen diaspora individuals who reside in North America. The Chosen Sisters on the other hand, have two members in the United States and a few others who live outside the North West region. Far from weakening the ties that bind members, migration has served not only to reinforce members' commitment to place (see Gupta & Ferguson 1992) but also the local idiom of celebrating one's success with one's community. In the next chapter, we see this in part how diaspora members collaborate with the Ntambag Brothers in carrying out hygiene operations prior to and especially during the Covid-19 pandemic.

CHAPTER FOUR

Sanitary Activism and Urban Renewal in Old Town

In Bamenda as in other towns and cities of Cameroon during the early 2000s, a day was generally reserved for cleaning up one's surroundings. Prior to its split into three separate municipalities, the Bamenda Urban Council (BUC) designated the last Thursday of each month for a city-wide clean-up operation which began at 8 a.m. and ended at noon. During this period, the circulation of taxis and other forms of public transportation were prohibited. Shops and business premises were also closed while citizens cleaned their domestic surroundings and public spaces particularly those beyond the reach of municipal authorities. Each year, the Ministry of Towns and Urban planning awarded a prize to the cleanest city or town as part of its agenda to promote a clean and healthy urban environment. Thus, it was that hygiene became part and parcel of the national discourse, just as it was a matter of daily concern for citizens and young people's associations in Old Town. The failure of municipal operations such as those of the BUC in dealing effectively with urban problems including hygiene and waste management created room for the appropriation of urban space and more importantly, what I have termed sanitary activism. Sanitary activism combines a plethora of rituals, dispositions, beliefs and actions on matters related to communal hygiene that aim to hold municipal government accountable, espouses self-reliance and participatory approaches to tackling the problems of waste management and general hygiene.

This chapter describes and analyses how young people in Old Town, acting through various associations inscribe their agencies on urban space through the politics of neighbouring (cf. Jerrems 2020) and sanitary activism. It details young people's preoccupation with and discourses on hygiene as well as their strategies and operations that seek to redress urgent health and environmental problems in their community. I show that young people's preoccupation with sanitary matters enables them to mobilise their resources, exercise power, and further their quest for visibility and influence in Old Town.

My interpretation of young people's mobilisation around sanitary issues sheds light on a range of issues, the most salient of which are that young people's associations in Old Town are equipped with sufficient knowledge to find solutions to the issues that plague their community and that such solutions must be homegrown. Their deep knowledge and daily experience of the predicament of living in a run-down neighbourhood earns them the designation of what William Easterly has termed "searchers" (2007:6). I show that a study of the daily life of "searchers" and grassroots movements is significant, in part because they illuminate the micro-processes of meaning production and how change on the ground takes place. Furthermore, the ethnographic evidence detailed in this chapter reveals the ways in which young men and women shape the meanings of social adulthood. For the young women in the United and Chosen Sisters, I show that social adulthood is primarily negotiated through women's empowerment pursued collectively, whilst for the young men, an almost militant approach to sanitary issues highlights not only their manhood but also their claims to pre-eminent status as fixers and "bricoleurs of community" life (Fuh 2020:5). Sanitary activism expresses one dimension of moral citizenship – that which focuses not so much on state-derived notions of rights and entitlements but rather, on what citizens are capable of doing for themselves, their community and the nation.

I also elaborate on the gendered dimensions of sanitary activism by showing how mobilising around hygiene issues may not only be understood as "doing gender" but also how the specific activities related to sanitary campaigns - constitute "resources for doing gender" (Aulette & Wittner 2015:72).

Modernity and Sanitary Activism in Old Town

My first visit with the NBA turned out to be a dramatic encounter with the association's preoccupation with hygiene and cleanliness in the neighbourhood. It seemed that an aspect of its agenda was to step in where local municipal authorities were perceived to have failed. With time, I discovered that the NBA was not the only association passionately involved with hygiene because I soon realised that all the three associations I worked with carried out elaborate programmes on sanitary issues. With time, it became obvious to me that "modernity and success" as aptly observed by Michael Rowlands "have elective affinities with hygiene and the removal of dirt in Bamenda" (Rowlands 1996:208). Rowlands observes that in Bamenda, cleanliness is not only associated with success but also enjoys strong allusions to power and modernity. A modern and clean neighbourhood constituted part of the collective imaginary of the young people's associations preoccupied with urban renewal. Reflecting on my observations at my first NBA meeting led me to identify traits of Rowlands' association between hygiene and modernity. Immediately after the opening prayers, two separate minutes that had been meticulously prepared were read out – the first concerning the last plenary meeting and a special one pertaining to the association's visit to the BUC premises in Ntarikon which had taken place during the week. While the secretary read out the "special" minutes of the trip to the BUC premises, a small pack of photos was circulated - photos of the brothers with important personalities at the municipal offices. Several of the photos revealed an elaborate display of 20 green trashcans freshly painted with the caption – "Keep Old Town Clean" and beneath it – "Donated by Ntambag Brothers".

FIGURE 4.1 A public garbage bin fabricated and donated to the Bamenda Urban Council by the Ntambag Brothers. Photo by author.

My curiosity was roused even more upon seeing the photos, profoundly amazed that a group of mostly unemployed young men should donate trashcans to the BUC. When the secretary finished reading the special minutes, one of the executive members announced that individuals who were absent from the ceremony without prior permission would pay the standard fine of 150FCFA. This immediately provoked protests from a member who insisted that he was neither aware of the planned visit nor the date of this activity. His excuses were promptly dismissed as the other members seemed more interested in discussing the substantive issues concerning the visit and its implications for BUC-NBA relations. What I had just witnessed was the culmination of a well-coordinated inaugural project of the NBA.

The NBA's proactive engagement with hygiene began when the association unanimously agreed to produce trashcans for its neighbourhood. It is probable that this initiative was inspired by hygiene lessons delivered by a patroness of the association who worked at the provincial department of health. She too had been thrilled to learn of the association's objectives; a factor that persuaded her to readily accept the association's invitation to become a patroness. Max, 33, an influential executive member observed that the municipal council's neglect and the growing problem of garbage disposal also prompted them to sensitise the community and to carry out hygiene operations in the neighbourhood: "we wanted to encourage hygiene in the quarter because the surroundings were always littered with garbage. We know from basic education that if garbage is well managed we can avoid mosquitoes and consequently have less malaria in the community."

Determined to procure and distribute garbage bins in the neighbourhood, the brothers were undeterred by the allegation that producing and/or distributing trashcans not endorsed by the government delegate or his assistant was considered a violation of municipal laws. The association opted to settle any doubts by seeking the permission of municipal authorities:

> When we contacted the government delegate, we were surprised that he wanted us to repair some of the council's garbage bins that had been abandoned. We rejected his request by explaining that we simply wanted to carry out an activity that would benefit our neighbourhood directly. We told him that we simply needed his permission to go ahead with our plans but because we were reluctant to do what he wished, he started making excuses each time we sought an appointment with him. Contrary to the government delegate's lukewarm attitude, his assistant gave us all the support we needed. You know, he's from Old Town and as a member of our community, we knew we could count on his support. He has visited our association twice. When he learnt of our initiative, he was very pleased and urged us to complete the project. Looking back at the situation, I think

it was thanks to him that we succeeded. (Max, NBA member)

The first step involved writing a formal request to the government delegate seeking permission to produce trashcans for exclusive use in Old Town. According to Max, the government delegate allegedly declared he did not understand the association's motive and instead requested further information on the project. "I think he was concerned that we wanted to add unnecessary burden on the council especially with respect to the collection of garbage from the interior parts of the neighbourhood." It is also probable that the letter was poorly worded or perhaps failed to state clearly that the project's aim was to place garbage containers at strategic areas in the neighbourhood in order to encourage citizens to adopt healthy practices of waste disposal.[1] Prior to this initiative, residents tended to dump their waste in streams, private gardens, footpaths or small bushes in the neighbourhood. The NBA's initiative was to establish collection points where accumulated garbage would be transported to the BUC's dumpsters at the main street. Although the BUC ought to collect garbage from the main street once every week, it hardly kept its schedule. "So we wrote another letter to the government delegate explaining how we intended to distribute the trashcans. We stated that users would sign an agreement with the association in which they will promise to take full charge of the garbage disposal and promise to handle the trashcan with care." Max and other members of the association confirmed that the government delegate eventually conceded to their wishes upon persuasion from his vice[2] who had taken a keen interest in the activities of the association, himself a resident of Old Town.

1. Several NBA members also insinuated that the government delegate's reluctance to endorse the project could be partly attributed to his personal differences with Max, who as a former president of the youth-wing of the CPDM in Old Town had confronted the delegate over party policy. The government delegate was a leading figure in the Mezam division section of the CPDM and was alleged to have resented the former youth-president who had dared to challenge him.
2. The vice, just like his superior, the government delegate, are both government-appointed municipal managers. Both are prominent members of the CPDM, presiding over an SDF-elected council. Hence, the SDF-elected mayor (council chairman) exercises little or no power over council policy. Several attempts have been made to unseat the government delegate by the SDF to no avail. He has also resisted calls to resign, insisting that as an appointee of the president of the republic, he would only leave office if the president terminated his appointment. See *The Post*, online edition, "B'da Councillors, Gov't Delegate Draw Swords Again" by Peterkins Manyong, accessed on March 16 2007; http://www.postnewsline.com/2006/01/bda_councillors.html. It is also evident from this background that the government delegate is not accountable to Bamenda residents and does not feel compelled to do so.

Upon approval of the project, the association set to work. Dues were promptly collected and committees established. Individuals and sub-groups were assigned various tasks. One of these was a committee tasked with the purchase of barrels commonly known as "casks". With the help of a welder, each cask was cut into two equal halves and painted green in and out. Iron rod handles were also welded on either side of the casks to facilitate transportation. The stage was now set for the NBA to display its credentials as an association with a difference. Dressed in their best and armed with the NBA's badge – symbolising the magnitude and official nature of this activity, the brothers hired a vehicle to transport the bins to the council premises where the spectacle was scheduled to unfold. Often excluded from "postcolonial munificence and its sites of sociability" as Diouf (1996) reminds us, the NBA was determined to join the show rather than remain spectators. This was its first opportunity to apprise the BUC of its existence and aspirations. Despite the government delegate's questionable and visible absence from the ceremony, his vice and the Divisional Officer (D.O.) or *Prefect* of the Bamenda Central sub-division legitimised the occasion with their presence. The NBA leader delivered a written speech in which he subtly denounced the BUC's neglect of Old Town thus highlighting municipal deficiency in Bamenda. The speech also underscored the NBA's self-assigned role as moral guardians and fixers determined to give Old Town a face-lift in both metaphoric and practical ways. Excerpts of the president's speech are quoted:

> Today seems to be one of those rare days in the life of a people who seem to have been forgotten, either by design or by deliberate misconception or prejudice. The Association of young Old Town boys, baptized Ntambag brothers, which was formed some eight months ago, had as its objective to bring Old Town to its original status, to make it resemble the area where life in the Bamenda municipality once began. This in a deliberate attempt to inculcate hygiene, sanitation, fight poverty, unemployment, fill pot-holes, organize seminars on sexually transmitted diseases and related topics on development etc. All these in an attempt to cancel the myth that Old Town is an area of school dropouts and other vices. Furthermore, this association is apolitical and known (sic) profit-making association. Its finances depend on the good will of its 40 members. Therefore, like a new born baby who depends solely on its mothers Brest (sic), the association has no budget of its own.

Ladies and gentlemen, distinguish (sic) guest, to achieve our objective is not an easy task but very possible one and that is why we are here today. The production of these cans to us has just come in a right time. Right time in the sense that sanitation in our area of Old Town is very poor. This poor sanitation brings ill-health, which might lead to death and other health hazards. Therefore, to fight against these, we have sensitized the residents of Ntambag on the importance of proper disposal of their garbage, and most importantly, to keep their toilets in good conditions. We have struggled to keep all our streets clean by constantly sweeping it. Moreover, we have held Seminars at the Impersonal Life Foundation in Old Town on the importance of good sanitation in our area.

Distinguish (sic) guests; the above is not the only objective we have in mind. We have tried in our own little way to maintain our seasonal roads, which are not in good shape, by filing (sic) most potholes to our capacity and strength. We also held different seminars to make our young ones know their importance in the society. We have a plan of sponsoring the little poor girls who cannot afford to pay their school needs as from next academic year, numbering of houses, planting of trees around our periphery, just to name a few.

These tasks cannot be successful as soon as possible without the help of our people, our community or our council. In this light, we are appealing to the Government Delegate to the Bamenda Urban Council, the administrative machinery for Mezam and people of good will to give us the necessary support we need to achieve these prime objectives.

Following the display of the trashcans to council authorities and the rituals such occasions entailed, the NBA returned triumphantly to Old Town and "installed" five bins at strategic locations in the neighbourhood to the overt cheering and commendation of residents, young and old. This event legitimised the NBA as an influential actor on two crucial counts– first, by establishing its credibility in the eyes of the local government and the community of Old Town as an important voice for youth, and second, by delineating Old Town as its terrain for the elaboration of moral citizenship. Following this event, the BUC's hygiene department allegedly delegated some of its supervisory powers to the NBA, urging the association to act as its 'eyes and ears' in the neighbourhood.

Not all the trashcans were allocated for public use. The NBA strategically reserved a couple of them for donation to select government institutions in Old Town such as the Public Security Offices and MIDENO (North West Development Authority), a public agency tasked with enforcing the state's modernist development agenda in the North West region. Both located in Old Town, the heads of these institutions had expressed interest in the NBA's activities and had informally invited the leadership of the association to their respective offices. When a decision was taken to donate one of the trashcans to MIDENO and a date set for the visit, I volunteered to accompany the appointed delegation. This move was inspired partly by the imperative to 'hang out' with the brothers as well as my desire to witness the anticipated encounter between the NBA and the director of MIDENO, who, being a prominent member of the ruling CPDM and former transport minister was widely known for his association with PRESBY, a pro-government youth association with branches in all ten provinces of the country (Fokwang 2006). It was alleged that he had benefited tremendously from the support of the Bamenda branch of PRESBY to establish himself as an influential political figure.

On Wednesday, 8 June 2005, a few minutes after mid-day I caught up with a small group of NBA members near Subi House, in the area popularly known as Seven Doors. When I arrived, the brothers seemed to be engrossed in a conversation on high speed cars and street racing. They had arrived about ten minutes earlier and were waiting for Aaron who was eating lunch at a nearby restaurant. Aaron was the one tasked with coordinating the visit. The discussion soon veered to a topic which initially seemed hard to decipher.

"That secret is dangerous" Ben said to Achu. "You know, my friend derives so much satisfaction just from looking at it. Recently, he told me he won't use it. Instead, he's looking for anyone willing to give him 20,000FCFA for it." "What secret are you boys talking about?" Kevin quizzed just when I was about to do so myself. Ben and Achu burst out laughing, apparently delighted at our inability to make sense of their discussion. "It's a pair of sneakers" Ben said. "Someone in Belgium sent it to my friend as a gift but he'd rather sell it for fear that the stuff will get damaged when used on our bad roads. He's a funny guy. Every now and then, he pulls out the shoes from his suitcase, examines it, assures himself that it still looks new and then places it back in his box." Then Aaron joined us, wiping the corners of his mouth, greeted us briefly and excused himself. After five minutes or so, he returned with a lad of about 13 carrying the trashcan in one hand. "Why don't you put it on your head?" Ben queried the little boy. "It would be easier for you" he added but the lad simply ignored him.

Four NBA members including myself were now ready to leave for the MIDENO office located on the eastern side of Old Town. Because it was a short distance, we decided to walk. On our way, the discussion shifted to a popular topic that has captivated most young people in Cameroon - emigration, known popularly as *bushfalling* (see Wanki & Lietaert 2019; Jua 2003; Nyamnjoh 2011; Tazanu 2012), discussed in chapter six. "I have a friend who was trying to hook me up into a certain programme in Switzerland but everything changed when he left for Germany. He said he couldn't find a job in Switzerland" Ben told his friends. Like many NBA members, he also nursed the hope of travelling abroad someday. He explained further that the fact that his friend dropped out of secondary school might have accounted for his inability to find a good job in Switzerland but the others disagreed with him. Ben spoke about his friend's difficulty in adjusting to life in Germany but added that it was thanks to his elder brother that the process seemed less terrifying.

We crossed the main road that separated Old Town into 'upper and lower quarters' and continued on a stony path, then descended on a narrow trail which led to Ayaba Street. The MIDENO office could be spotted below as we descended the stony path. It was an imposing two-storey building undergoing renovation, freshly painted as well. But seeing the number of builders and carpenters moving in and out, it was certain that there was still a considerable amount of work inside the building. We crossed the road and entered the premises of the heavily fenced building – after identifying ourselves at the gateman's security station. The lad who carried the trash can was tipped with 200FCFA and he left promptly, visibly excited.

Parked in front of the building was a brand new green Toyota Prado, a luxurious Four Wheel Drive V8 sports utility vehicle with brown leather seats. "It looks very new" Kevin commented. "Yes, it's about three weeks old" Ben concurred. Based on my observation of the young men's reactions, the car's owner was unquestionable – it was the director's, formerly transport minister and prominent politician of the ruling party who had been dismissed from his ministerial position after occupying the office for just several months, allegedly for his mismanagement of government funds. When he fell from ministerial grace, he simply returned to his position as director of MIDENO, which he had held concurrently. "The man is slowly exposing the money he stole during his tenure as minister" one of my companions whispered. "Yes" agreed another, "he could not show off the money immediately after his dismissal; he had to take his time. We pay taxes so that people like him can ride in expensive cars like this. You might not know, but this car costs between 60 and 70 million francs." There was definitely a feeling of bitterness and resentment in the young man's voice. Nevertheless, it was evident that the director had only lost his ministerial portfolio but not the trappings of power and the propensity for ostentatious consumption at the expense of the masses so characteristic of the postcolony (Mbembe 1992:3).

Aaron went upstairs to meet the director but returned sooner than expected to explain that he was unsuccessful. The director's assistant descended from the balcony and met us near the gate. One of the brothers still held the trashcan and they all looked exasperated. The director's personal assistant then apologised for his boss' unavailability. "Is there anything I should tell him when he comes out of the meeting?" he inquired. "Not much," Aaron responded, handing over the trashcan to him. "Normally, when we give out something like this, we expect that the recipient would have some small thing for us." The director's assistant then thanked us for our gesture and promised to convey our message to him. Everyone looked disappointed. "He was really keen on meeting us" Aaron remarked, sounding consolatory. Aaron had personally negotiated this appointment with the director and was confident he would receive the delegation with paternal excitement. "He was really impressed by our activities and wanted to know our source of funding. He wanted to know how we're able to carry out things like this" Aaron added. Our companions urged Aaron to return the next day to enquire if the director left a "small thing" for the association. On our way back, Kevin expressed concerns on the dangers of a working relationship with the director: "our greatest fear is that he should not become too close to the association because he might bring politics into the whole show." When Aaron eventually met the director a few days later, he acknowledged having seen the trashcan and requested a detailed record of the association's members in order to identify potential persons for inclusion in future projects sponsored by his agency. Aaron also reported that the director had requested the association to submit an application for funds to his office towards the production and distribution of more trashcans in Old Town.[3]

---

3.   In 2005, the African Development Bank awarded the sum of 15 billion FCFA towards sponsorship for the Northwest Grassfield Participatory and Decentralised Rural Development Project, GP-DERUDEP, a programme of the Northwest Development Authority, MIDENO. The funds were intended to finance socioeconomic and agricultural projects in the Northwest Province. See *The Post*, online edition, "ADB Disburses FCFA 372 Million For Grassfield Project" by Chris Mbunwe & Peterkins Manyong, accessed on 16 March 2007; http://www.postnewsline.com/2005/06/strongadb_disbu.html. The NBA anticipated to benefit from these funds through its garbage can project.

The emerging alliance between the NBA and the MIDENO director, echoed partly by Kevin's remarks above, highlights the patron-client relationship that has established itself so firmly in Cameroon and many other African countries. A patrimonial network as defined by Bangura is:

> a system of resource distribution that ties recipients or clients to the strategic goals of benefactors or patrons. In the distribution of 'patrimony', or public resources, both patrons and clients attach more importance to personal loyalties than to the bureaucratic rules that should otherwise govern the allocation of such resources (Bangura 1997:130).

Patrimonial relationships particularly those involving "big men" and youth tend to flourish in "shadow states" (cf. Murphy 2003) or in circumstances of social moratorium (cf. Vigh 2006) where securing entry into a patrimonial network, young men anticipate "a way" out of the foreboding terror of social and physical death. Aaron's explicit request for a "small thing" in reciprocity for the trashcan underscores the NBA's search for access to a potentially rewarding patrimonial network with the director, despite the fact that the association represented itself as "non-political".

Although the prospective patrimonial relationship between the NBA and the director did not blossom during my fieldwork in Old Town, the association has not shied from building relationships with prominent personalities in both the public service and private sector[4]. Nevertheless, the NBA's strategic donation of a trashcan to MIDENO challenges the postcolony's established monopoly of dramatizing benevolence – that is, a situation where gifts flow in a unidirectional mode from the state or big man to the masses (Diouf 2003). Besides this challenge, the NBA's sanitary activism also reveals its agency in circumscribing space for itself in Old Town – that is, by staking its claim to urban space through markers such as trashcans and by acting on behalf of a deficient municipal authority as will be seen subsequently.

Gendered 'Work" and the Performance of Cleanliness
The NBA was not the only association preoccupied with hygiene operations in Old Town. In this section, I elaborate on sanitary activism by describing

---

4.   For example, the association has welcomed high profile visitors to its meeting venue such as Bishop Michael Bibi and accepted donations from Felix Mbayu, a junior minister with residential ties to Old Town.

the strategies employed by two of the three associations to improve the sanitary conditions in their neighbourhood. The discussion below highlights the gendered dimensions of sanitary activism as witnessed in the different ways in which respective associations harnessed sanitary campaigns. I show that for the women's associations, sanitary campaigns are primarily seen to serve associational goals and women's empowerment whilst for the young men in the NBA, hygiene operations provide a broad scope for them to perform productive masculinity, thus shaping their own meanings of social adulthood.

The salience of sanitary campaigns among young people's associations in Old Town was reinforced the first time I attended the United Sisters' meeting. At this gathering, frequent reference was made to 'work' – loosely translated as a form of human investment or 'manual labour'. 'Work' entailed a sanitary campaign of some sort executed with the use of implements such as brooms, mops, machetes, hoes and spades. This could be carried out on private or public premises and involved clearing small bushes, weeding off wild plants from domestic spaces and sweeping the streets. Such work was often undertaken on invitation by potential patrons or when the association solicited selected patrons to request a special clean-up service. During my first official session at a United Sisters meeting, a member submitted a motion for 'harsh punishment' to members who had failed to show up for 'work' without prior permission. Upon hearing this, a lady who sat opposite me rose suddenly from her seat, displayed her blistered palms and spoke in support of the motion: "we should really give heavy fines to those who did not show up because I think the usual fine is nothing compared to the amount of work we did." She was referring to the physically exhausting 'work' the association had carried out, proof of which could be seen in their blisters. Claude, the patron who introduced me to the association also showed his blisters to the ladies and urged the house to ensure that absentees should pay heavily. At a subsequent meeting, the president of the United Sisters was accused of having skipped a clean-up operation. She was not absolved of her excuses but fined despite her protests that she had mixed up the addresses and had ended up at the wrong site.

Although the United Sisters occasionally organised small-scale sanitary campaigns in Old Town, the above references to 'work' involved activities carried out specifically to raise funds for the association's 4th anniversary celebration scheduled for November 2005. Between July and October 2005, the United Sisters undertook more than a dozen 'work' operations aimed at raising funds for their 4th anniversary. Each campaign began with identifying potential areas for clean-up. This was followed by the preparation of application letters which were delivered to government offices, business premises, and private homes. If approved, the sisters descended on the premises with an army of implements and with clinical devotion, swept, mopped, and dusted the site to the best of their ability. Such work often included removing weeds from the premises and ensuring the site was left in the best sanitary state possible. Upon completion of their tasks, the young women were rewarded with a cash amount decided exclusively by the beneficiary of their 'work'.

Such proceeds were often used to cover associational expenses such as refreshments for their functions and occasionally, purchased gifts to be donated to the needy (covered in the next chapter). For these young women, sanitary operations furthered their goals of empowerment and agency in positioning themselves collectively as social adults. One sense in which empowerment may be understood relates to the ability to make choices and agency as the "processes by which choices are made and put into effect" (Kabeer 2005:14). Kabeer further observes that agency "in relation to empowerment...implies not only actively exercising choice, but also doing this in ways that challenge power relations... It encompasses not only 'decision making' and other forms of observable action but also the meaning, motivation, and purpose that individuals bring to their actions; that is, their *sense* of agency. Empowerment is rooted in how people see themselves – their sense of self-worth. This in turn is critically bound up with how they are seen by those around them and by their society" (2005:14-15). If resources are the medium through which agency is exercised, then the proceeds acquired by the United Sisters from their sanitary campaigns constitute important resources for exercising agency. The acquisition of such resources enables them to make choices as a group and to define how they see themselves, their self-worth and role in society. Such agency undermines the age-old perception which in the past recognised the attainment of reproductive maturity and eventually, marriage as key markers of adult status for young women.

Unlike the United Sisters, the NBA gradually established a solid reputation in the community for its frequent and rigorous sanitary campaigns which combined 'work' with the inspection of private toilets and domestic spaces. Manual work consisted of activities such as sweeping the streets, the maintenance of unpaved roads in the neighbourhood by filling up potholes and clearing bushes. These activities were often executed on Wednesdays, the NBA's reserved day for manual work. Every Wednesday, as early as 5:30 a.m., the brothers assembled at Subi House (their regular meeting venue) from where they moved as a unit to the identified site and laboured for an average of three hours. Communal approval and praise for the NBA's operations were shown through verbal expressions; occasionally, residents would join the brothers in carrying out a given sanitary operation or by donating cash to the association. For instance, in May 2005, the Police Commissioner for Public Security in Old Town rewarded the NBA with 5000FCFA for cleaning up the police station. During one of its road maintenance campaigns, residents of the area chipped in coins and bank notes into a small plastic bowl on the road side in appreciation of the NBA's work. Upon learning of the NBA's maintenance work in his area, the local councillor for Ntambag II, Oumarou Sanda donated 1000FCFA. At the end of that session, the brothers had been gifted with over 5000FCFA from various community members. On a separate occasion, someone donated 1000FCFA to the brothers for sweeping the streets.

FIGURE 4.2 Members of the NBA clean up the neighbourhood and erect a banner wishing community members a Merry Christmas and Happy New Year, December 23, 2005. Photo by author.

If we draw on Judith Butler's framework of "gender as performance" (Butler 1990), it becomes apparent how young men in the NBA "perform" their roles not only as "fixers" (Fuh 2020) but also as proper men who take care of their wards and community. Richard Waller (2006) has referred to this sort of performance as "productive masculinity". I show that productive masculinity is partly tied to the attainment of social adulthood amongst young men in Old Town, measured by their pursuit of the ideals of responsible behaviour, proper citizenship and marriage (Waller 2006:78). It should be emphasised that in precolonial Grassfields society, marriage was not a sufficient cause for the attainment of adulthood. The achievement of independence as household heads was generally emphasised.[5] However, we see that young men in Old Town have reshaped the "traditional" meanings previously associated with social adulthood by emphasising their productivity as key markers of what it means to be a social adult in the contemporary Grasslands. This interpretation becomes even more salient when we examine the NBA's sanitary activism on toilet hygiene, Covid-19 mobilisation and involvement in community health-care matters discussed in the next section. I show that these practices may be understood as "resources for doing gender" (Aulette & Wittner 2015:71) – that is, activities and social processes by which the young men not only distinguish themselves from their female counterparts, but also position themselves as productive men and social adults in the community.

Operation Clean Toilet: Hygiene and Municipal Authority by Proxy in Old Town

Of all the activities undertaken by the NBA, none was as decisive as the "operation clean toilet" which generated considerable debate within the association. At issue was the existence in certain parts of Old Town, of dilapidating pit latrines whose putrid smell made life unbearable for residents. Kevin, who raised the issue at a Sunday meeting, was particularly concerned about the dreadful smell of a neighbour's latrine that had compelled him and others to discontinue the use of a footpath that led to his home. He roused the brothers to make use of the informal "authorisation" given them by the sanitary department of the BUC for the common good of the community.

"Fellow brothers" he began, "we really have to do something about these stinking toilets. Maybe some of you are not affected by this problem but I'm seriously affected and so I urge you to think of what we need to do." Max was the first to respond to Kevin's concerns. "I suggest that we should inform the

---

5.   A young man could be married but still lived in his father's compound and as such was considered a dependent. In the Cameroon Grasslands, it was not sufficient to be married in order to be considered an adult. Warnier (1996) maintains that a young man remained symbolically impotent until he was able to participate in procreative reproduction.

council of this problem and then give deadlines to the owners of these toilets. We'll inform the owners of such toilets that their neighbours have complained about the state of their toilets and that they must do something about it." Pierre rose suddenly from his seat to speak. Because of his confrontational approach to things, listeners, myself included, expected him to counter Max's point. He wore a stern look and raised his finger as if it to warn his interlocutor:

> We're not sanitary officers in this quarter. I think there are individuals who are charged with such functions. I would suggest that let's mount pressure on the councillors who are in charge of this quarter to do their job. They can channel our complaints to the rightful quarters. We cannot carry out this job by ourselves. Never mind the fact that the council gave us permission to carry out certain activities in the neighbourhood. We don't have any proof or written document which shows that we are permitted to assume such functions in this quarter.

The discussion got fiercer and although only a few people had spoken, the topic seemed to generate a lot of excitement. While some appeared incensed by Pierre's doubts about the credibility of the association to undertake a campaign to root out 'stinking toilets' from the neighbourhood, others seemed to agree with him, evidenced by the nod of heads as he spoke. Despite the fact that several hands were up, Max ignored them and rose speedily to respond to Pierre's commentary:

> I wish to differ with you. We produced trashcans to sensitise community members about the need to keep our environment clean. When we went to the council to present the trashcans, the council gave us permission to carry out projects in the neighbourhood that we believe could contribute to better health in our community. They also told us to seek their assistance in carrying out any sanitary activities in the neighbourhood. My advice is that let's go out during the week and instruct people to do something about their toilets. We'll tell them that if they did nothing about the state of their toilets, the council would be forced to break down their toilets.

Max's view initially seemed appealing to a majority of members until Abong, the day's chairman expressed his reservations:

> My fear is that people in the community will question our authority. They

would like to know who gave us permission to take the law into our own hands. This might also cause problems for specific Ntambag brothers who might be accused of having identified their toilets for destruction. My fear is that we are neither councillors nor sanitation officers.

Abong's concerns cast a shadow of anxiety over the room. Judging by the whispers around me, it was apparent that the brothers were becoming apprehensive. Kevin, who had raised the issue rose to support Abong's cautionary view.

It's true. I think we should be careful because when people start pointing fingers, you might hear of something else. In fact, you might hear that so and so did this and died because of this matter. I don't think we should do this by ourselves only. We should invite the councillors or sanitation department to inspect the toilets.

In support of Kevin's perspective, Pierre took the floor once again. He appeared even more solemn, moved forward from his seat and raised his finger as usual.

Is there any written document which shows that the council has granted us permission to carry out sanitary operations in this community? We cannot go just by ourselves to sensitise people about the state of their toilets. We must take at least one councillor with us.

Chairman Abong agreed and insisted that staff from the sanitation department of the council should be approached prior to further action. Elias, 32, who had been relatively quiet during most of the discussion sought permission to speak. He looked calm but had an uneasy grin:

No one will show these toilets because of fear. People don't want to run into trouble with their neighbours because things might turn out differently. I remember we had a problem in my compound. There was a mango tree next to our compound whose fruits used to fall on our roof, sometimes destroying the zinc. We reported the matter to the council. When the council workers came, they simply asked for the owner of the mango tree. They didn't tell him that neighbours had complained about the destruction caused by his tree. They simply told him that it was council policy to fell tall trees in town. The council workers did not say so and so reported this matter to us. So it simply looked like the guys were doing their job around the area when they came across the tree. I think we should employ a similar method with this toilet issue. We should see the councillors and push them to take up the matter. We really have to be careful because we all know how people are; you might hear that someone has fallen because of a small issue like this.

Elias' speech seemed to have brought the matter to a fair conclusion, but before he could take his seat, Ernest's hand was already up.

In the past, when we were growing up, sanitation officers used to move around to carry out the inspection of toilets but these days, nobody cares. They're not doing their job any more. So my suggestion is this; that we should report to the sanitation department that the entire Ntambag area has bad toilets and that we need them to do something serious about this. If we generalise the issue as a problem faced by the entire quarter, then we have a bigger scope to solve the crisis and many people whom we don't even know stand to benefit from the project.

Elias seemed moved by Ernest's suggestion and immediately sought permission to speak. "What Ernest has said is true. This is a serious problem" he insisted "even in my compound, I know people who don't have toilets anymore. You might not believe this, but there are people who relieve themselves in plastic bags and dispose of them in small bushes or by the road side." Some members could not contain their laughter upon hearing this. "It's good that we should speak the truth, instead of dying in shame. We need to act urgently on this matter, it's serious", he insisted, provoking even more laughter. The chairman then recommended the appointment of a small committee to raise the matter with the council.

This issue resurfaced three weeks later when members sought feedback on the delegation's trip to the council. Contrary to everyone's expectations, the executive had resolved during an extraordinary meeting to sensitise the community prior to seeking the BUC's intervention. According to the executives, it was resolved that residents and landlords in particular whose properties did not have toilets or whose toilets were below sanitary standards should be told unequivocally to do something about the state of their toilets. According to this new logic, the NBA would act as messengers by informing residents of an impending crackdown by the council on properties that had poor or unsanitary toilet facilities. The executives concluded by requesting members to come out en masse on an appointed date to sensitise residents. It was now universally agreed among the young men that all homes, rather than isolated households would be targeted for the campaign. This new logic was expected to be beneficial to all and sundry, first, by providing immunity to NBA members from being identified as ring-leaders and second, by forestalling any potential backlash among residents who may feel that they had been targeted.

Once this agreement was arrived at or subtly imposed by the leadership, a date was fixed for the inspection. The brothers agreed to assemble in front of Subi House at 6 a.m. on a certain Wednesday, not with work implements but with their badges – symbolic of an official operation. To facilitate the task, Old Town was divided into about 10 partitions, each constituting about 50 households. They would tackle each partition over several weeks until a full circle was accomplished. On the first day of the tour, a group of about 15 NBA members set out and inspected a total of 15 households. The operation went successfully except at the house whose dilapidating toilet had ironically prompted the operation. The owner allegedly asked the brothers to report him to the council and resisted their recommendation to construct a new toilet. He went further to claim that his toilet served many households in the neighbour-hood that had no toilet facilities and even allegedly embarrassed the brothers by naming two NBA members who benefited from his "open-door" policy. Although the campaign for the most part was deemed to have succeeded, the NBA saw this as the commencement of a worthy cause with potential for further sanitary development in the community. "There are at least three compounds on this street without toilets" Simon told me one sunny afternoon, pointing to a set of houses about a hundred metres west of Subi House.

Consequent on the initial inspection tour, the association began to receive handwritten and verbal complaints from residents urging the NBA to intercede with council authorities on their behalf. One of the complaints concerned a resident's grievance against his neighbour whose toilet was prone to flooding during heavy rainfall. According to the complainant, particles of excrement and debris from his neighbour's toilet often ended up in front of his house, provoking an extremely foul and unhealthy atmosphere. He alleged that com-plaints to his neighbour had fallen on deaf ears. Another resident complained about the poor location of his neighbour's toilet just beneath his bedroom window. He claimed that the stench from his neighbour's toilet had made his life miserable. He too had complained to no avail and therefore beseeched the

NBA's assistance in resolving the problem.

The NBA won tremendous credibility on account of its engagement in this sanitary campaign. News about the inspection tour spread far and wide and before long, each household anticipated the NBA's visit. Even elderly women in the neighbourhood commended the NBA's 'work' and urged them to leave no stone unturned. Evidence for this occurred when Carlson accompanied me to interview one of their members' mothers. She was busy tending a garden in front of her house and when she saw us approaching, she dropped her hoe and started to talk about the toilet problems in the neighbourhood: "my children," she began, "you should really do something about these toilets in our community." Then she pointed to a small garden across the street which she claimed belonged to her. "Each time I plant crops over there I can't harvest them because of excrement. People use that area for their toilets. The smell keeps me away and that's how I lose a lot of my crops" she lamented. Carlson suggested that the tall weeds around the garden should be cleared off in order to render the space "open". "No one would have the courage to squat in open view" he said, "except at night" I added. "Seeing that you guys are handling this issue, I would be very happy if you try to solve this problem" the woman stated.

The weekend after the initial inspection tour, the NBA held its regular Sunday meeting to assess the operation. "Since we've sensitised the people and many already know that something is going on, it is imperative to get the council involved" recommended Collins, one of the executive members. The meeting's agenda was dominated by discussions on the inspection tour. Some members expressed disappointment on what they perceived was a low turn out. "Those who didn't show up are the same individuals who hardly show up at other human investment operations" Carlson queried. But these concerns did not dampen the NBA's resolve to pursue the operation to its logical conclusion. In pursuit of its goal, the association resolved to undertake a trip to the BUC to demand the council's intervention. To this end, the brothers took with them a formal letter addressed to the director of the Health and Sanitation Department at the BUC:

> Our group that was led by the Health Committee [of the NBA] inspected toilets around the periphery of Old Town on the 27th of July 2005. The condition in which we met the toilets calls for a cause of concern from your office which caters for the good health of our people in Bamenda.
>
> To start with, there are very many compounds without toilets. It is in this light that people staying in such compounds excrete anywhere they

think good for them. With such situations, it is very likely very many people will get sick.

- Secondly, we discovered that most toilets are not built. People passing by can easily see and discuss with another who is easing himself. This system is really deplorable.
- Thirdly, toilets around this area are very stinky. The smell coming out from most toilets makes the quarter unbearable to live in.
- Some toilets are already full. The owners care very little to see how they can dig up another or how they can even empty the toilets.
- Other toilets surroundings are so dirty. This makes it possible for mosquitoes to come out from such places and bite the people living around these places, thus leading to malaria.

Also included in the letter were two specific requests to the council authorities: a) to send sanitary staff to Old Town to collaborate with the NBA in 'sinking' toilets that posed a health risk to its owners and the community and, b) appealed for chemicals to assist in the treatment of pit toilets in the community.

Contrary to their expectations, the NBA met with uncooperative staff at the council. "They wanted us to provide them with transport money before they could come" Carlson reported. "But after explaining to them that we are simply a voluntary group without any sponsor, the guys accepted to visit us on Tuesday at 8 a.m." He then appealed to members to come out in their numbers to welcome the sanitary staff and to enable them see "how serious" the operation was. "I would like that after our discussion with them, they should not hesitate to help us when next we go to the council. That's why I'm appealing to all members to come out on Tuesday morning so that the council people can see we are a serious group" urged Carlson. Tuesday went by without the anticipated visitors. After several weeks of waiting, the NBA unanimously resolved to contact Pa Njikam, the vice government delegate, hopeful that he would assist the NBA once again as he had done with the "trashcan operation". This yielded crucial results, thus vindicating the NBA's claim as a proxy of the BUC in the community of Old Town.

Upgrading the Community Healthcare Centre

Since its founding in 2004 and its reincarnation as a common initiative group, the NBA has been at the forefront of health initiatives intended to benefit the Ntambag community. The NBA's efforts in these respects highlight another dimension of what I have previously described as productive masculinity.

Although a national government directive created a community centre for Old Town since 2007, it only started operating in 2015. In a bid to meet its commitments on goals #5 and 6 of the Millennium Development Goals (MDGs), health centres were established in areas of desperate need throughout the country. However, these facilities often existed on paper, and where physical structures existed, they were often understaffed and heavily under-resourced. Their upkeep predictably is left to the community. At its inception, it was headed by a senior nurse who single-handedly, oversaw the health centre. Due to security concerns and with growing demand for healthcare, the Ntambag Brothers lobbied a Yaounde-based government official with ties to Old Town who played a part in the relocation of the centre to its current site – the Ntambag Community Hall.

Overwhelmed by the increased number of patients under her care, the senior nurse turned to the NBA for help. This call for assistance led to what the brothers consider one of their greatest accomplishments – they hired a family doctor in 2016 who had completed his residency and was awaiting deployment. For the first two years, the physician was paid a modest stipend of 100,000FCFA exclusively from the Ntambag Brothers' coffers. Subsequently, a partnership between the Ntambag Brothers and the Joseph Ncho Foundation, a US-based non-profit enabled the hiring and payment of successive medical doctors.[6] While the nurse was on the government's payroll, the Ntambag Brothers along with several donors ensured that volunteers who served at the facility were paid a small stipend.

Besides upgrading the status of the health centre by hiring a physician, the Ntambag Brothers also invested in the procurement of a blood screening equipment in 2019. When the need for this machine arose, the NBA diverted a prior donation of 1 million francs CFA from their patroness and embarked upon an aggressive fundraising campaign, targeting especially its diaspora members. Today, the NBA takes exceptional pride in the "uniqueness" of its health centre that is unlike any other facility in the region.

Mobilising During the Covid-19 Pandemic

When Covid-19 struck the community of Old Town in March 2020, residents were initially skeptical about the reality of the disease. According to

---

6.   These employees are generally recent graduates who have completed their residencies and awaiting government appointments to public hospitals.

my friends in the NBA, the association decided to intervene after three Covid-related deaths were reported in the community. Members agreed to carry out a sensitisation campaign that would hopefully, prevent further spread of the disease and possibly, death. Each member was obliged to contribute 5000FCFA from which 300 masks and 20 buckets for hand washing were procured. During the campaign that ran for three days, NBA members assigned themselves into small groups to maximise time and outreach. In their outreach, they emphasised the benefits of social distancing, demonstrated to community members how to wear their face masks and the importance of washing one's hands frequently.

FIGURE 4.3 Temporary bucket taps on display prior to distribution in the community of Old Town by the NBA. Photo by the NBA

FIGURE 4.4 The brothers install temporary bucket taps around the community to enable frequent handwashing in a bid to stem the spread of Covid-19. Photo by the NBA

FIGURE 4.5 The NBA educate community members in Old Town on how to correctly wear their facial/mouth masks during the Covid-19 pandemic. April 2020. Photo by the NBA

The initial supply of face masks and buckets quickly ran out and the association galvanised for a second campaign. This time, the Joseph Ncho Foundation provided additional funds and diaspora members contributed towards the purchase of 5000 face masks, 20 buckets and thousands of personal hand sanitisers.

Empowerment and Reshaping Social Adulthood

I have shown in this chapter that sanitary activism amongst young people in Old Town provides a rich repertoire through which to theorise the significance of young people's mobilising and the politics of everyday life. One of the questions raised in development studies circles includes how collective actors build collective identities and how they create new cultural models (Escobar 1992:30). We see from the foregoing that everyday life "involves a collective act of creation, a collective signification, a culture" (Escobar 1992:30) that sheds light on the micro-processes of how people reshape their identities and give meaning to their lives. This chapter offers an account that explains how collective actors build collective identities while engaging with and challenging existing structures. The NBA's sanitary activism – from its manufacture of trashcans, to the sensitisation campaigns during the COVID-19 pandemic, underscores the view that change may be understood not from the perspective of "grand structural transformations" but rather by examining the ways in which grassroots movements construct identities and seek "greater autonomy through modifications in everyday practices and beliefs" (Escobar 1992:31).

We may further our understanding of the significance of everyday life in Old Town by highlighting two ways in which young people appropriate urban space. First, the *implantation* of the NBA's trashcans in public and private spheres of Old Town enabled the group to *insert* itself into the urban landscape of Old Town. The trashcans for instance, expressed in a symbolic and potent manner, their "capture" of urban spaces that previously were perceived to be the exclusive domain of the state and municipal government. According to Diouf, the postcolony has tended to treat urban public space "as an adult territory off limits to youth at the same time that it denies them a private space" (Diouf 1996:226). This exclusionary practice is informed by the logic of tradition that conceives the subordination of the young as a traditional imperative. Thus, by inscribing their activities on urban space, young people in Old Town challenge the postcolony's exclusionary practice.

Second, young people's physical presence, their human investment through 'work' and frequent sanitary operations highlight the appropriation of urban space in a context where the municipal government was perceived to have withdrawn or abandoned its duties. Through the implantation of its symbols and 'work', young people's associations in Old Town, particularly the NBA, positioned themselves at the forefront of communal affairs, posing not only as crusaders for communal hygiene but also as alternate sites of power, armed with the capacity, real or imagined, to broker communal needs with local government and civil authorities, even if achieved through emerging or existing patrimonial networks.

Young people's sanitary activism in Old Town also challenges popular constructions of "urban youth" as decadent and moral failures, perhaps not unlike the physical atmosphere of decay they inhabit. Often depicted as the postcolony's *enfants terribles* and perceived as more prone to breaking than making (cf. Honwana & de Boeck 2005), young people often find themselves victimised by urban renewal programmes, particularly those designed and executed by national government or municipal authorities (cf. Samara 2005). This is partly because many young people creatively eke out their livelihoods in the informal sector as hawkers. Urban renewal programmes carried out in Bamenda in the late 1990s and early 2000s attest to this sort of government myopia and arrogance when young people were cleared off the streets as part of the BUC's programme to reclaim control over the streets. However, we see in this chapter how young people constructively challenge the marginalising practices of the BUC. Indeed, their engagement with matters of sanitation enables us to gain insights on municipal corruption, lethargy, greed and the chronic manifestation of decay that characterises the Cameroonian postcolony (Mbembe 1992, 2001; Schmidt-Soltau 1999). Note for example, the bitter remarks of the young men concerning the MIDENO director's luxurious vehicle and the NBA's exposure of the government delegate as a liability to the citizens of Bamenda. It is therefore not surprising that young people in Cameroon like their counterparts in many African countries tend to interpret their predicament through a moral prism by contending that the "elders" have betrayed or abandoned them (cf. Abbink 2005). However, by opting to act differently, young people have also "enunciated a new sociability, contradictory to the norms that have presided over the postcolonial compromise" (Diouf 1996:247). By acting differently, young people highlight their yearning for more democratic, egalitarian and participatory models of social change. Importantly, their quest for greater autonomy and less dependence on the state sum up the their redefinition of social adulthood.

This chapter has also shown that sanitary activism, while providing pathways for young people to assert their claims to social adulthood, is nevertheless a highly gendered activity. It is gendered in the sense that embedded in its ideals and practices are "resources for doing gender" – that is, practices that produce or reinforce gender ideologies in society. Aulette and Wittner (2015) suggest that *doing gender* "reinforces the illusion that there are essential differences between women and men when, in fact, the *doing* is what creates these very differences" (2015:72). We see these differences in the kinds of sanitary operations carried out by the women and men's associations in Old Town. Whilst the women's campaigns have predominantly occurred in private homes, the NBA's operations have in the main taken place in public spaces such as main roads, public buildings, direct engagement with public officials and other popular campaigns that aim to sensitise the community as a whole. This doing of gender has reinforced the idea of a hierarchy of young people's associations in Old Town that places the NBA at the pinnacle, on account of the scale and public dimensions of its operations. That it has also won the recognition and praise of many "elders" in the community, is drawn upon by the NBA to highlight its pre-eminence in a patriarchal hierarchy of credibility and influence where "men" always carry out the most valued tasks (see Seidler 2006). Thus, sanitary activism inadvertently reproduces gender inequality and stratification as the young men claim greater prestige and visibility on account of their civic engagements through the performance of productive masculinity. Remarkably, sanitary activism provides a platform through which young men not only prove their manhood (by showing physical strength, endurance and responsibility towards their community) but also as constitutive of their status as social adults. I also show that women's sanitary activism on the other hand enables them to exercise agency by gathering resources to empower themselves as young women.

Young people's collective responses to urban decay in Old Town reveal the mechanisms through which citizens challenge municipal exclusion and the marginalising practices of national and local governments. In pursuit of their ideals for a sanitised neighbourhood, young people stake claims not only for their recognition as social adults but also enable us to appreciate the processes through which grassroots movements redefine state-centric notions of citizenship and civic engagement. By substituting the neighbourhood for national territory as the canvas for elaborating the symbolic and the imaginary (Diouf 1996), young people's local actions assume national significance. The ethnographic details recounted in this chapter further reveal not only young people's disillusionment with the postcolonial state but also their dreams of a renaissance and the values of solidarity and the micro-processes of social transformation. Preoccupation with sanitation in Old Town also mirrors a similar enterprise carried out on a moral landscape which comes under focus in the next chapter.

CHAPTER FIVE

Cultivating Respect, Gendered Spaces and Moral Transformation in Old Town

This chapter describes and analyses the ways in which young people in Old Town position themselves as moral citizens by constructing a moral community circumscribed by highly gendered notions of respectability, self-care and charitable action. The moral community forged by these young people is in part driven by their shared desire to root out social ills –perpetrated either by delinquent members or other "youth" in the community – pursuits that affirm their collective will to social adulthood through practices perceived by them to bring respect and honour. I argue that by deploying a variety of technologies of self-care, by cultivating virtuous selves through collective charitable pursuits as moral citizens, these young people transform not only themselves but also their social and material spaces. However, I also show that these processes and actions are not only gendered but also tend to normalize various forms of oppression, thereby reinforcing some of the very "social ills" they seek to root out. I foreground my analysis by showing how these young people's *moral subjectivities* – that is, their sense of self and self-world relations (Holland & Leander 2004) are shaped by the social and material spaces they inhabit. In other words, one's subjectivity rests on the basis that as individuals, we bear not only rights, but also duties and obligations in our personal and intimate relations with others. Our subjectivities are therefore shaped by a combination of our duties, rights, obligations as well as our personal dispositions (Werbner 2002:2-3). This chapter analyses how young people's moral subjectivities are deployed in a range of social settings and practices while accounting for the contradictions in their pursuits.

I show that young people in Old Town aim to position themselves and to be seen and respected as social adults in a social landscape where traditional pathways to these identities and statuses are no longer predictable. Having come of age in a country characterised by multiple and prolonged crises (Fokwang 2014; Roitman 2014), the young people in this ethnography are shown to be creative and dynamic as individuals and as members of gendered associations who seek moral transformation for themselves and their community. Their practices are framed within what I call moral citizenship – that is, the pursuit of ethical actions that combine the cultivation of virtuous character and self-care in fulfilling one's obligations towards the moral and physical transformation of one's community. Unlike conceptions of citizenships that prioritise membership within a political community, one's entitlements or status in relation to the modern state (Henn & Weinstein 2006; Jones & Wallace 1992; Wallace & Helve 2001), moral citizenship advances the idea of the common good (Chomsky 2013; Regh 2007), conviviality, mutual indebtedness (Nyamnjoh 2017) and one's obligation to community.

But what factors drive these pursuits? I show that the "day-to-day technologies of self-care" (Mattingly 2012:4) deployed by young people in Old Town are in part, responses to local discourses that paint a sordid image of the neighbourhood. In the popular imaginary, Old Town is perceived as a neighbourhood replete with bandits, drug addicts, prostitutes and morally depraved persons of all shades and flavour. Contemporary Old Town is akin to colonial and postcolonial literary representations of the African town that embodies "corruption, moral, sexual, and social deviance" in which Africans have lost their souls and sense of community (Diouf 1996:228). What we see in this chapter is not only ethnographic descriptions of how young people are grappling with the soiled image of their community but also, how as individuals and collectivities, they seek to redefine and give new meaning to it.

I develop these ideas in three main sections – first, by providing ethnographic evidence to substantiate what it means to pursue collective goals with and on behalf of a community. Next, I show how associations contribute towards the cultivation of virtuous character amongst their members and the contradictions these practices hold for social transformation. I then detail the life histories of selected individuals, showing the micro-processes that inform how their moral subjectivities intersect with or contradict their associations' goals. A brief analysis of the data concludes the chapter – showing the gendered implications and beyond of these processes and actions.

The Collective Basis of Achievement

As previously discussed in this work, a popular Grassfields trope compares elderly male notables to vessels brimming over with vital substances required for social reproduction (cf. Warnier 1996:121) while social cadets on the other hand, are perceived as "empty vessels" with little to offer besides their labour and deference. Because of their possession of vital substances, elders command and enjoy respect and social power over social cadets. However, changing notions of personhood and respectability in the Grasslands have enabled young people to draw on local idioms to position themselves as social adults – the most salient of which is the pursuit of success on behalf of a group. Another popular metaphor that reinforces this ethos is tied to hunting in the wild. A daring young man or hunter who ventures into the "deep bush" and returns with a formidable game deserves recognition. It is this same worldview that has morphed and powered the notion of "bushfalling" today whereby young people unable to achieve economic citizenship at home risk the arduous task of seeking greener pastures abroad with the intention to bring back their "catch" to celebrate with kith and kin (Fokwang 2003; Jua 2003; Nyamnjoh & Page 2002; H. Nyamnjoh 2021). Thus, by redistributing one's success or pursuing a charitable cause on behalf of a group, one demonstrates maturity and in consequence, wins honour and the symbolic capital of respectability. Francis Nyamnjoh sums up this popular discourse when he asserts that in the Bamenda Grasslands "achievement is devoid of meaning if not pursued within, as part of, and on behalf of a group of people who recognise and endorse that achievement. For only by making their successes collective can individuals make their failures a collective concern as well" (Nyamnjoh 2002:115). This is akin to the kinds of exchange relationships Jennifer Cole describes for young Tamatavians who pursue full personhood and social adult status by fulfilling the needs of their ancestors and living kin (Cole 2010).

I show in this chapter that young people in Old Town pursued a range of altruistic actions within and beyond their communities – moral practices that won them honour, visibility and prestige. To this end, all three associations undertook charitable activities such as visiting the sick in their homes and hospitals, donating food to prisoners and contributed to urban renewal through sanitary activism. My friends in Old Town affirmed that these moral causes were not only intrinsically worthy in themselves but also enhanced their social standing in the community. In other words, the pursuit of these causes insofar as they contributed to the transformation of society, ultimately shaped the way society also saw them – that is, as mature, moral citizens whose accomplishments were being pursued "within, as part of, and on behalf of a group of people." These claims will be illustrated by describing the planning and execution of three major public events or schemes carried out by two of the associations, namely, a prize award ceremony at a local public school, a hospital visit to support individuals living with various disabilities and the development of a scheme to sponsor underprivileged children.

The Prize Award Ceremony

During one of its Sunday meetings in May 2005, the NBA resolved to organise an end of year prize award ceremony[1] at the Government Primary School (GPS), Old Town. Many of the NBA members had attended this primary school and therefore felt proud to organise such a pioneering event at their alma mater. Although initially intended to encourage pupils to take their studies seriously, the NBA anticipated that this event would boost the association's standing in the community and contribute towards transforming the damaging stereotypes about its residents. A young man who sat next to me during the meeting underscored this sense of optimism when he whispered confidently: "after this event, people will know that Old Town has changed." To achieve their objective, the leadership of the association demanded a contribution of 1000FCFA from all members. The unanimity with which the brothers agreed on this sum initially puzzled me, partly because financial issues often suffered endless arguments particularly if the required contribution was above 500FCFA. To emphasise the urgency of the impending event and to encourage members to meet their financial obligation, the NBA suspended other contributions and fines. Besides the required contribution of 1000FCFA, the association also invited individual members to sponsor prizes of their choice to be awarded to deserving pupils.

After consultations with the school authorities, the NBA scheduled the event for 10 a.m. on Friday, 10 June 2005, which incidentally was the designated date for all primary and secondary schools to close for the summer vacation. Invited to the event were the patrons of the association as well as the divisional Inspector of Basic and Secondary Education[2]. Upon arrival at the school premises at 9:45 a.m., I met up with a group of five NBA members chatting at the school entrance. Pupils in their blue uniforms were dispersed in every nook and cranny of the school premises, screaming, playing and chasing each other.

Unlike the previous days that had been rainy and cloudy, this Friday glowed

1.   Prize award ceremonies were common in nursery schools (kindergarten) and gradually introduced in private primary schools in the 1990s. However, this was generally rare in public schools, something the NBA initiated in Old Town.
2.   Equivalent to a school district superintendent in the USA.

in beautiful warm sunlight, exuding an aura of optimism and the joyful anticipation of a long break from academic affairs. Indeed, by 7 a.m. that morning,
the sun was already fully visible in the clear blue skies, and when I arrived at
the school, it was already scorching, evidenced by the strips of sweat on the
young men's faces whose company I immediately sought. One of the brothers
who could no longer bear the heat suggested we move into the school premises where he was certain we would easily find a shade from the blazing sun.
Without protest, the group moved into the inner quarters of the school and
predictably, found refuge on the veranda in front of the headteacher's office.
Inside the schoolyard, the population was even bigger and noisier – about
600 or more. It was in brief, a scene of joyful chaos – which reminded me of
my own days in elementary school in the early to mid-1980s. On the last day
of school, pupils would receive their report cards, bid farewell to friends and
classmates and head off for the long summer vacation.

Attendance at public functions such as this was mandatory for all NBA
members. Individuals who failed to attend without prior permission were
fined even if they had contributed the required due. Although I was confident
that a majority of the NBA would attend, I was equally convinced that they
would not be time conscious. Upon arrival at the veranda, I was pleasantly
surprised to find a few NBA members arranging the prizes. One of them was
Ernest, who was particularly fond of me. He frequently invited me to visit
him at his house where we had long conversations on a variety of topics. He
was arguably the liveliest of all the NBA members I had befriended during
my fieldwork. From the vantage point of the veranda, we faced the assembly
grounds and watched the children as they played. When I met up with Ernest
and Philip, another member, they were talking about a little boy whom they
pointed out in the crowd. I had some difficulty locating him and once I did,
Ernest whispered to my hearing that the little boy's father was a well-known
thief. "He's one of those who gives our quarter a bad name."

"I caught that kid and one of his friends smoking marijuana" Philip claimed.
The little boy would have been about eight or ten years. His left eye was swollen,
and his forehead revealed an untreated wound. I was immediately driven to
pity upon seeing him and before I could comment, Ernest added that he was
certain the child's family had come from far away: "that kid looks like a terrorist,
I think he's a Chadian; there's no way he can be a child from this area." "What
do Chadians look like? You simply can't tell his origin by looking at them," I
queried. Ernest and Philip simply ignored my protests and insisted on their
view that most of those who contributed to the sordid image of Old Town were

"foreign" to the community. Their claims then were not uncommon and still prevalent today where contestations over who belongs within the body politic still informs public opinion, whether in Cameroon (Geschiere 2009; Geschiere & Nyamnjoh 2000), in southern Africa (Comaroff & Comaroff 2001; Everatt 2011; Nyamnjoh 2006; Vale 2002) or Euro-America (Fetzer 2000). What my friends' statements hold in common with popular discourses elsewhere is the tendency to blame the community or nation's woes on immigrants, refugees and/or foreigners – a major contradiction of globalisation which, as aptly described by Peter Geschiere is characterised by the "dialectics of flow and closure" (Geschiere & Gugler 1998; Geschiere & Meyer 1998).

Ernest and Philip were both former pupils of this school and offered to brief me on the history of the school. Opened in 1981, GS Old Town rapidly gained the reputation of being one of the unruliest schools in Bamenda. My friends insisted that this ill-reputation was due to the predominant Muslim population of its pupils, coupled with the fact that the school was located within the bounds of what is known as the Hausa quarters in Old Town. In this part of the country, the ethnic category, Hausa is synonymous to Muslim, sometimes invoked by non-Muslim populations to stereotype fellow citizens as violent and ruthless – akin to the stigmatization of Arabs and Muslims in the West especially after the terrorist attack of September 11, 2001. My attempts to challenge their characterisations, as before, failed woefully. To substantiate their claims, Ernest went on:

> In those early days, the pupils were much older than they are today; so pupils used to beat up primary school teachers or fight with them. Some teachers were afraid of pupils and when they realised how difficult it was to work in this environment, they would apply to be transferred elsewhere. There were stories of teachers who came to class and found excrement in their drawers. Those Hausa kids used to do terrible things. The worst mistake was for a teacher to beat up an unruly Hausa pupil. On several occasions, children who were punished by their teachers simply went home, brought their friends, neighbours and parents who entered the school premises and beat up the teacher.

Things allegedly improved, Philip recalled, when the school saw an increase in the non-Muslim population. "Today, the Hausa are a minority in this school, so they've opened a new school just down there in the valley." As we chatted, one of the association's patrons arrived and shook hands with us and alerted us to the fact that the event was about to begin.

It was a few minutes past 11 a.m. by now and the ceremony was finally going to begin. The grey-haired headteacher, dressed in a green suit with black shoes came out of his office and stood at the middle of the veranda. He moved from one end of the assembly line to the other, brandishing a cane. From time to time, he threatened to use his cane on the pupils who kept pushing and shoving each other to gain a front position. The headteacher wanted them to step back about a metre from the veranda, but each attempt yielded the same result because those behind kept pushing their friends. Determined to win their attention, the headteacher instructed the pupils to raise their hands. "Clap five times", he declared, and the children responded. A female teacher tuned a song for the kids to sing but the chaos was still in full swing. Frustrated, the headmaster yelled instructions at three female teachers to organise the pupils. Each grade ought to form four straight lines, two for boys and two for girls. However, only the older pupils in senior primary could organise themselves without the teachers' assistance. The female teachers looked haggard in the scorching sun. One of them left defiantly and retreated into the shade of the veranda. The headmaster stood still and without uttering a word, pretended to ignore the defiant teacher. "Raise your hands", he instructed. "Clap five times" and the pupils obeyed. This trick seemed to work because after several claps, the kids became attentive. Finally, he asked them to be quiet. "Put your finger across your mouth" he yelled, and the kids placed their index fingers against their mouths.

"Today is a special day unlike yesterday and unlike other closing ceremonies", he began, once calm had been established. "It is special because you have seated in front here, a group of youths who have come to encourage you to work hard. They will give prizes to deserving pupils and those who go home with nothing will work harder next time so that they can win prizes in future." After speaking for a few minutes, the headteacher gave the floor to the NBA's organising secretary who came forward and read out the details of the programme. He proceeded to invite the NBA's president to deliver his speech. Carlson rose from his seat and greeted everyone and then began by thanking the teachers for performing an excellent job during the academic year and promised to organise a prize award function specifically for teachers the following year. This time, he declared, the association had decided to begin with the pupils. Finally, he urged the Inspector of Basic Education to address teachers' concerns because pupils' success depended largely on the working conditions of teachers. On his part, the Inspector expressed surprise and delight at seeing what the NBA was doing for its community. "If there are more associations like yours, then Bamenda would be a better place. Through you, I hope, Old Town will become New Town", he declared, and a thunderous applause greeted his words. He urged the teachers to participate in future seminars organised by his department to strengthen their professional skills. Following the inspector's speech, the NBA's organising secretary invited respective personalities and NBA members to hand out the prizes. Each prize consisted of an exercise book, a ruler and varying amounts of pencils. The top four pupils from each class received a prize. The NBA donated a total of seventy-two prizes after which, serving as the event's photographer, the laureates and the brothers were invited to come forward for a photoshoot.

FIGURE 5.1 Pupils of the Government Primary School, Old Town at the assembly ground on the last day of the academic year, June 2005. Photo by author.

FIGURE 5.2 Pupils of the GPS pose with their prizes donated by members of the Ntambag Brothers Association, June 2011. Photo by NBA

A Day at SAJOCAH, Bafut

The United Sisters, like their counterparts, the Chosen Sisters, and the NBA carried out small and high-profile charitable activities within and beyond Old Town. To commemorate its fourth anniversary, the United Sisters organised a visit to the St Joseph's Catholic Hospital (SAJOCAH), a renowned mission hospital specialised in the care of persons living with various kinds of physical disability, located in Bafut about 20km north of Bamenda. The event was sched-uled for Sunday, 6 November 2005. Although the dry season had just begun, the harmattan winds were powerful and the earth, dry and dusty. Susan, who was tasked with organising transportation for the members turned up that morning without a vehicle. She also offered no coherent explanation why there was no vehicle. Frustrated by this development, the sisters settled for a pickup truck popularly known as *Cargo* – owing to its use for the transportation of merchandise or hardware. Dressed in their sparkly, colourful uniforms, the ladies mounted the pickup and sat on benches brought from their meeting venue. They were soon joined by two young men who would assist them in carrying the gifts they had pooled for their trip - a 50kg bag of rice, a box of soap tablets and a 20kg bag of salt. The sisters appeared undeterred by the prospect of enduring a windy, open ride to Bafut. Except for a little delay provoked by Bella who wanted a seat in the driver's cabin – even though four of us were already cramped in that compartment, all was set for the trip. At 12:30 p.m., the truck throttled off from Old Town while onlookers taunted them for dressing so beautifully and then dirtying themselves by riding in an open *Cargo*. Soon after our departure, the sisters burst into song, occasionally accompanied by claps.

FIGURE 5.3 Members of the United Sisters pose with gifts for residents of SAJOCAH, November 13, 2005. Photo by author.

Upon arrival at SAJOCAH, we proceeded to the reception hall where Rev. Sr. Cecilia, the resident manager of the hospital welcomed us. Residents of the institution were soon assembled to perform a welcome song, followed by a short speech by the president of the United Sisters who briefed them on the association's objectives – one of which was to care for the underprivileged. Sr. Cecilia thanked the United Sisters for their generosity and most especially for thinking of the poor and the disabled. She urged them to become ambassadors of SAJOCAH and to sensitise people about the institution and its need for support. Sr. Cecilia further insinuated that due to the stigma associated with disability, some families tend to hide potential patients in their homes where they are treated poorly or denied access to medical assistance. "SAJOCAH[3] is the place for them" she added.

FIGURE 5.4 The United Sisters in their uniform back in Old Town to celebrate their anniversary following a successful trip to Bafut. November 13, 2005. Photo by author.

Education for the Underprivileged

One of the areas in which the NBA has won tremendous admiration is its development of an education initiative whose primary beneficiaries are children from extremely poor households in Old Town. The NBA's involvement arose from the association's concerns about the alleged high rate of school dropouts in Old Town[4] - a phenomenon exacerbated by sharp economic downturns

3.   For over three decades, the institution has established a solid reputation for its care for the blind, children with rickets, providing physiotherapy for victims of stroke and other conditions.
4.   Although education is one of the most valued markers of success in the Grasslands, statistics in the 2000s revealed that an increased number of households could not afford to enrol or maintain their children in primary school. This downward trend was in part related to the prolonged economic crisis that has rocked the country since the mid-1980s. For instance, government records show that net primary enrolment rate declined from 76.2% in 1989 to 61.7% in 1997 (Government of Cameroon 2002). Although the 1996 Constitution provides for compulsory primary education for Cameroonians, the government only declared its intention to provide free primary education in 2001– a promise whose substance has remained largely empty because parents still bear the cost of providing their children with uniforms,

faced by the country in general and the North West Region specifically.[5]

A couple of weeks after the award ceremony, the NBA designed a small-scale sponsorship programme for underprivileged female children on the assumption that this category of the population faced specific cultural impediments to primary education – particularly among the Hausa (Muslim) populations. Many NBA members who knew about the Millennium Development Goals (MDGs)[6] considered this initiative as their contribution towards some of its objectives. The Cameroon government on its part, had set the objective of eliminating gender disparities in primary and secondary enrolments by 2005. It was therefore remarkable that the NBA's new scheme was in synergy with the national government's objectives.

First, a questionnaire was designed by a small committee headed by Collins, one of the association's university graduates. The questionnaire elicited socio-economic data from residents as well as cultural attitudes towards education in general. After a month of data collection and analysis, the NBA resolved to sponsor a maximum of four pupils. The shortlisted candidates included several children abandoned to their grandmothers by their single-mothers and little Fulani boys pulled out of school by their parents for lack of funds. Drawing on the experience of a member who was then a sponsor of two children in a local primary school, the sum of 20,000FCFA was budgeted for each child. Further brainstorming led to the NBA settling for only two pupils. However, one of its self-employed members volunteered to sponsor a third child on behalf of the association. With a budget of 40,000FCFA, the association purchased notebooks, the required textbooks, a pair of uniforms and sandals for each child. Eventually, the leadership of the association sought and obtained admission for the selected pupils at the GS Old Town. They subsequently notified the headmaster of their initiative and of the pioneer beneficiaries.

Between 2005 and 2022, the association has sponsored over a hundred students including a seminarian and at least two university students. Some of the beneficiaries have enjoyed sponsorship from primary through high school,

books and school supplies.
5.   Things took a turn for the worse in 2016 when a protest movement led by lawyers and teachers morphed into full-scale civil war in 2017. The conflict has displaced hundreds of thousands of people and deprived over 500,000 children of education for several years.
6.   The eight Millennium Development Goals (MDGs) – which range from halving extreme poverty to halting the spread of HIV/AIDS and providing universal primary education, by the target date of 2015 – formed a blueprint agreed to by UN member nations. The MDGs have since been succeeded by the Sustainable Development Goals.

thanks to a standing committee within the association tasked with fundraising exclusively for education.

***

The three cases above substantiate the enactment of young people's moral subjectivities across various domains of social life. Members participate not only in fulfilling their obligations to their respective associations, but we also see that their individual contributions reveal the ways in which collective resources and objectives are mobilised within, as part of and on behalf of their associations in the service of community. Indeed, as members of various associations, their participation in these causes is akin to anthropological conceptions of the principle of reciprocity, especially the potlatch – where resources are pooled by community members and subsequently redistributed (see Carrier 1995). If we extend Warnier's metaphor of the empty vessel – we see that young people are actively filling their cups, not necessarily dependent on the exclusive vital substances from notables as it were, but by legitimising their actions and causes, in part by seeking communal approval and praise – "vital substances" that also engender social adulthood. By donating food and other necessities to the needy, awarding prizes or establishing a scholarship scheme for underprivileged children, members of these associations fulfil not only the responsibilities associated with social adulthood but also, contribute towards the moral transformation of their community. However, I also show that these pursuits, especially those that entail ethical self-care and the cultivation of virtuous character embody contradictions that warrant further explanation.

Ambiguous Virtuosity and Gendered Responses to Deviance

In pursuit of their goal to root out social ills from Old Town, members of the three associations also turned their focus within – enacting new rules and behavioural norms that would epitomise the adage that charity begins at home. In this section, I detail these practices, showing how they sought not only the transformation of their community but also in reforming their members. One of the first issues that struck me about the Chosen and United Sisters, concerned their punitive sanctions against members accused of various transgressions. For example, both associations took a very tough stance against abortion[7]– an act most members perceived as contrary to Christian morality.

---

7.   The Cameroon Penal Code, Section 266, Article 1 stipulates that abortion is a criminal

Abortion, many argued, undermined their objectives and invariably resorted to meting what they perceived to be hard punishment or expulsion for guilty individuals. To this end, the Chosen Sisters and NBA for instance, clearly outlined proscribed behaviours in their bylaws with corresponding penalties. For example, Article 2 of the Chosen Sisters' constitution outlines as such:

- Without being exhaustive, the following acts shall be punishable.
- Gossiping or spying into peoples' private lives destructively (500FCFA).
- Misconduct during in-and outdoor activities tarnishing the image of the group (1000FCFA).
- Disturbance during meetings. e.g., eating, talking or drinking, unnecessary in and out movement, sleeping, and late coming (50FCFA).
- Quarrelling i) during meetings (300FCFA). ii) out of the meeting (1000FCFA).
- Unceremonious departures (French leaves) from i) Meetings (100FCFA). ii) other activities (500FCFA).
- Wearing of group's uniform at the wrong time (1000FCFA).

The article concludes by stating that the "embezzlement of group funds will be recollected by proper legal action." Two items in this article that I found intriguing were– "spying into peoples' lives destructively" and "misconducts that tarnish the image of the group." With time, I would understand why these items were central to the association's attempt to reform the moral lives of their members. An adulterous liaison that involved a member of the association illustrates such conduct that "tarnished" the good name of the association.

The story goes that a member of the association was involved in an adulterous relationship – brought to light when the wife of the cheating husband caught the two lovers red-handed in the boys' quarters of their house. Gravely offended and angry, she shared the news with a friend who, like her husband's mistress was a member of the Chosen Sisters. When the scandal eventually made its way into the association, a couple of members were appointed to investigate the matter who established that the accused had indeed been

---

act. Procuring an abortion according to Cameroon law is punishable with imprisonment between 15 days and (1) year and/or with fines that range from 5000FCFA to 200,000FCFA. However, abortion is widely available through private medical facilities. Women who are unable to afford safe abortions resort to crude methods. There has been hardly any mobilisation for women's reproductive rights that include access to safe abortions. Most members of the United and Chosen Sisters expressed their opposition to abortion, drawing on Catholic teaching which considers it a mortal sin.

involved in grave misconduct – and had consequently tarnished the association's reputation. Initially suspended from the association for two months, the accused eventually lost her membership after she refused to comply with the punishment. Her sister's objection (also a member of the association) to the punishment led to her dismissal as well.

A second case of suspension and eventual expulsion involved a member accused of having procured an abortion. "We were scandalised by this incident because one of the objectives of our association is to fight against abortion in the entire community", a member told me. According to several Chosen Sisters, this incident was considered even more scandalous because the accused had allegedly administered herself an unknown potion to induce the abortion. Instead of seeking medical assistance when she began to bleed, she reportedly locked herself up in her bedroom, anticipating that the bleeding would subside. However, when she realised she may lose her life due to the excessive bleeding, she screamed for help. "We were terrified that she may die" my interviewee said. "When I got there, she had opened the door and her mother was helping to clean the blood." An act, initially conceived to be a private affair had ended up in the public eye, leaving not only the Chosen Sisters but also the entire community horrified. According to my interviewee, the community was scandalised even more so by the fact that the young woman was a mother of two and had allegedly resorted to an abortion upon her boyfriend's persuasion. A few weeks after the incident, the Chosen Sisters received a letter from an anonymous individual calling on the association to discipline the accused member. In a letter dated 8 June 2005, the anonymous writer emphasised that she was not a member of the association but had deep respect and admiration for the association especially after the departure of "some notorious feel-big members". She also admired the Chosen Sisters due to the absence of "competition as in the United Sisters; no enemies and hatred, low gossiping rate" although she added that it was impossible to eradicate "gossiping" completely. Referring specifically to the abortion incident, she reminded the association: "One of your group's objectives is to fight against unwanted pregnancy and abortion. What are you going to do about [...] case with the accomplice of [...] your VP? "Shame". It is not strange but do the right thing." Summoned to a disciplinary hearing, the accused was questioned during a special session scheduled to discuss the matter. She was eventually found guilty and suspended from the association for two months. In addition, she was required to mop the meeting venue every Wednesday throughout the period of her suspension. While she acknowledged having wronged the association, she allegedly disagreed with her peers on how the matter was handled. According to another interviewee, the suspended member "wasn't impressed with the way they spoke to her" and eventually, refused to comply with the association's sanctions. Her accomplice who incidentally was an office holder in the association was relieved of her portfolio and an election organised to fill the position. The suspended member's refusal to comply with the sanctions resulted in the association's decision to expel her after two warnings. In the letter of dismissal addressed to her, the association stated as follows:

> Accept the peace and love of Chosen Sisters!
>
> It is rather with a heavy heart that we write to you. As you well know, our sanctions range from fines to suspension and at times to DISMISSAL especially in the absence of cooperation from the person in default.
>
> *As you already know, you committed an act contrary to Article 2 of our Group's Constitution.* Be reminded that the Constitution in any group stands as a norm to which every other oral or written law must draw its validity....
>
> Since all attempts to bring you to reason failed. You are hereby officially DISMISSED from Chosen Sisters Social Group! We however wish you the best of luck.
>
> We would love to part company amicably. We seize this opportunity to exhort you to make sure you settle your debts with us. You still owe 1000frs for the recent uniform as well as soap for those members who contributed for you. Please be responsible and let them reach us as late as two weeks from this date (emphasis mine).

While most of the members agreed with the expulsion of the accused, the demoted executive opposed her removal from office and allegedly denounced her successor using abusive language. She was served with a warning by the association and urged to comply with the group's decisions.

According to Helen, an ex-member of the Chosen Sisters, the association faced a hard time enforcing its moral code without undermining one of its core values. For example, meddling in members' private affairs was interpreted by some as "spying into peoples' lives destructively" – a constitutional clause (the dreaded Article 2) punishable with a fine of 500FCFA. It was precisely because of this unresolved tension that Helen purportedly left the association because:

> people were bringing personal problems into the meeting which generated a lot of misunderstandings. Our initial goal was to love, care and

show concern for the welfare of each member and our community as a whole. But abortions were rampant and promiscuity fairly common – the two are closely related as you know. When we tried to talk about these issues, people said we were delving too much into people's private lives and advised that we back off which we did initially.

However, the association also resolved that it would not turn a blind eye to some of the problems affecting their peers and the community. It was because of these "social ills" that the association had found its place and voice as a moral vanguard, speaking out against sexual promiscuity and abortion. Abandoning this issue would be an admission of failure on the association's part and the executives would not tolerate any accusation of failure on their part. According to them, it was their responsibility to maintain the integrity and honour of the association's name as best as they could without "spying" on anyone.

The United Sisters also took a tough stance against abortion and sexual promiscuity. However, unlike the Chosen Sisters who expelled two members, two cases handled in the United Sisters simply resulted in the suspension of the accused for a month each. They were further exhorted to write an apology to the association and to clearly express remorse for having soiled the association's name. Attempts to see or read some of the letters proved futile. Besides the suspension of members, I also observed that some members would admonish suspected peers during Sunday meetings on the importance of discretion in their sexual relationships.

Once, I witnessed in astonishment when members took turns to denounce two siblings who were allegedly involved in wanton acts. This came to light when Manka, a leading member of the association reported that someone had complained to her about the behaviour of the two sisters. Their behaviours, she alleged, had brought so much shame to the association and as 'sisters' they had resolved to discuss the issue openly rather than do so behind the backs of the accused. Manka recounted that the two sisters were notorious for dating men for easy access to beer and money. One of the sisters, she claimed, was well known in the community for asking beer from young men who often interpreted such requests as an indication of her availability for sex. Manka further alleged that "a certain person in the quarter has told me that he loved [the accused] but each time he invited her for a drink, he realised that other men would come up to her and ask her to repay the drinks she had consumed." The accused sisters sat quietly while members took turns to voice dissatisfaction with their behaviour. At the end, none of them responded to the accusations which was interpreted as an acceptance of their guilt. One of the speakers appealed for them to cultivate self-pride and to learn to say no to both beer and men. "There's a deadly disease out there", she yelled; "if you girls are not afraid, I'm certainly afraid" she said. "How many people in this house can beat their chest with pride and say they've lived decent lives? Please, dear sisters, stop taking beer from men, because it's not everything that we must accept; it's not every man who proposes to us that we must sleep with." When she concluded and sat down, an uneasy calm seized the room for a while.

On a separate incident in the summer of 2005, a visitor distributed a bunch of flyers to members of the United Sisters during a Sunday meeting. Targeted at teenage girls and young women in their 20s, the flyer aimed to conscientise this demographic against the phenomenon of sugar daddies.[8] Referring to them as *yoyettes,*[9] the flyer unequivocally denounced "cross-generational sex", arguing that any relationship with "sugar daddies" was doomed to fail. One of the flyers carried the following caption printed in bold: "sexual relations between young girls and aged partners are dangerous and they increase the spread of HIV/AIDS." On another page, it stated, "Sugar daddy + Yoyette = A dangerous Mixture". Contrary to my expectations, the flyers did not provoke any further discussions on HIV/AIDS or the phenomenon of sugar daddies. Determined to carry on with the adopted agenda, members were encouraged to read the flyers privately and to direct their questions to *100% Jeune,*[10] the non-profit responsible for circulating the flyers.

8.   Public campaigns against sugar daddies have included protest marches, public talks amongst other activities. See *The Post*, D. O. Bans Protest Against 'Sugar Daddies', accessed on allAfrica. com, July 25, 2005. According to the news story, the divisional officer for Bamenda banned a planned protest march organised by the Cameroon Association for Social Marketing on the grounds that its application was late. The newspaper reports further that following the failure of the planned protest, over 120 youths met at the Bamenda Congress Hall to listen to public talks on the devastating health, moral and social effects of cross-generation sex. Also see *Cameroon Tribune*, "North West: Girls Train to End Cross Generation Sex" accessed at http://allafrica.com/stories/200707050282.html on 4 July 2007.
9.   The term likely has its origins in what has come to be known as Camfranglais; – *yoyette*, I conjecture is the feminine equivalent of *youth* while its masculine counterpart is simply *yo!*
10.   100% Jeune was a popular youth Magazine that covered issues of sexuality, friendship and matters of general interest to youth. Sold at just 100FCFA, it was arguably, the cheapest and most widely circulated magazine in the country, especially attractive because of its glossy colour.

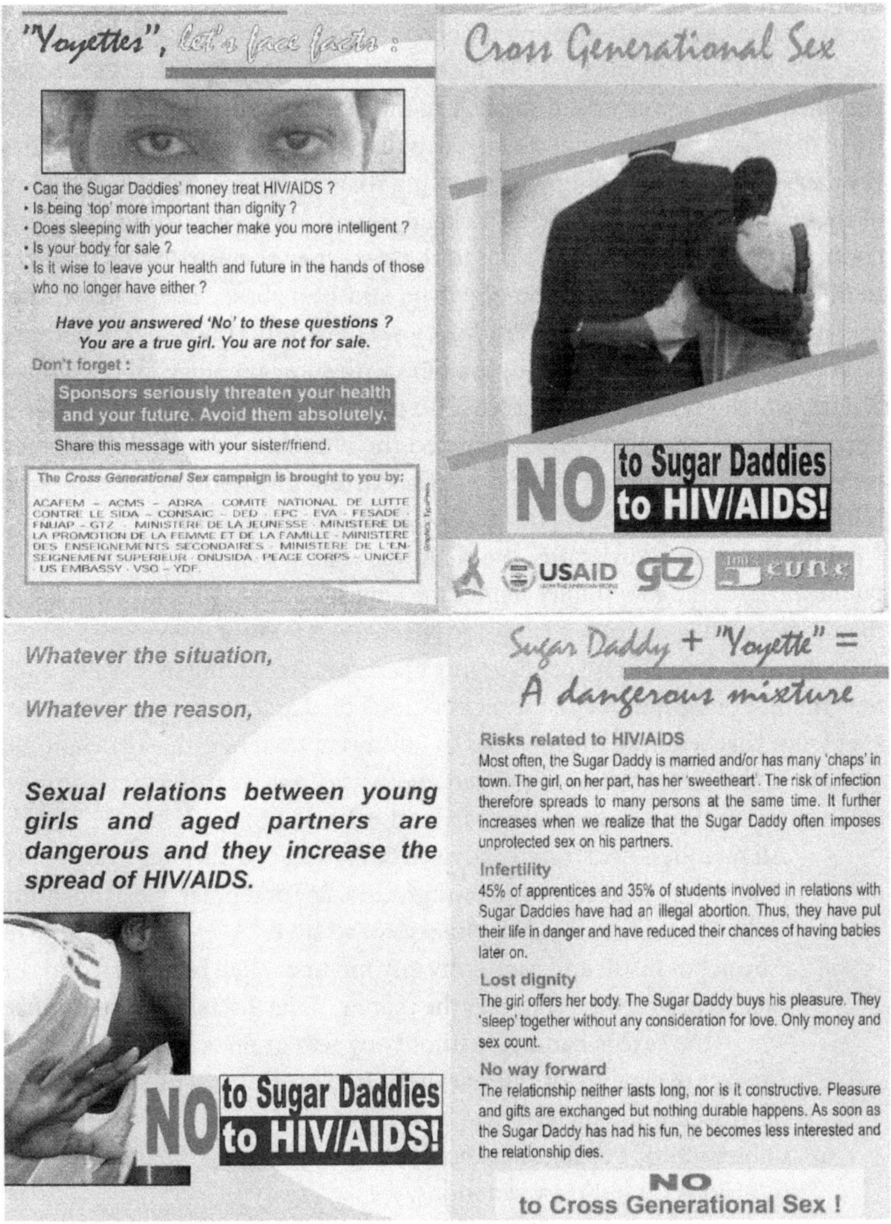

"Voyettes", let's face facts :

Cross Generational Sex

- Can the Sugar Daddies' money treat HIV/AIDS ?
- Is being 'top' more important than dignity ?
- Does sleeping with your teacher make you more intelligent ?
- Is your body for sale ?
- Is it wise to leave your health and future in the hands of those who no longer have either ?

Have you answered 'No' to these questions ? You are a true girl. You are not for sale.

Don't forget :

Sponsors seriously threaten your health and your future. Avoid them absolutely.

Share this message with your sister/friend.

The Cross Generational Sex campaign is brought to you by:

ACAFEM – ACMS – ADRA · COMITE NATIONAL DE LUTTE CONTRE LE SIDA – CONSAIC · DED · EPC · EVA · FESADE · FNUAP – GTZ · MINISTERE DE LA JEUNESSE · MINISTERE DE LA PROMOTION DE LA FEMME ET DE LA FAMILLE · MINISTERE DES ENSEIGNEMENTS SECONDAIRES · MINISTERE DE L'EN-SEIGNEMENT SUPERIEUR · ONUSIDA · PEACE CORPS · UNICEF · US EMBASSY · VSO · YDF.

NO to Sugar Daddies to HIV/AIDS!

USAID gtz Jeune

Whatever the situation,

Whatever the reason,

Sexual relations between young girls and aged partners are dangerous and they increase the spread of HIV/AIDS.

NO to Sugar Daddies to HIV/AIDS!

Sugar Daddy + "Voyette" = A dangerous mixture

Risks related to HIV/AIDS
Most often, the Sugar Daddy is married and/or has many 'chaps' in town. The girl, on her part, has her 'sweetheart'. The risk of infection therefore spreads to many persons at the same time. It further increases when we realize that the Sugar Daddy often imposes unprotected sex on his partners.

Infertility
45% of apprentices and 35% of students involved in relations with Sugar Daddies have had an illegal abortion. Thus, they have put their life in danger and have reduced their chances of having babies later on.

Lost dignity
The girl offers her body. The Sugar Daddy buys his pleasure. They 'sleep' together without any consideration for love. Only money and sex count.

No way forward
The relationship neither lasts long, nor is it constructive. Pleasure and gifts are exchanged but nothing durable happens. As soon as the Sugar Daddy has had his fun, he becomes less interested and the relationship dies.

NO to Cross Generational Sex !

FIGURE 5.5 Flyers circulated during a United Sisters meeting aimed at sensitising young women against sugar daddies.

Although members of the United Sisters did not discuss the issue of sugar daddies following the distribution of the flyers, my subsequent interviews with members revealed their ongoing preoccupation with enforcing a moral code against sexual promiscuity. One of them voiced this during an interview when she alleged that about a third of NBA members had had affairs with some of their members. My interviewee was also disgusted by the fact that Ntambag Brothers were not only guilty of "corrupting" their members, but also that some of these brothers were so reckless to keep several girlfriends within the same community. These claims were put to the test when the association resolved to fill a vacancy for the position of patron and Barnabas, a Ntambag brother was nominated. However, his candidacy was unanimously rejected because he was alleged to have had multiple affairs with some members of the United Sisters, which predictably, had provoked interpersonal strife amongst members. The lady who allegedly nominated the Ntambag brother was shamed for her proposal. It turned out she was the current girlfriend of the disgraced NBA member.

Like the other associations, the NBA was concerned about its honour and public image in the community. Unlike the female associations that preoccupied themselves with issues of sexuality, the NBA's quest for morality centred on the cultivation of virtuous and gentlemanly character. According to its rules, each new member ought to recite the association's pledge upon formal admission – a pledge that required the member to "always uphold her [the association's] Honour and Glory wherever the need may arise." Article 5 of its constitution for instance outlined a series of proscribed behaviours:

- All members are strongly advised to respect one another irrespective of position, education and background, age and other social position. Culprits will face the disciplinary committee.
- Any act of insult and assault by any member shall be reported to the executive who then transfers the matter to the disciplinary committee where the case is handled without any fear or favour.
- Any act of stealing or burglary reported against any member will be dismissed immediately.
- Other acts of misconduct reported against any member shall result in serious disciplinary sanctions.

The above-mentioned disciplinary committee dealt with cases referred to it by the executive. Typically, these were cases that involved alleged breach of moral conduct such as physical fights between members, of which I witnessed a few. Despite a few brawls and alleged interpersonal rivalries, the NBA did not have records of any expulsions.[11] Perhaps, this was partly because the NBA was a relatively younger association compared to the Chosen and United Sisters. Another probable explanation was that the disciplinary committee was unexpectedly dormant.[12] This notwithstanding, I recorded several cases of members suspended from associational activities for owing fines. Such persons could return to the fold upon completing their fines. However, it was not unexpected to see members resume normal activities after a few absences without having paid or arranged to pay their fines. In this respect, it is fair to say discipline was lax – a trend many justified by invoking their 'brotherliness'.

It turned out that football was a universally loved pastime amongst the Ntambag Brothers and no misconduct however grave was sufficient to prevent a brother from participating at a Saturday game. The pre-eminence of football in associational life was underscored by the fact that they had two sports coordinators. Initially introduced as a mere leisure or "keep fit" activity, football eventually became a key frontier for combating negative stereotypes about youth in Old Town and as a platform for building the association's reputation (Fokwang 2009). Until the early 2000s, residents of Bamenda held on to the perception of Old Town youth as a lot of ruthless and vicious thugs who could not be invited to mix and play with polite society. One story recounts an incident when Old Town youth, facing certain defeat at the hands of their opponents, stopped the match a few minutes to the finish time and fled with the ball. Another story recalls the actions of Old Town youth, who, facing imminent defeat against a visiting team from Ntarikon, stirred up a fight and beat their opponents in a deliberate show of supremacy. These incidents gave the youths of Old Town such a bad reputation that many athletic associations in Bamenda expressed reservations about playing against any team from that area. My friends in the NBA acknowledged they had witnessed such "wild" manners in their teens but were now determined to rehabilitate the image of the community by enforcing strict protocols during football matches. Thus, each "friendly encounter" with a guest team was an opportunity to project a reformed and positive image of themselves. Members who failed to observe the rules of the game were punished with a fine. It was thus that sports gradually

11.   However, there were at least five cases of people who had left the association voluntarily or were no longer actively involved.
12.   Evidence for this is contained in a letter addressed to the NBA executive by a member of the disciplinary committee accusing its chairman of inertia. In this letter, the member threatens to withdraw from the disciplinary committee if no action is taken against the inactive chairman.

became an instrument of the NBA's broader goal to "fight against social ills" and to promote sportsmanship in the community. Persons accused of indiscipline were fined and expected to apologise to the assembly at regular Sunday meetings. I witnessed such an incident at one of their meetings when Claude, who incidentally was the day's chairman decided to fine himself following sustained criticisms against him for improper conduct during the previous day's football match against the *Brasseries Football Club*. At issue was the claim that Claude had unjustifiably and aggressively tackled a few opponents during the match at which the NBA was defeated 8 to 3. Submitting to the barrage of criticisms, Claude declared proudly, "I find the chairman guilty of the accusations and request that he should pay a fine of 1500FCFA" – a statement that drew thunderous applause amidst laughter and confusion. Although it was fair and indeed remarkable that Claude should fine himself, many considered the amount rather excessive particularly as most members traditionally opposed heavy fines. It was customary for individuals found guilty of misconducts to be fined an amount that ranged from 200FCFA to 500FCFA. No one could recall if anyone had ever been fined 1500FCFA for the kind of misconduct Claude was accused of. His inability to pay the fine later strained his relationship with the association for which he was suspended for a couple of months. Nevertheless, it became routine to fine individuals who were guilty of having breached the rules of fair play. This trend notwithstanding, the association had an uneasy relationship with fines. Members received fines for non-attendance of sports activities, for not showing up for sanitary campaigns, lateness at meetings, improper conduct at outdoor activities and unruly behaviour during meetings. Drawing inspiration from disciplinary strategies employed in the school system, an executive member was tasked with the responsibility of recording transgressions and the names of defaulters read out at the end of each meeting. No one looked forward to that moment – one that was always characterised by shock, and protest by individuals who either denied any prior knowledge of owing a fine or outrage at how much the amount had been inflated.

All three associations believed that their integrity was directly tied to individual members' conduct. However, they differed in the kind and magnitude of transgressions that warranted sanctions. Amongst the Ntambag Brothers for instance, hardly anyone cared if a member had a dozen affairs and did not see a link between their members' romantic affairs and the association's reputation. The female associations on the other hand linked their associations' honour and respectability to members' sexuality. At least, one NBA member felt that young men should be discreet about their affairs. Irked by allegations of sexual impropriety among some members, David, one of the few university graduates prepared and delivered a talk to the association entitled: "Who am I as a Ntambag Brother?" In his presentation, he deplored his peers for having multiple sexual partners whilst projecting themselves as vanguards of moral change in Old Town. "One of the objectives of our association is to fight against social ills" he stated, "but we're the ones who corrupt teenage girls. What social ills do we claim to be fighting? How can we claim to have the moral authority to advise our younger brothers and sisters when we ourselves have failed to lead by example?"

FIGURE 5.6 NBA members play soccer in the morning at the St. Joseph's Cathedral grounds, June 2007. Photo by Divine Fuh.

"Something Useful" and Moral Transformation

One of the many practices that captured my interest during my time with the United and Chosen Sisters was a slot known as "something useful". A parallel activity among the Ntambag Brothers was known as "formation time". This activity was characterised by spontaneous motivational speeches, moral anecdotes, and discourses on topics of varying themes based on the disposition of the speaker or pertinent issues within the association or community. In all three associations, this was often the last item on the agenda. A slight difference between the female associations and the NBA consisted in the latter's preference to assign specific individuals to deliver a talk on a prepared topic, at least a week prior to the meeting. *Something useful* or *formation time* provided its members with a platform for "ethical reflection and self-creation" (Mattingly 2012:5). The topics covered included the cultivation of virtuous character, the prevention and management of HIV/AIDS, how to nurture romantic relationships and tips on how to run a successful business. The female associations specifically emphasised the acquisition of basic skills that could help them cope with the prolonged economic crisis - skills that enabled them to prepare homemade toiletries, various items for personal hygiene, hairstyling, and even healthy food recipes they could make at minimal cost. In the following paragraphs, I present three episodes that reveal the moral subjectivities of Old Town's young people as they grappled with the challenges of self-creation and communal transformation.

Money, HIV and its Victims

The United Sisters' vice president delivered the session's *something useful* on the topic of HIV and AIDS[13]. She began her talk with a personal testimony stating that during the months she spent in the hospital taking care of her sister, she witnessed the reality of the ravages caused by the AIDS pandemic. It was not obvious if her sister had been an AIDS patient or if she had witnessed patients afflicted by the disease while caring for her sick sister. "Many young people are dying of this terrible disease, especially young women. That's why I wish to advise my fellow sisters today to abstain from practices or persons that may leave you vulnerable to HIV infection. I say this especially because I know how the phenomenon of sugar daddies has become popular. They come around and flash money and they know we love money. Let me tell you my sisters, money is evil. Yes, I repeat, money is evil" she emphasised, her face darkened with fright. No one stirred or dared to interrupt. "I want you to think about your future. Think about your future, not about the ways to satisfy short-term financial needs because you may end up in your grave prematurely. That's the little thought I had for you today", she concluded and returned to her seat. Just the previous Sunday, members had received literature from 100%

13.   Although it is widely believed that the principal victims of the HIV/AIDS pandemic are the young and poor, conflicting studies carried out by the Cameroon government maintain that the rich and educated are the most affected. According to the Demographic and Health Survey of 2004, the national HIV prevalence rate is 5.5%, a majority of whom are young women between 25 and 29. Critics have contested this study on the grounds that its results were based on data obtained from two cities only. See *The Post*, "HIV/AIDS Highest Among Educated, Rich Cameroonians" No. 0693 of Monday August 22, 2005, p. 7.

Jeune aimed at raising awareness on the dangers of sexual liaisons with sugar daddies. It was therefore remarkable that the topic should come up two weeks in a row and since there was little reaction to the literature when it was initially shared, I anticipated that members would no longer shy away from the topic. Moved by the vice president's talk, several members took turns to support and contribute to the topic. Most tended to focus on the need for behavioural change. Charlotte, probably the group's most garrulous member was the first to react. "Today, I want to discourage this phenomenon of jumping from one man to the next in search of money. You all know me very well" she declared proudly, hitting her chest. "For several years now, I've been frying *puff puff* from which I make enough profit to buy myself a beer" she added, provoking considerable laughter among the sisters because she was a notorious drinker. "Must you talk about beer?" someone queried. She simply ignored the question and continued her denouncement of sugar daddies. "I was saying that I don't ask money from anyone before buying myself a bottle of drink. Today, men lure women because of two things, beer and fish. Yeah, that's what they call us – fish" amidst giggles. "How did my mother raise us? She used to sell food and still does so today. We survived and we're still struggling to manage the little we have. So, I just wish to tell my sisters that they should learn to earn their own income and not become the next HIV victim because they were searching for money from one man to the next."

The Debate on HIV Transmission

Aaron gave the day's talk on HIV/AIDS, which provoked a most animated discussion amongst the brothers. It was not clear to me then if he had any expertise on this topic or if he had simply read extensively to prepare for this presentation. His talk began with an explanation of how HIV was transmitted and concluded with prevention methods. According to his presentation, HIV was transmitted by blood transfusion or contact with an infected person, from mother to child at birth or through breastfeeding and lastly, through sexual intercourse. The use of condoms, he said could help to prevent someone from contracting HIV. Given that a significant proportion of the membership was Catholic, I was struck by the fact that his presentation did not mention the techniques of abstinence or fidelity as alternative prevention methods – techniques that were being pushed by the church at the time. Although his presentation was clear, albeit undermined by omissions rather than any false claims, it provoked a major debate in the house about the transmission methods of the virus. On the one hand, a group of young men argued that a key vector of HIV transmission was by blood contact, excluding bodily fluids, especially semen. Aaron and others, including myself maintained that the virus could be transmitted through bodily fluids. Our opponents remained unconvinced and demanded evidence to support our claims. Kevin on his part looked shaken. "If it is true that HIV is transmitted through bodily fluids, then we're all dead" he screamed. "We're all dead" he repeated. He was one of the sceptics who believed that HIV was transmitted exclusively through blood contact. According to him, one did not need a condom insofar as one's partner did not have any sores. While the discussion unfolded, Mohamed, a young man from the Local AIDS Control Committee (LACC) entered the meeting venue. His visit was co-incidental, and he was pleasantly surprised to learn that a major debate on HIV/AIDS was underway. Despite attempts by a few NBA members to get him to say something about the debate, he refused to be drawn into the argument. Instead, he insisted on explaining the purpose of his visit: "I'm glad to see that young people are taking the HIV/AIDS issue seriously because it concerns us a lot. Today, I've come to communicate a programme being run by the Ministry of Health through the LACC in Ntambag. The committee has sent me to invite you to a free voluntary HIV screening event. You won't have to pay for anything. Just endeavour to be there and you'll have answers to some of your questions from the experts. We'll also distribute other materials which you can read at your leisure." Simon thanked Mohamed for his message while others nodded in acknowledgement. Simon was also one of the sceptics who had demanded evidence from the opposing camp. He jokingly asked Mohamed or anyone in the gathering to bring a cure for AIDS as a condition for him to go for a voluntary HIV test. Others expressed panic at the prospect of knowing their HIV status.[14] "Someone will have to tie me up first before I would consider doing an HIV test", whispered a member who sat next to me.

How to get Hitched and Other Matters

Mary, 31, gave a talk on the theme of marriage to her peers in the Chosen Sisters. Although her talk sounded incoherent, the topic attracted considerable

14.   The young men's fright contrasted sharply with my general observations in Bamenda with respect to young people's participation in voluntary HIV screening events. On several occasions, I witnessed long queues on the Commercial Ave where the provincial health department had set up a temporary office to test citizens. The North West Province is also alleged to have the highest HIV prevalence rate in the country. Those who accept these statistics, however flawed, contend that the rates are allegedly high because the educated population of the province tend to attend screening exercises compared to other provinces in the country.

interest. Although unmarried herself, her talk sought to equip her unmarried sisters with the proper techniques on how to choose a suitable partner for marriage. "Learn to be friends with the person and make sure you understand each other very well" she began. "I should also add that you should ensure that you are compatible because if both of you are so different in many ways, your marriage would be a difficult one. Also learn to take your partners for who they are, and learn to be welcoming, soft and understanding. As many of you know, husbands like a welcoming home, one in which they can look forward to coming to and this home is not the physical structure but the attitude and warmth of the inhabitants of the house, especially the wife." Although a member jokingly took exception with Mary for raising a topic about which she knew nothing (because she was unmarried and still lived under her father's roof), most of the ladies seized the opportunity to discuss and share their individual experiences. A few members criticised Mary for implying that if things did not go well in a marriage, then the woman was necessarily to blame. Speaking as a married woman, a member rose to Mary's defence, stating that indeed, an old adage states that the woman is the cornerstone of every household. She added that it did not mean women should not voice their concerns when faced with inappropriate behaviour from their men. Sirri added to the discussion by emphasising the importance of compatibility, drawing on her personal experience. One early morning, she claimed, she paid a surprise visit to her fiancé's and discovered an aspect of his lifestyle that led her to question everything she thought she knew about her future husband. He had been drinking and smoking all night. "He still had a bottle of beer in his hand and the house smelled of cigarettes. I just knew this was a bad case. I knew I would never cope, and I walked off that relationship for good."

Something useful occasionally spilled over into words of encouragement or denouncement of members who were believed to have strayed. Seminars and workshops were also broadly understood as extensions of this practice owing to the moral and intellectual formation derived from participating at such events. With respect to denouncements, I witnessed an incident among the United Sisters at one of their Sunday meetings during which Charlotte reprimanded Carmen, a young single mother for negligence towards her son. Earlier in the meeting, Carmen had been rebuked for wearing flip-flops and a dirty T-shirt to the meeting. According to her critics, Carmen had disrespected the association by dressing poorly but this time, Charlotte had strong concerns about her qualities as a mother. "I believe that when sisters have a problem, they should bring it to the house rather than talk about it behind each other's back", she said. "Young girls, your child is your pride. You were not forced to become pregnant. If you don't want a child, please don't sleep with men" she yelled. "Even if your child has no father, you have to take care of the child in every way possible." She further alleged that Carmen frequently left her 20-month-old son undressed and exposed to the elements. "Even if this should make us enemies for life, so be it. I'm advising you as a sister, that you should show some love to your son. If any of you saw him yesterday, you would have wept. Everyone is complaining. He's always running to the main road and might be hit by a vehicle; he spends half of the day naked, lacks food and often does not have anything warm to wear." Susan, a young single mother herself picked up from Charlotte and made an appeal to all mothers in the house. "I wish to thank Charlotte very much for raising this issue in the house instead of taking it outside for gossip. This is the kind of behaviour we applaud and of which I have spoken about before." She then urged young mothers to provide clothing for their children before thinking of themselves. "Give priority to your children before anything or anyone else."

FIGURE 5.7 A cross section of seminar participants in Old Town, Bamenda. In attendance are members of all three associations including community members.

A rare type of *something useful* included seminars that brought all three associations together. One of these joint sessions was organised by the NBA on 13 March 2005 on the topic, "The Importance of Women in Society" to which the United and Chosen Sisters were invited. Through this seminar, the Ntambag Brothers aimed to sensitise young men in the community about the important role women played in society The NBA further justified this seminar as its contribution towards celebrating the International Women's Day that had taken place a few days prior on 8 March. In July 2005, the NBA organised another workshop on youth leadership, which also brought both female associations together.

Cultivating Virtuous Characters

I have argued in this chapter that a primary preoccupation of the young people I interacted with in all three associations was to assert and be seen as social adults in their community. I have also shown in previous sections that these objectives were generally pursued within and on behalf of their respective groups. What remains to be seen are the specific individual trajectories that enabled or facilitated the pursuit of these group objectives. In this section, I show that these broad associational goals were only meaningful insofar as individuals were ready to embrace the day-to-day technologies of self-care and moral transformation of self. I do so by exploring the lives of five individuals, foregrounding their moral subjectivities, life histories and the circumstances under which they became members of their respective associations. Through each case, I demonstrate how these individuals understood and articulated the moral objectives of their associations and the sort of ethical self-formation that contributed to their self-perception as worthy members of their associations. Through these cases, I show the ambiguities of the moral projects undertaken by the respective associations while highlighting the ways in which individual agencies shaped them.

Thelma's Path to Motherhood

Thelma, 23, was one of the leading members of the United Sisters. She was the youngest in a family of four, two of whom had died – her father and a male sibling. She lived with her mother and her two-year-old son. Due to poor academic performance, Thelma had dropped out of secondary school in Form 2 (8th Grade): "I guess I had bad company which influenced my performance," she said. When she left school, she assisted her mother at her small business. "My mother used to make fish rolls (pies) and I assisted her in frying the rolls. The boys who used to sell the fish rolls in the market left for their village to attend a family function and never returned. This affected the business; so, my mother eventually stopped frying the fish rolls because it was difficult to find reliable persons to sell for her."

After living with her mother for several years without acquiring additional skills, one of her friends (also a member of the United Sisters) advised her to enrol as an apprentice at a hairdressing salon. "Before I became a member, I had been at home for three years doing nothing. Some of our members advised that it was not okay for a young woman to have no skills. Some of them persuaded me to learn a trade, which I did. When I complete my training, I'll set up my own salon." She sounded determined to do something with her life from the lessons she had learnt in the association. "The group has changed me a lot", she said confidently. "At first, I didn't have any skills but after becoming an active member of United Sisters, I was made to understand that I can learn a trade and fight for my future. The association gave me a sense of pride in myself, and my friends made me feel I could still do something with my life again." Her self-esteem had fallen to its lowest when she became pregnant with her son. "I felt bad about the fact that I had a child with someone who didn't marry me. I would have loved to be his wife, like any other mature woman but from the current situation, it is not possible because he's already married to someone else. I wouldn't have loved to be a mother without being married". Despite her regrets, she remained optimistic about her future goals and potentials. "I'm no longer unskilled like before. I'm not just staying at home doing nothing. I'm proud of myself and proud of my child. Not all young women today can afford to take care of their offspring or even give birth to a child. I feel proud because I didn't abandon my child with my mother like other young women do. I have the full support of my mother and my baby's father."

Thelma also acknowledged that thanks to her membership in the association, she now saw herself as morally transformed: "I think the group has changed my ideas on certain things. I used to depend a lot on men for financial assistance. When I saw my peers doing things to earn their own income, however small, I knew I needed to do the same. The members often warned us about being financially dependent on men. I used to date a person depending on the size of his wallet. I had no time for people who had nothing. Now, I know I could start with someone who has nothing, and we build together."

***

The Reluctant Old Towner and Manager

Pierre, 27, the first in a family of five was born and raised in Old Town. When he completed his Advanced Levels, he left for Yaounde where he majored in geography at the University of Yaounde. However, his ultimate ambition was to travel to Europe. He would simply use his time in Yaounde to explore opportunities that would expedite his departure from the country. University studies in Yaounde was therefore a temporary measure, an excuse to get money from his parents to provide for his needs. Two of his friends had already travelled to Europe and he was desperate to join them. Things did not work as planned; his mother became ill and eventually died. His father had preceded his mother in death just a year prior. Pierre was compelled to abandon his studies and return to Bamenda to fend for himself and siblings. It was also at this stage that he shelved his aspiration to travel to Europe, at least temporarily. "We grew up in a strict household", he recalled. "We were not allowed to mix with a lot of people around here. My parents taught us not to rely on this uncle or auntie, so we really stuck to ourselves." He found employment as a salesperson in a local firm and gradually rose to the position of branch manager due to the firm's expansion. "I usually don't like to tell ladies that I'm a manager because they'll think I've got a lot of money" he said with a chuckle. "I just tell them I work for this company." Contrasting his achievements with his peers in the community, Pierre claimed that they were not hardworking; "they are lazy; they prefer to spend time having fun. That is why you can never see me in the evenings hanging out with the guys drinking beer. I prefer to stay indoors with my siblings. I don't interact with lazy people" he said and named a few individuals known to me with whom he associated. One of them was a Ntambag brother who ran a very successful small business. "You see, people here are not motivated. Those who are financially handicapped often resort to picking up things in their homes to sell in order to have cash." Pierre claimed he would move out of the neighbourhood as soon as he had the means – "I hate this Old Town; I really hate it; I plan to move out if I have a way. It's not a good quarter. When you compare Old Town kids with those that grow up in Foncha Street, you see that those in Foncha Street are smarter."

Compared to other Ntambag Brothers I interacted, Pierre had never been a member of an association, not even the defunct Yorkaaz. "I'm an unusual person, perhaps funny. I've never really liked groups, especially those in Old Town." He reluctantly joined the NBA only after a few friends explained the association's objectives and its potential social benefits. "When I spoke to a few people, I learnt that some of my friends did not show up for my parents' funeral because they claimed my family didn't participate in other people's funerals in the neighbourhood." Pierre admitted that his parents had indeed been strict and had isolated them from the rest of the community. He thought it was beneficial to be part of the community and did not want to repeat the "errors" of his parents. "In my opinion, the most important thing about being a member of Ntambag Brothers is just for company, in order not to feel isolated and stressed. I don't really go there for friends or to make new friends because I have two dear friends and both of them are in Europe."

Although he was unmarried and a father of a 20-month-old son, he remained highly critical of his peers: "There's no ambition, no encouragement for young people in Old Town. Every young person wants to leave for Europe or survives on remittances from their relatives already in Europe. Do you know that you can acquire AIDS from stress?" he asked, much to my surprise. In his view, the lack of opportunities and young people's low motivation contributed to high levels of stress, which could result in poor health and eventually to AIDS. "Besides, young people here drink too much and many don't practice safe sex, so I think there's a great danger here." He would enrol his son into pre-nursery, marry his son's mother if he could raise enough money by the end of that year. "I want to legalise everything" he emphasised.

Pierre claimed his community had a very high incidence of AIDS although he knew only one person living with the disease. "Her lifestyle will not leave you in doubt about the fact that this rumour is true" he said. This was only rumoured, he repeated, since no one knew exactly what the lady was suffering from. "The thing is that many people are hiding it and nobody wants to talk about it. Those health workers are wasting their time. People are reluctant to do HIV tests and I know many people who have multiple partners. I was born in this quarter, so what I'm saying is true."

Pierre seemed even more critical of his peers in the association: "Our group is not doing what it is supposed to be doing. We cannot develop our quarter without first developing ourselves." He didn't think he had learnt much from the association or changed his moral convictions because of his membership in the association. "I've just learnt to understand people more, to know how to deal with people elsewhere" He did not sound enthusiastic about the sanitary campaigns the NBA had mandated: "I do it to avoid problems" he said unapologetically. "The only thing that has inspired me is the sponsorship project to assist disadvantaged children in the neighbourhood. But it's a dangerous idea. How can you educate people when you don't have that education yourself?" he queried. "Does it make sense to you that young men who dropped out of school, and who still hang around their parents' homes reducing their siblings' rations, can appear serious to these kids?" He was convinced young people had lost faith in education because it led them nowhere. "The most important thing for a young man", he claimed, "is independence. Many of our fellow members aren't independent. A majority of them are unemployed."

***

A Single Mother with Big Dreams

Nicole, 20, unlike most of her peers in the United Sisters was born in Douala, Cameroon's economic capital where she lived with her mother until they moved to Bamenda when she was 10. She joined the association at 17, a rare occurrence in the association, because in principle, they only accepted members who were at least, twenty. Nicole claimed she had been granted an exception because she was too talkative and assertive. "I was so mouthy, and the president even considered expelling me from the group soon after my admission. It was thanks to her that I was permitted to join in the first place, but on second thoughts she allowed me to stay" she said, laughing. This revelation reminded me of remarks I had overheard by some members about the extent to which Nicole had matured during the three years of her membership. At the time she was admitted, she spoke rudely to community members and easily resorted to invectives if anyone offended her. It was precisely because of this "condition" that the president had thought she would be a good candidate for reform. No doubt, everyone pointed to her as a success story.

Like some of her friends in the association, Nicole had dropped out of secondary school. After spending several years at home, her mother enrolled her to study dressmaking in Old Town. It was during her apprenticeship that she became pregnant and gave birth to a daughter, then 19 months. She eventually completed her training but was unable to set up her own shop due to the cost of rent and taxes. "So, in order to make ends meet, I sew clothes at home. People who know me bring their clothes to my house and I deal with them there. I specialise in school uniforms and other kinds of female dresses. I even sewed some of the United Sisters' uniforms."

During my interviews, I often sought to know how individual members understood the objective of their association. This question turned out to be quite insightful as it revealed the different perspectives shared by members of the association. For instance, Nicole responded that the association's main

objective was to "fight against prostitution", by which she meant sexual promiscuity among young women. She later added that the association also fought
against unwanted pregnancies and abortion. "We are not saying we've wiped
out that phenomenon, but I think we've succeeded to reduce it" she added. "We
are not really opposed to abortion as such, but we know it's bad and we try to
educate our members to avoid getting to the situation where abortion becomes
an option." She recalled that the association had felt deep embarrassment when
a member was accused of having aborted her pregnancy of six months. "The
pregnancy was at an advanced stage and she told us she did not have money
to abort much earlier. We thought of expelling her but reflected on the issue
and concluded that an expulsion would not help her. So, we decided to talk
to her and she wept bitterly. She confessed and promised she'll never do it
again." When news of this members' abortion spread in the community, all
the members were ridiculed unfairly. "The boys in the quarter ridiculed us a
lot. Some of them once claimed that one of the conditions for membership in
the United Sisters was a minimum of five abortions."

Nicole thought of herself highly, especially in terms of the moral transformation she had achieved. "I'm proud of myself because I don't move from
place to place," she said. "What does that mean?" I asked. "I don't date more
than one person. I'm not a promiscuous woman like the other girls in Old
Town. I'm also confident of myself" she added, meaning that she knew her
HIV status was negative. "You can never hear my name in any gossip. I don't
gossip and my friends respect me a lot for that." Nicole claimed she and two
other members of the United Sisters were amongst the few who could hold
their heads high because they had proven themselves decent.

She also went on record as an opponent of the use of fines in the association
as a disciplinary measure, arguing that it was counterproductive. "We are here
to change, to become better persons. Sometimes, the fines are too much and
you find that some people have to "prostitute" themselves in order to pay their
fines." In her view, if some members had to resort to sugar daddies in order
to pay their fines in the association, then it contradicted the core objectives
of the association.

Like many disillusioned young people in Bamenda and beyond, Nicole
dreamed of migrating someday to the USA in search of greener pastures. "If
I can get enough cash, I'll get a visa and leave for the USA to work and then
return to Cameroon and build a good house for myself and my daughter."

***

Franklin, the Entrepreneurial Casanova

I met Franklin, 27, for the first time at a 'born house' ceremony during the early days of my fieldwork. He caught my attention because unlike most of the young men at the function who drank beer, he drank a soft drink. He recounted a tragic incident he had witnessed as a child when a drunken man fell into a stream and died. The memory of this incident always haunted him. "But I buy beer for my friends although I don't drink". "Do you mean you've never tasted any alcoholic drink?" I quizzed. "No," he insisted, "my alcohol is women" he emphasised, jokingly, and then added that he had reduced the number of women he dated to 40%.

Franklin was born and raised in Old Town. Like most of the NBA members, he lived in a detached single room within his parent's compound, commonly referred to as the boys' quarters. Franklin's room was classy and very modern compared to other rooms I had seen in the area. He had a JVC stereo system, a 14-inch TV, a Video CD player and high-quality speakers. The latter were strategically spread in the four corners of the room to produce a surround sound effect. At the centre of the room was a large queen-sized wooden bed.

Franklin dropped out of school after failing his high school exams. He then travelled to Douala where he lived with a relative and made two desperate attempts to travel abroad with the assistance of his family. Eventually, he returned to Bamenda and started a small business, which involved supplying customers with home video cassettes, DVDs, and audio-visual accessories. During the period of my fieldwork, he had suspended his business due to low demand and survived on the remittances his elder sister sent from France.

He joined the NBA several months after the association had been formed. Although he had attended the preliminary meetings to discuss the possibility of starting an association for young men in the neighbourhood, he was sceptical about its viability. "I don't like rowdy gatherings" he said, having feared that the proposed association would turn out to be a talking house. "When I discovered they were serious, I joined them on the day elections were held to choose the executive." At the time of our interview, he was not only an active member but also held the health and sanitation portfolio. "I enjoy the company of the brothers in the quarter which is very important," he said. With the brothers, he shared ideas and played football. It was thanks to the association that he had widened his circle of friends in the community. "Now, I'm friendly with a lot of people and when I'm on the road, I greet most of the people since the number of persons I know have grown so much."

Franklin made no secret of his multiple girlfriends. During my fieldwork, he reportedly had three girlfriends and was trying to recruit a fourth, whom I knew. He justified his philandering by claiming that he neither drank nor smoked, and that his only God-given talent was to win over the hearts of women. The last time I met up with him, he was about to transport one of his electronic gadgets to his "official" girlfriend's apartment who lived out of Old Town. Franklin insisted that his private life had no bearing on his moral standing in the association or community and it was nobody's business to tell him how he ought to live his life.

***

A Bouncer, turned Petty Trader

Claude, 33, was born and raised in Old Town. He was one of the few with whom I first established rapport when I started attending NBA meetings. At the end of my first meeting, he walked up to me and gave me his mobile phone number. He eventually became a key participant and friend. He rented a single-room apartment where he lived by himself. He spoke proudly of the fact that he had rented his apartment for 14 years and was regular with his rent.

Claude completed his primary school education at GS Old Town but did not proceed to secondary school. "I didn't see the need" he said, but when I spoke to him a couple of days later, he clarified that his father had died when he was still very young, and the burden of raising their young family had fallen on his mother whose means were very limited. He had therefore felt the pressure to support his mother rather than proceed to secondary school. He soon found employment at a bakery where he worked for two years. One sunny afternoon, when I sat with him chatting in a local pub, he showed me a long scar on his hand which he said were burns from the time he worked at the bakery. "I've suffered my friend. You see, my case is different because most of the brothers still have their parents to support them, but I didn't have anyone."

When he left the bakery, he ran a mobile restaurant for a couple of years. This entailed transporting food in a hand-pushed cart (popularly known as truck) around town. Being mobile assured his business greater visibility and this enabled him to sell more than he would if he rented a fixed space. Tragically, he went out of business when thieves broke into his house and stole his savings and the cart. He was unemployed for months until a primary school mate who was then the manager of a popular bar/casino at the Commercial Avenue recruited him as a security guard. "I was paid 5000FCFA and with time,

I rose to the position of bouncer and my salary was increased to 10,000FCFA." By the time he left his casino job, he had risen to the position of manager and earned a monthly salary of 25,000FCFA. He reminisced how lucrative his job as manager was, in part because he and his colleagues knew how to "manipulate the casino machines" which earned them extra money. "I even turned down a job offer to work as a bouncer at Ayaba Hotel although they had proposed a salary package of 70,000FCFA." Some months at the casino, he earned up to 300,000FCFA because he knew "how to get around things". It was thanks to his ability to "get around things" that he was able to save enough to assist his younger brother to emigrate to Europe. Claude reminded me frequently that his destination of choice would be the USA. "If I go to America, I would like to join the US Army or become a truck driver" he once said. Concerned that he would have exceeded the age limit to join the US Army if he ever got to the USA, he ended up dreaming of his life as a truck driver, driving cross-country. He said he would count on his half-brother who had lived in the US for over 30 years to support his own emigration.

In early 2000, Claude lost his job when the casino was temporarily closed. He then started his own home-based business – producing and selling ice pops commonly known as Alaska.[15] He bought a second-hand deep freezer to store the ice pops and also earned a bit of income from freezing people's groceries.

Claude revealed he was a father of two with separate women. He had custody of one of the children – the one whose mother had tragically died soon after giving birth. This child, he said, lived with his grandmother in the village and was then in his second year in secondary school. In addition to supporting his children, he was also the principal sponsor of two nephews who lived with his mother in Old Town.

Claude joined the Ntambag Brothers several months after it was founded. "I realised that most of my mates were members, and this prompted me to find out what was going on. So, I was permitted to attend the meetings for three weeks as an observer and eventually, I applied to become a member." I sought to know what he had learnt as a member of the association. "I simply became a member in order to share ideas with my peers so that we can develop our quarter" he responded. "Oh, let me add that I've also benefited from one thing - I spend less money now on Sundays than I used to do when I was not

---

15.   The origin of this term is unknown but I have speculated that it may be connected to the extreme cold temperatures associated with Alaska, USA. This was popular with people seeking to cool themselves from the scorching sun during the hot dry season.

a member." Prior to joining the association, he would go into town on Sunday afternoons where he ended up buying drinks for his friends. "I don't drink too much, myself. With two bottles of beer, I'm okay." He was also convinced the association had reformed certain members. "We've also helped some persons to change for the better. It's not good to call names, but there was one guy who was a notorious thief in the neighbourhood. We accepted him into the association and brothers advised him on alternative things to do to get income. He's changed so much and everyone in the community credits his change to our association."

The Ambivalence of Moral Citizenship

This chapter aimed to deepen our understanding of the moral practices that engender social adult status among young people in Old Town. The ethnographic evidence thus far supports my interpretation of young people's pursuit of social adulthood as a moral quest. Rooting out "social ills" was not the sole preoccupation of the associations; what they also sought was honour, respect, prestige, visibility, leadership, and empowerment. While individuals sought these qualities as moral subjects, their fullest expressions were in the associations to which they belonged. Associations required certain qualities of its members; that is, to be in good standing, individuals ought to pay their membership dues, contribute towards associational objectives and causes, respect the internal rules and regulations as well as promote the "fictional kinship" ties that bound them as brothers and sisters in the community. I have equated these individual dispositions with what Mattingly has referred to as the "day-to-day technologies of self-care that people draw upon to cultivate, or try to cultivate, virtuous characters" (Mattingly 2012:4). I show that it is by actively cultivating these virtuous characters that members achieve their individual and collective goals as agents of change – that is, as moral citizens capable of bringing about some form of material transformation.

This chapter has made the case that we must take seriously the efforts young people make to "maintain productive relations with each other" (Simone 2014:33) and the ways they seek to position themselves in a precarious urban landscape and postcolonial world characterised by "waithood" (Honwana 2013) and "arrested adulthood" (Côté 2000). While the ultimate "reward" for this *positioning* is social adulthood, I argue that a close reading of the ethnographic data holds at least two significant insights for what it means to be a young person in Old Town. First, we see that social adulthood is rooted in reciprocal relationships. It rests not only in maintaining productive relationships with each other, but also in recognising that individuals and collectivities are mutually indebted to each other. Although differentiated by seniority and gender, all three associations are united in their shared goals of ridding their community of "social ills", in caring for members' welfare and most significantly those whom they identify as even less privileged than themselves. Individual members are also mutually indebted to each other and to the association – for the tips they get from "something useful" or "formation time", the time they spend together playing soccer or celebrating a "born house". Not even Pierre, the Ntambag Brother I brand as the "reluctant Old Towner" is ungrateful for the companionship he derives from his membership. Thelma, the young mother who dropped out of school and only dated men with deep pockets admits to how much her membership in the United Sisters transformed her life. Thanks to the support of her "sisters", her self-esteem was not only restored, but she also acquired vital skills that could generate income for herself and baby. This understanding of social adulthood, grounded in reciprocity contrasts sharply with capitalist conceptions of the autonomous rights-bearing individual who seeks and celebrates "independence" as the ultimate marker of achievement and adulthood. On the contrary, young people's moral practices in Old Town remind us of what Francis Nyamnjoh has referred to as the incompleteness of our being. His theorising is a reminder that we inhabit a world of "incomplete beings, constantly in need of activation, … and enhancement through relationships with incomplete others and by means of embodied and external technologies" (Nyamnjoh 2017:195). I show that membership in their respective associations provides individuals with tremendous scope for the enhancement or activation of their fullest claims to social adulthood.

Related to our elaboration of social adulthood as a moral quest is the notion of personhood. I argued earlier that the constitution of personhood and the attainment of social adulthood are processes that are manifest in collective as well as individual agencies. In the Cameroon Grasslands, the attainment of social adulthood is a major milestone in the journey towards full personhood. This phase is tied to the fulfilment of certain roles or social obligations – marriage, parenthood, employment, and the ability to redistribute one's resources or "success" – achievements that come to fruition through and in relation with others. For the young men and women I befriended in Old Town, their claims to social adulthood are manifest not only in parenting their biological children, but also in the extension of their parenting to children and individuals beyond their community, despite their limited resources. From the prize award ceremony at G.S. Old Town, to the donation of food items at

SAJOCAH, or the payment of tuition for the underprivileged, members of the studied associations assert their claims to social adulthood through the fulfilment of culturally sanctioned obligations. *Becoming* rather than *being* a person in the Grasslands is therefore intricately related to fulfilling one's sociocultural obligations, amongst which is membership in social clubs – whether these clubs are driven by ties to neighbourhood, ethnicity, *njangi*, scholastic or other common interest (cf. Ndangam 2014 for the significance of social clubs in Bali Nyonga). Whilst the primary locus of meeting one's social obligations is within one's kin group (to the living and the living-dead) – membership in associations or social clubs extend and reinforce one's personhood because they are the channels through which personal success is domesticated into collective achievements and individual failure entertained as communal pain.

A second implication worth considering are the gendered dimensions of these processes. All three associations are united by their common quest to position themselves and fulfil their sociocultural obligations as social adults. However, there are stark differences in what issues are emphasised and in their conceptions of virtuous character. We see from the ethnographic data that the women's associations are preoccupied with cultivating respectable femininity – that is, a feminine personhood steeped in self-controlled sexuality, fidelity, modesty and the fulfilment of culturally assigned gender roles. Respectable femininity is the antidote to the stereotypical Old Town woman – hypersexual, unfaithful, uncouth, and unmarriageable. Virtuosity in the women's associations is living up to the image of the respectable woman who eschews abortion, sugar daddies, affairs with married men and holds a job. She is also a woman that takes proper care of her baby or children, does not depend on men entirely for their upkeep and cares for herself and the community. We see in this cultivation of virtuous character, parallels with Jessica Ogden's study of migrant women in Kampala who "actively generate the means and meanings by which they can obtain respect and respectability, and be identified as Proper women" (Ogden 1996:165). These ideals and practices inform our understanding why members are disciplined for having an abortion, extra-marital affairs, or for providing inadequate care to their children.

Whilst the cultivation of respectable femininity could be seen as empowering – in terms of expanding one's power to make their own choices (Cornwall 1997), we also see how it could be disempowering in its tendency to normalise gender oppressive beliefs, and practices. That women's respectability and honour have frequently been tied to their sexuality in many African contexts is not new (see Johnson-Hanks 2006 for south Cameroon; Ogden 1996 for

Uganda; Smith 2010 for Nigeria). However, less attention has been paid to the ways in which oppressed women enact and perpetuate their own sub-jugation within patriarchal systems. We see how this plays out among the Chosen and United Sisters when members penalise conduct that transgresses their understanding of reproductive rights. Rather than advocate for access to reproductive healthcare as one mechanism to deal with unwanted pregnancies, members instead focus on further criminalising abortion without offering any real solution to victimised members. Similarly, both groups' preoccupation with fighting "promiscuity" among young women, while well-intended, ends up reinforcing the double standards that ignores men's philandering. This is evident amongst the United Sisters who nominate (although eventually rejected) a Ntambag brother with a track record of philandering; members' opposition to heavy fines because they would have to "prostitute" themselves to pay such fines. These concerns enable us to appreciate how the technologies of self-care initially intended for good could be instrumentalised to normalise and discipline members, thereby perpetuating deprivations and undermining women's capabilities and freedoms (Nussbaum 2000; Sen 1999).

Amongst the Ntambag Brothers, the pursuit of social adulthood reso-nates with what earlier in this work, I referred to as productive masculinity. Although many of the Ntambag Brothers were unemployed in the formal economic sector, they were resourceful as we see in Claude's example – the bouncer turned petty trader. From the puny income they earned, members were able to meet their financial obligations towards the association as well as support junior kin members. By fulfilling these multiple obligations, members not only positioned themselves as social adults but also as productive males.

It is also significant to contrast the women associations' conceptualis-ation of honour and respect with the Ntambag Brothers'. For the Chosen and United Sisters, their conception of honour was not dissimilar to what Jennifer Johnson-Hanks found among Beti women in south-eastern Cameroon who emphasise financial success, sexual restraint, certain forms of self-perception, particularly pride and self-respect (Johnson-Hanks 2006:86). While the Ntam-bag Brothers emphasised "respect for one another irrespective of position", financial success and responsibility were highly prioritised – that is, for the payment of one's fines, dues and other associational demands. Unlike the women's associations, sexual restraint hardly preoccupied the deliberations of the brothers. In fact, a contradiction worth noting is that whilst the Ntam-bag Brothers sought to root out social ills, toxic masculinity did not seem to be one of them. Toxic masculinity refers to ways of behaving as a man that is harmful towards other men and women such as engaging in risky sexual behaviour, aggression, excessive use of drugs and alcohol, bullying, etc. When Franklin, a Ntambag Brother whom I captioned earlier as an "entrepreneurial Casanova" proudly declares that "my alcohol is women", he does not perceive this as having a negative repercussion on the association's standing. Even when David, a member of the association, delivers a forceful criticism of his fellow "brothers" about their alleged multiple romantic liaisons, this is hardly seen as damaging to the association's reputation. This may be contrasted with young men's disparaging statements about the United Sisters whom, they allege, require a "minimum of five abortions" as a precondition for admission into the association. Similarly, we see a member of the Chosen Sisters sanctioned for admitting to an adulterous affair and shamed by members for having tarnished the image of the group.

The above analysis reveals the gendered dimensions of the ways in which the associations not only pursue their shared goals of ridding Old Town of social ills, but more significantly, how these processes normalize and in fact reinforce certain attitudes and beliefs that sometimes, contradict their objectives. Young people's associations continue to play important roles as mediators of their identities, aspirations, accomplishments, and failures, without necessarily being reduced to any of these particularities. The young people whose lives and actions we see in this ethnography are far from perfect, just like human beings elsewhere. Their "incompleteness" notwithstanding, the details recounted in this chapter enable us to see the extent to which they seek to maintain productive relations with each other while aiming to transform themselves and their community.

CHAPTER SIX

Alternate Pathways to Social Adulthood and the Economy of Faux Dossiers

Home Boy – going by his name on Telegram, is a Cameroon-based seller of Covid-19 vaccination cards. Each card sells for $170 and he claims to deliver within 48 hours. Home Boy alleges to have worked with more than 250 people in the past three months (August-October 2021). Responding to a Guardian journalist's concern if he is a scammer, Home Boy proceeds to share "proof" of vaccine cards he has made and insists on the importance of trust: "If we have to work together we have to start by building trust," he says.[1]

Home Boy is most likely a young man, possibly unemployed or underemployed in Cameroon, computer savvy and proficient in the use of social media. He is most likely a constituent of what Jean and John Comaroff have referred to as the "counternation" – that is, "a virtual citizenry with its own twilight economies, its own spaces of production and recreation, its own modalities of politics…" (Comaroff & Comaroff 2000:308). I show in this chapter that central to these "twilight economies" is the illegal production and circulation of forged documents. I refer to these creative and recreational practices as the *economy of faux dossiers*. Drawing on ethnographic data from my fieldwork in Bamenda, Cameroon, I describe the inner-workings of the economy of faux dossiers, and their roles as mediators of global processes of flows (migration). I show that both the producers and users of faux dossiers seek to negotiate their way out of socioeconomic exclusion and precarity in a neoliberal and SAPped[2] Cameroon, internally held hostage by a college of neo-colonial gerontocrats

---

1. Samira Sadeque, 'They tell you what you want to hear': people buying fake vaccine cards get scammed themselves, *The Guardian*; 11 Nov 2021, accessed on April 12, 2022.
2. By this, I refer to living in a structurally adjusted world (derived from the IMF-backed policies of the 1980s and 90s known as the Structural Adjustment Program (SAP).

and externally by the IMF and its associates.

The Economy of Faux Dossiers

A topic that frequently came up in casual discussions with young men in Old Town was not only the prevalence of *faux dossiers* but precisely their "power" to make things happen and to transform the lives of its bearers. *Faux dossiers* are forged documents, that is, counterfeit papers whose legitimacy is supposedly underwritten by government or private institutions. Such documents include drivers' licenses, visas, police clearances, birth, marriage and death certificates, bank statements, vaccine certificates and even school report cards etc. Fabricated by individuals operating from the "margins", faux dossiers enable a multiplicity of flows in the local, national and global economy. It echoes recent advances in scholarship to understand the quotidian in Africans' experiences of the economy, democracy and the state (Adebanwi 2022). In this chapter, I focus on its centrality in the migratory practices of young Cameroonians. This by no means implies that most or all young Cameroonians' travels are facilitated by "faux dossiers". The narratives that follow therefore do not seek to stereotype young Cameroonians, but rather, aim to capture and analyse an aspect of their lives that has so far been neglected in the ethnographic literature.

One rainy afternoon in July 2005, I sat with several Ntambag brothers chatting about football and local politics when the theme of faux dossiers emerged. "With the proliferation of computers, one can do anything these days," Max began. He was referring to the claim that the widespread availability of computers had vastly facilitated the fabrication of *doki* – a synonym for faux dossier. Ben corroborated this claim with an anecdote about his talented friend who was not only a prolific fabricator of faux dossiers but could also replicate the signatures of some of the most influential government officials in the region and beyond. "There are many talented young people around but they're not able to use their skills effectively," Awa added. In response, Max said he knew how to make "dry stamps" – that is, stamps that could be used to authenticate documents with the seal of government authority. Ben interjected, claiming to know a young man who allegedly rivalled Max's talents. "There was this guy at the Commercial Avenue who used to carve stamps" he said. "He even carved government stamps for individuals who used it for their private businesses. He was eventually picked up by the police and guess what happened; they ended up employing him in the government service. Now he carves stamps for the government."

"Sometimes, these *dokis* go through", Max said, sounding elated. "I know people who have used these documents and travelled abroad. Could this be the reason why the British embassy in Nigeria is now refusing to issue visas to young people below 30?" he wondered. "No, they're still issuing visas; it depends on your motive" Achu responded. In April 2005, the British government imposed a ban on entry visas for young Nigerians aged 18 to 30 who intended to travel to the UK for the first time. Questioned about this policy, the British High Commission in Nigeria claimed its embassy was unable to deal with the high number of visa applications, which had nearly doubled in two years.[3] Contrary to the High Commission's explanation, many of my friends in Old Town tied the visa ban to the proliferation of forged documents in both Cameroon and Nigeria. Although the fabrication and distribution of forged documents carried high risks, involving arrests and detention,[4] none of my research participants thought fabricators should be punished. If anything, they all agreed that individuals who resorted to producing faux dossiers were being productive, resourceful and providing a much-needed service. Some of them pointed out that the police only arrested fabricators if they failed to pay a bribe. It was against this backdrop that I came to understand that the economy of faux dossiers has its moralities, values and norms. Although primarily operated by young men experiencing "waithood", they also had partners within formal institutions including government agents such as the police.

My friends recounted stories about visa applicants known to them who would arrive for visa appointments in Yaounde, armed not only with faux dossiers but also pose as important personalities such as members of the clergy, traditional rulers, businessmen and artists – convinced that these carefully staged personas would readily convince reluctant visa officials about the veracity of their intended trip. Max substantiated this trend with the story of a young man whom he met at the US embassy dressed in the legendary Bamenda regalia posing as a traditional ruler from the North West Province. "He staged quite a convincing show. I knew this guy but was unaware of the fact that he was faking his identity. So, I approached to greet him, but he refused to shake

---

3.   See BBC News – 'UK visa delay for young Nigerians' http://news.bbc.co.uk/2/hi/uk_
       news/4425079.stm accessed on 29 May 2007.
4.   See *Cameroon Tribune*, online edition, 'GCE Certificate Fraudsters Detained in Bamenda'
       accessed on December 11, 2006 concerning the arrests of two young people for forging GCE
       certificates amongst others. Both the accused were technicians who owned computers which
       they had allegedly used for the production, printing and distribution of forged certificates.
       http://allafrica.com/stories/printable/200612111371.html

my hands."[5] Bernard added to the conversation by referring to the thriving economy of faux dossiers in the popular student neighbourhood of Bonamoussadi in Yaounde. "That's a dangerous quartier", he said, "really dangerous" he emphasised. In Bonamoussadi, he claimed, you would find producers of all sorts of "official" documents, including those that carried President Biya's signature. "There, you'll find middlemen who make a living as peddlers of faux dossiers. They take the commands, return to the producers whose identities are highly protected and then return with the expertly forged documents."

The economy of faux dossiers was not something that happened elsewhere or somewhere remote. It was deeply embedded in Old Town and other suburbs of Bamenda. I knew several young men who were experienced and smooth operators within the faux dossier economy. William, 28, for example, nicknamed the *inspector* was considered one of the most reliable entrepreneurs in this sector. A university dropout whose employment status had been unsteady, William once told me he discovered his talent for forging documents back in secondary school. "I used to help students with their report cards. I made new report cards for students who had failed their exams. They would use their new report cards to get admission elsewhere. It really helped; you know." William could accurately forge any signature after a brief practice and had earned the nickname, *inspector* for his ability to replicate any government document needed by his numerous clients. He also provided bank statements and life insurance policies to a growing clientele of people seeking visas to travel abroad. Ironically, his numerous attempts to travel abroad had failed.

One morning, I met Lawrence, an NBA member who had commissioned several faux dossiers from William to apply for a US visa. He pulled out a bank statement from a manilla envelope, professionally prepared on a Union Bank of Cameroon letterhead, stating that he had about 12 million FCFA in his account. With no prior travel experience outside the country, Lawrence believed I would be well-placed to advise him about one of his major concerns; the amount on the bank statement seemed too much for his "framed" persona. "Do you think those guys might be suspicious? Willy had second thoughts about the amount. He thinks the money is too much." Lawrence was also concerned that his supporting documents showed he had worked for two years as a sales assistant and that it was unlikely he had earned such an amount of money during his two years in that position. "I must leave for Yaounde tomorrow to submit these documents. Willy has promised to do

---

5.   Traditional rulers from the Bamenda Grasslands do not shake hands with their subjects.

another bank statement for me." He then proceeded to pull out all the other documents from the brown envelope and requested that I examine them and tell if they were credible enough. Without hesitating, I took the package into my hands and flipped through, stunned by the claims of its contents. I was particularly intrigued by the title deed of a piece of land he supposedly owned in Bamenda; an affidavit from the CEO of his company granting him leave for the period of his visit, emphasising that he would resume work at the company upon his return.[6] Lawrence's story introduces us to the intricate nexus between the economy of faux dossiers and migration – a trend that was as significant during the period of my fieldwork as it is today.

Imaginaries and Trajectories of Migration

In precolonial southern Africa, the ultimate protest against a despotic chief was desertion or the threat to desert one's chiefdom. Such threats or desertions were often taken seriously because the adage that "a chief is a chief because of his people" was vital to a chief's legitimacy and credibility (Fokwang 2009). A deserted chief was not only prone to attack by his rivals or enemies, but it was also suggestive of the chief's failure to meet his obligations to the living and the living-dead (the ancestors).

While studies of young people's migratory aspirations and adventures have increasingly focused on the effects of migration on social stratification (Pelican 2011, 2012), their ambitions for graduate education (H. Nyamnjoh 2021) or the identity politics and imaginaries that fuel migration (Alpes 2013; Nyamnjoh & Page 2002), few studies have examined the nexus between the economy of faux dossiers and migration. While more and more young Anglophone Cameroonians have fled the country because of the ongoing civil war[7], many were already leaving out of desperation in the 1990s and early 2000s. Many young people felt betrayed by their leaders, like the despotic chief from whom they must flee, if only to return at a much later period. While many left,

---

6. It is mandatory for applicants of travel visas to the USA to demonstrate ties to their country of residence and to show proof they would return at the end of their visit.

7. The following sources and more have documented the brutal conflict in the Anglophone territory of the country: "A new surge of people fleeing Cameroon's Anglophone regions" https://www.dw.com/en/a-new-surge-of-people-fleeing-cameroons-anglophone-regions/a-50186298; It is also estimated that over half a million citizens have been displaced as a result of the conflict, with more atrocities being reported in 2022. Also see "Conflict in Cameroon's Anglophone regions forces 430,000 people to flee" https://reliefweb.int/report/cameroon/conflict-cameroons-anglophone-regions-forces-430000-people-flee both articles accessed on June 9, 2022.

concerned about their safety in an increasingly hostile and intolerant political environment, a significant number of these departures were facilitated by faux dossiers issued by equally disillusioned politicians or activists, especially within or allegedly on behalf of the Southern Cameroons National Council (SCNC).

Many young people in Old Town expressed the desire to leave Cameroon, disillusioned with the Biya regime's 40-year rule that has yielded little in terms of socioeconomic progress. For many of these young people, emigration would enable them to attain a status they have long been denied - social adulthood. From a sample of 60 young people in the three associations I studied, 91% of them stated their wish to leave Cameroon if they had the means and opportunity. Also significant was that a majority chose the USA as their destination of choice.

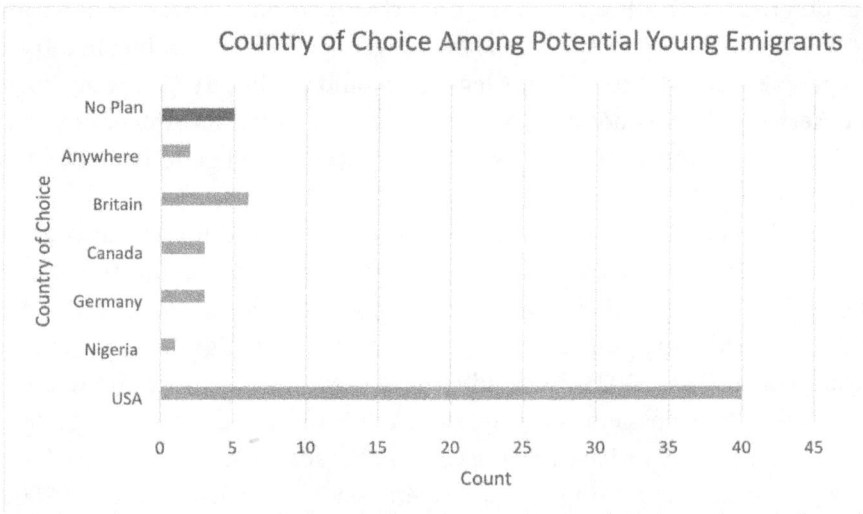

FIGURE 6.1 Chart showing country of choice among potential young emigrants.

Why such overwhelming preference for the US? First, many claimed to know someone already living in the USA (friends, family etc.,) who could assist with settling in a new country. They would also not need to learn a new language given their fluency in English. Most importantly, many were attracted to the idea of the American dream - the idea that it did not matter where one came from and that if you worked hard enough, you would reap a bountiful harvest in the land of endless opportunities. For many young people who grew up in the 1980s when television was introduced in the country, popular sitcoms starring black people like the *Cosby Show* and the *Fresh Prince of Bel'Air*, just to name a few, portrayed the prosperity and boundless material abundance that awaited its potential arrivals (also see Mbaku & Awasom 2004).

Even more attractive than these sitcoms was the introduction of the Diversity Immigrant Visa Program (DV Program) in the mid-1990s by the American government.[8] This program offered a genuine pathway for young people to emigrate and as such, was received with unprecedented euphoria, particularly among the Anglophone populations who felt treated as second-class citizens in a Francophone-dominated state. Figure 6.2 shows the steady increase since 2004 in the number of DV winners of Cameroonian nationality.

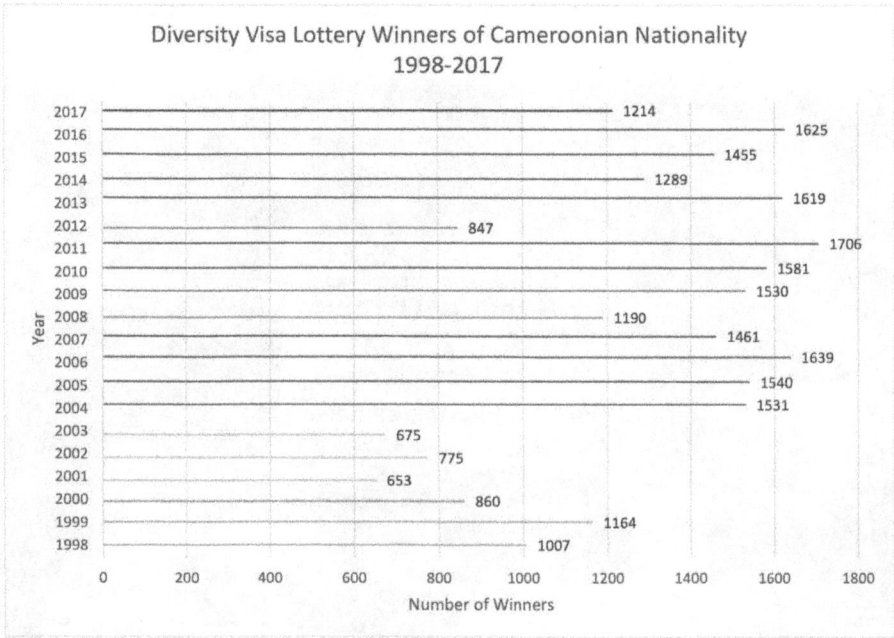

FIGURE 6.2 Diversity Visa Lottery Winners of Cameroonian Nationality 1998-2017.

8. "The Diversity Immigrant Visa Program (DV Program) makes up to 50,000 immigrant visas available annually, drawn from random selection among all entries to individuals who are from countries with low rates of immigration to the United States. The DV Program is administered by the U.S. Department of State (DOS)." https://www.uscis.gov/green-card/green-card-eligibility/green-card-through-the-diversity-immigrant-visa-program

Knowledge about this program was far reaching.[9] For some, submitting their application had become an annual ritual, including many members in the associations who had played the "lottery" at least once. In 2003, legislation governing the organisation of the DV program stated that effective from 2004 and henceforth, all submissions would be electronic – that is, through the internet. This did not dampen the popularity of the programme or diminish aspirants' hopes of winning a "Green Card" ticket to the USA. The period between October and November/December became popularly known in town as DV lottery season – a time when internet cafés and photographers cashed in because of the volume of people seeking to take a chance with the DV program. During my fieldwork, especially in November 2005, I was frequently requested by my friends in Old Town to take digital photos for their DV "lottery" applications.

FIGURE 6.3 An ad for the American DV lottery in front of a popular shop on the commercial avenue, Bamenda. Photo by author.

9.   Knowledge of the DV programme was also widely circulated in local newspapers, especially in *Business and Marketing*, an affordable monthly newspaper that published the results and information on the DV programme. Every month the paper also carried eye-catching front-page headline such as 'Have a foreign job in 45 days' or 'Become an international volunteer today.' See Issue No. 063, August 2005.

Despite the tremendous popularity of the DV program, most young people I interacted with sought to widen their options beyond hoping for a randomised process that would alter their fate. Traditional options such as invitations from family and friends already resident abroad as well as "staged" business trips and increasingly, political asylum were very promising options. Many members in the NBA had tried at least one of these options and were very familiar with the visa application and interview protocols at various embassies in Yaounde.

Max had made numerous trips to the US embassy and recounted his experience with a female official at the American embassy who had become notorious for her harsh treatment of visa applicants. "That woman does not care", he said. "If she speaks to you for a minute, then you could nurse the hope that you might have a visa. What she normally does is to look at your invitation letter for a few seconds, then she pulls out a certain form and stamps your passport at the back, sometimes without a word." Despite the extremely high rejection rate, few people were willing to give up. "These guys are making a lot of money from us because their application fee is non-refundable" Achu remarked. "The sad thing about the process is that applicants are interviewed to the hearing of everyone. Even those seated in the hall can see and hear your discussion with the officials" he said, "but the British provide some privacy." It was at this juncture that Achu recounted his experience at the British embassy. "You get into a small room in which there's a desk with lots of paper and a laptop. Then a white man comes in and appears to be in a hurry. They always seem to be in a hurry," he joked, and the young men laughed noisily. "He then asks you to answer some questions. 'If you don't understand a question, don't answer', the white man advises. While you speak, he's busy typing away into his sophisticated laptop. If he is satisfied with you, he asks you to return at 2 p.m. If he's not, he gives you a letter of appeal. It's a long paper which he inserts into your passport and apologises for not being able to grant you a visa."

Of all the young men I hung out with, Kevin's experience was most extraordinary. He did not only own four passports, but had also received at least six visa rejections – a story of hope and perseverance which he painstakingly shared with me.

After completing high school, Kevin was determined to travel abroad with the assistance of his elder brothers and sisters who were already resident in three different European countries. "While in school, I had lots of financial difficulties and wanted to begin earning my own money. My brothers were ready to assist me if I could find a way out of the country" he said, sipping from a bottle of Top Orange, a popular Cameroonian soft drink. Instead of an alcoholic beverage, Kevin had opted for Top Orange because he was still recovering from a brutal hangover – thanks to a party he had attended two days prior. "Actually, my elder sister in Denmark brought up the idea. She suggested that I should travel abroad and look for a job. I had no plans of continuing school." With the financial assistance of his older sister, he travelled to Douala in search of reliable persons versed in the business of 'trafficking' people abroad. "While in Douala, I lived with some relatives and eventually got employment with a certain *doki* expert." He soon discovered that Douala was replete with young men specialised in the business of furnishing clients with forged documents to travel abroad. "It's big business" he said, noting that most of the *doki* guys were also involved in feymania.[10] "My employer, Moukoko was a feyman" he recounted. Moukoko's office was equipped with a landline phone, fax machine and a computer – equipment that vastly facilitated his business. "I was paid 3000FCFA per day, but as you know, Douala is an expensive city. It was just enough to survive. Moukoko's company was registered at the Chamber of Commerce in Douala and part of my job was to go there regularly to pick up catalogues of businesses in Europe. At the time, the internet was not yet very popular as it is today. When we got the information we needed, we then communicated with a potential business organisation in Europe and requested an invitation letter, expressing interest in establishing a partnership with them. It was a lengthy process to obtain invitation letters for clients." Kevin further clarified that although Moukoko's business was registered as a sales agent for imported products, none of such transactions ever took place. His real business was 'trafficking' clients abroad as 'businessmen' in return for a hefty fee. His network included among others, a government agent at the customs department in Douala who was responsible for the supply of passports on demand and bank agents who supplied a variety of traveller cheques etc. A typical transaction proceeded as follows: Moukoko's company writes to company X in Europe, introducing itself as a giant retail company in Douala with Y million FCFA as its capital and that they would like to purchase company X's products for re-sale in Cameroon. Excited at the prospects of a new market, company X dispatches its most recent catalogue by UPS. After reviewing the catalogue, Moukoko and his boys would then order a large quantity of goods but would not proceed to payment. Moukoko then convinces the sales department at

10.   Feymania refers to the practice of scamming. It is equivalent to the Nigerian 419 scam (Apter 1999). Feymania has attracted the attention of a growing number of ethnographers including Basile Ndjio (2006) and Dominique Malaquais (2001).

company X that sending the payment through the formal banking institutions would be a costly affair due to prohibitively high processing fees and a poor exchange rate. He would rather that one of his employees or agents should undertake a business trip to company X to complete the transaction. His agent would also use the opportunity to explore further business partnerships with company X. Often, company X would issue an invitation letter, convinced that they were dealing with a credible counterpart. Such letters would serve as a key document for a visa application.

Kevin revealed that he was employed at a period when Moukoko's business had suffered a major setback owing to the introduction of stringent visa regulations at the French embassy, which had been his principal port of transaction. Kevin recalled excitedly how he successfully helped Moukoko to diversify his business to other countries where business was carried out in English. "You know, Moukoko was Francophone and couldn't speak English. I assisted in writing letters to these European companies, especially those in the Schengen zone."

Kevin made a total of six attempts to obtain visas from various embassies - once at the Greek embassy, twice at the German embassy, once at the French embassy and once at the Spanish embassy but none of his applications had succeeded. "My brother said I had bad luck. He could not understand why I could not get a visa." Faced with rejection, he sank into depression and lost a lot of weight. "I completely lost focus. I didn't know what to do with my life. I started discouraging people not to put all their plans to travel abroad." He even insinuated that he would deliver a talk about the perils of migration during *formation time* so that others could learn from his experience. "That's how I wasted an entire year of my life." His pain was accentuated by the fact that many of Moukoko's clients had succeeded while he always met with rejection. "After a year of trying and failing, my sister asked me to return to Bamenda which I did. She said I needed to take a break." Even more crucial was the advice given him by Moukoko to seek the services of a diviner to 'find out' what was "tying" or blocking his path[11]. "I simply laughed when he told me this. My people don't believe in those things, so I didn't bother. They simply told me that perhaps, it was not yet my time and everyone asked me to exercise some patience."

11. In such a context, individuals believed to be suffering from ill-luck were encouraged to seek the services of a diviner who would determine if such ill-luck had been masterminded by a malevolent person or spirit. Divination, it was believed, would not only diagnose but also provide spiritual cure and further protection from harmful persons and spirits.

Reflecting on his experience with Moukoko, Kevin recounted that his boss' business was extremely profitable. "Clients were charged about a million francs, but I can say with certainty that it cost less than 200,000FCFA to carry out the entire transaction." He said a majority of the clients came from the South West Region (one of the two Anglophone regions in Cameroon) and approximately eight persons successfully travelled each month. Such clients would travel as businesspersons supposedly going to participate at trade fairs or to shop for merchandise to resell at home. "If I had continued with school, I would have completed my undergraduate studies by now" he said, disappointedly. "Now, I'm not sure what I'll do and my family is very concerned."

During my fieldwork, at least three NBA members were involved in arrangements to emigrate, but none had materialised at the time of my departure. Since then, dozens of NBA members have emigrated and now live in Europe and North America. Their dispersal accounts for the global credentials of the association. Such migration – whether by harnessing the opportunities afforded by the faux dossier economy or through the DV program – have vastly accelerated many young people's attainment of social adulthood.[12]

In the past two decades, an unprecedented number of young Cameroonians have sought political asylum in the global north – now a popular and speedier trend to obtain legal papers in Western countries. Whilst some of these claims are based on spurious grounds, a growing number of young Cameroonians affected by the ongoing conflict have indeed fled to neighbouring Nigeria while others have sought refuge in the USA[13] and across Europe. In 2022, the US government finally granted Temporary Protected Status (TPS) to Cameroonians fleeing the conflict in the Anglophone regions, protection that activists and

---

12.   Even those with limited financial means have chosen to go through the ordeal of crossing the Sahara Desert. See *The New York Times*, 'Migrants reported found in desert' By Craig S. Smith Friday, October 14, 2005, http://www.iht.com/bin/print_ipub.php?file=/articles/2005/10/14/news/morocco.php accessed on 8 December 2005. The news article reveals that Cameroonian youth were amongst other West African youth en route to Europe via the desert. In 2005, a French photojournalist, Olivier Jobard, documented the crossing of a young Cameroonian man, 23, now available as a documentary on http://www.mediastorm.org/0010.htm

13.   See for example: "A Cry for Cameroon: How the United States Failed Refugees" by Lauren Seibert https://www.hrw.org/news/2022/03/28/cry-cameroon-how-united-states-failed-refugees, accessed on June 9, 2022. Human Rights Watch has also reported that some of the deported asylum seekers have been put into harm's way following their return to Cameroon; see https://www.hrw.org/news/2022/02/10/us-deported-cameroonian-asylum-seekers-suffer-serious-harm accessed June 9, 2022.

human rights organisations had been lobbying for.[14] It is expected that over 10,000 Cameroonian refugees will benefit from this program. This designation lends credence to what scholars and activists have claimed about Cameroon – a brutal dictatorship that has consistently masked itself as a democracy. In the years leading up to the conflict, the United Kingdom alone had received over 2000 applications for political asylum,[15] especially by alleged SCNC activists who accused the Biya regime of harassment and brutal killings.[16] Similarly, the Cameroon government also expressed moral panic about the growing involvement of young Cameroonian women in 'cyber-marriages' with European men.[17] Such marriages were perceived by young Cameroonian women as a pathway to migration and consequently the attainment of social adulthood. Cyber marriages are indeed implicated in the faux dossier economy – given the ways in which young women construct, manage, and present their persona on cyberspace with the aim of attracting potential or gullible suitors.

Conclusion

In previous chapters, I described and analysed how young men and women in Old Town leveraged their respective aassociations in pursuit of social adulthood status. This chapter has focused less on the actions within associations. What we see instead is an unpacking of the connection between the faux dossier economy and migration. I use the example of a few of my friends to highlight the allure of migration as an alternative pathway to social adulthood. By travelling abroad, often with the aid of faux dossiers, these young men and women hope to accumulate the material resources that will enable them to establish independent households and also extend support to kith and kin back home – key indicators of social adulthood. That many young people have been unsuccessful in achieving their desired goals of relative autonomy underscores the crisis of citizenship in a postcolonial state such as Cameroon.

Through the prism of these young people's lives, we see the "inconsistencies

14.   See "Secretary Mayorkas Designates Cameroon for Temporary Protected Status for 18 Months" https://www.uscis.gov/newsroom/news-releases/secretary-mayorkas-desig- nates-cameroon-for-temporary-protected-status-for-18-months accessed on June 9, 2022.

15.   See 'Longing for Asylum without Persecution' in *The Post* No. 0672, Friday, June 3, 2005, page 9.

16.   A growing number of Francophone asylum seekers also allege to be SCNC activists.

17.   See 'Girls Told to beware of Cyber Marriages' in *The Post*, No. 0668, Friday May 20, 2005, page 6 and 'Internet marriages fuelling prostitution in Europe' in *The Herald*, No. 1645, Monday 23-24 May 2005, page 8; also see *Cameroon Tribune*, 'Hidden Side of Internet Mar- riages' accessed at http://allafrica.com/stories/200609290250.html on September 29, 2006.

and contradictions" of citizenship, namely that "not all individuals have equal access to the state, that citizenship is a mediated relation determined at least in some measure by social positioning" (Werbner 1998:7) and that migration provides a "lens through which to understand the key dynamics around ine-quality and social change" (Paret & Gleeson 2016:277). A growing number of young people see themselves trapped between what Jones and Wallace (1992) have termed *semi-citizenship* and *deferred citizenship* and are frequently reminded by state leaders to wait for their turn (cf. Biya's 1998 Youth Day speech). Not many young people are contented with either semi-citizenship, deferred citizenship or even waithood. They are actively and creatively involved in negotiating their exclusion by positioning themselves at the leading edge of appeals for the reconfiguration of the postcolony. They are also determined to use the technologies at their disposal to forge the necessary "dossiers" that would facilitate their travels abroad. These experiences are far from isolated. There are striking parallels between the young Cameroonian women who resort to cyber marriages and Jennifer Cole's (2010) observation of young women's survival strategies in Tamatave, Madagascar. Similarly, ethnographers of women's migration contend that such mobilities point to and are produced by structural inequalities within the country (see Mills 2002 in the case of Thailand), an observation that has remained true of Cameroon for over two decades.

This chapter has brought together three strands of issues that may initially appear isolated – migration, the economy of faux dossiers and social adulthood. I argue that for many young people experiencing "deferred" or semi-citizenship in Cameroon, migration offers them a viable pathway towards the pursuit of their personal dreams and ultimately the attainment of social adulthood. Furthermore, for those without the means to secure "legitimate" documents as part of their travel plans, procuring "faux dossiers" provides an opportunity for them to negotiate their way out of structural violence and exclusion.

Personhood, Moral Action, and Social Adulthood in the Cameroon Grasslands

This ethnography has described and analysed the lives of dozens of young men and women in the community of Old Town, the cradle of the sprawling city of Bamenda, Cameroon. A central concern in my analysis has focused on how these young people, previously positioned as "youth" despite their attainment of biological maturity – have sought to re-position themselves as social adults – this, against a backdrop of diminishing state resources, prolonged economic crisis and more recently, raging armed conflict. Although the processes of *becoming* social adults are fraught with ambivalence, I show that they deserve to be analysed because they enable us to appreciate the specific ways in which identities, subjectivities and social transformation are brought about in society. Becoming social adults entails labour-intensive processes that could be easily ignored and indeed, often ignored in the literature. This ethnography, I hope, illuminates how young people in Old Town "are heavily implicated in each other's lives with the day-to-day work that is necessary in order to maintain functional relationships with neighbours, co-workers, and extended family members" (Simone 2014:33). I contend that in their quest for social adulthood, an aspect of personhood in the Grasslands, young people embark upon individual and collective practices of self-care that entail cultivating virtuous character aimed not only at their own moral transformation but also their community. In elaborating this argument, I have drawn on the concepts of personhood, subjectivity, social adulthood, gender, and moral citizenship as important building blocks.

What does it mean to be a person? The answer is not as obvious as many may assume. In North America and the global north broadly, the person is often conceived as an autonomous rights-bearing human being irrespective of age, sex, creed, social race or national origin. Nevertheless, there is considerable anthropological agreement that societies differ in how persons are conceived and that these conceptions are linked to their forms of social institutions and how things work in society. This means that socioeconomic, political and religious life are organised based on each society's conception of personhood, shaping what roles are available to the "persons" within that society. Not everyone or anyone can occupy certain positions or fulfil certain roles. For example, the US Constitution prohibits naturalized citizens from running for the highest office in the United States. Similarly, other rules and norms govern who can occupy the presidency of the United States, one of which states that a so-called candidate must be at least thirty-five years.[1] Personhood, therefore must be understood cross-culturally, while paying attention to those elements that are emphasised when defining a person and whether one's personhood changes overtime.

In the Cameroon Grasslands, personhood is not a fixed entity. Rather, the individual is always in a state of *becoming* a full person through sociality with others as one traverses significant stages in the life cycle. For instance, in many precolonial kingdoms in the Grasslands, unmarried cadets (young men and women) irrespective of their age, were considered "children" and therefore could not fulfil roles meant for "adults". While women could become "adults" through marriage and childbirth, the same was not true for young men who were believed to lack "transmissible life essence" that could only be properly acquired through their service and symbolic blessings from notables and chiefs (who were always men). These *social cadets* – to borrow from Jean-Pierre Warnier, were akin to empty vessels that lacked the capacity to fill themselves. Through participation in both social and more importantly, biological reproduction, these cadets could attain *social adulthood* as a major step in becoming persons.

In contemporary Old Town, I show that becoming persons is tied to young people's sociality and their participation in social reproduction. Their sociality as members of various associations is evident in how they pool their social and material resources together which are then redistributed within and beyond these associations. Participation in associational life is a first step in this process. It is within associations that young people ruminate on their collective predicament as individuals whose citizenship in relation to the state is "deferred". It is also within associations that members are invited

---

1.   See ArtII.S1.C5.1 Qualifications for President; https://constitution.congress.gov/browse/essay/artII_S1_C5_1/

to cultivate certain technologies of self-care - rooted in the wisdom that one cannot give that which one does not have. Morally conscious or transformed individuals can give of themselves in ways that would accelerate communal transformation. To this end, we see young people as they participate in maintaining a sanitary environment, donating to the needy and undertaking the sponsorship of underprivileged children in their community. It is through such forms of sociality that we see young people in Old Town becoming persons in contemporary Grassfields society.

The modernity of their personhood is tied to new of forms of subjectivities that may be contrasted with precolonial Grassfields conceptions. By subjectivity, we mean one's sense of self and self-world relations – or put differently, one's interactions with society. Evidently, one's subjectivity is shaped by the social and material spaces we occupy –in terms of how we understand our duties and obligations in our dealings with others. I show that becoming persons in Old Town entails practices on two fronts; first, the duty to one's self and the cultivation of moral virtue and secondly, the duty towards one's fellows in the associations and the community at large. If subjectivity is created by experiences of being positioned and of positioning, this ethnography has detailed how young people in Old Town continuously seek to position themselves as social adults, away from being positioned as "youth" or social cadets. We see that youth and social adulthood are different kinds of subjectivities and that social adulthood is actively sought because it advances one's personhood within the cultural context of the Grasslands. Modern social adulthood is underpinned by the fulfilment of certain cultural expectations. Certainly, marriage and parenting are highly coveted factors, but they are not exclusive or sufficient in the processes of positioning oneself as a social adult. Other elements that are emphasised in the construction of social adulthood include self-control (ethical self-care), interdependence and conviviality. As members of various associations, we see how self-care transforms into communal care as they take up responsibilities that should otherwise be borne by either the state, local government, other parents or community actors.

I also show that although social adulthood and moral citizenship are intricately connected, they are nevertheless different kinds of subjectivities. Moral citizenship is the vehicle through which social adulthood is affirmed. I formulate moral citizenship as a subjectivity that requires the pursuit of ethical actions geared towards the moral and material transformation of one's community. Moral citizenship advocates and advances the idea of the common good, conviviality and mutual indebtedness. As anthropologists have observed, cities are the lived spaces where the "uncertainties of citizenship are experienced" but they also provide the locus against which "emergent forms" of citizenship are expressed (Holston & Appadurai 1999:3). One of these emergent forms of citizenship that remains underexplored is what I have referred to as moral citizenship. This kind of citizenship does not derive its legitimacy from the state but rather, its association between persons and is expressed in a diversity of practices. In Old Town, these practices are evident in the domains of sanitary activism, the cultivation of virtuous character at the individual and associational level as well as the pursuit of charitable causes believed to be intrinsically worthy.

Although moral citizenship affirms young people's positioning as social adults, I also show how ambivalent and gendered this subjectivity is. While the attainment of social adulthood was traditionally different for men and women in the precolonial Grasslands, practices related to moral citizenship are embedded in power relations and gender ideologies that undermine the sort of ethical and material transformation they seek in the first place. In becoming moral citizens, the young men and women in Old Town cultivate and deploy specific kinds of femininities and masculinities that end up being counter-productive. For example, in their quest for honour and respectability, young women in both associations run up against members whose lack of access to reproductive resources puts them on opposing sides of the moral divide. On the other hand, the young men's enactment of productive masculinity through sport, "work" in public spaces and an elaborate child sponsorship scheme overlooks the existence or perpetuation of toxic and hegemonic masculinity within its ranks. Hegemonic masculinity legitimates and values among other things, hierarchy, risking taking and the privileging of physical strength (cf. Connell 1995; Haenfler 2004). Toxic masculinity on the other hand refers to ways of behaving as a man that is harmful towards other men and women such as engaging in risky sexual behaviour, aggression, excessive use of drugs and alcohol, bullying, etc. These practices are gendered in the sense that embedded in their ideals are resources for *doing gender*. By doing gender, these young men and women reinforce the illusion that the differences between men and women are essential and natural, whereas it is their cultural construction in specific ways and spaces by *doing* that these differences become actualised.

If cities are the prime locus for the expression of emergent forms of citizenship, I show in this monograph that associations provide the enduring platforms within which specific kinds of subjectivities are fashioned and lived out. The study of associational life in African communities should be taken seriously in part because they show the labour-intensive mechanisms through which people seek to maintain productive relations with each other, especially in contexts of precarity.

Community or voluntary associations in Africa have played vital roles in the socioeconomic development, not only of its members but also of the constituencies or areas these associations claim to represent (Kerr 1978; Little 1972; Little & Southall 1973; Wallerstein 1964). Many urban sodalities such as the associations covered in this monograph often seek to contribute to the general welfare of its members by providing socioeconomic support to members (see Lentz 1995 for similarities in north-western Ghana) and the community at large. With limited or diminishing access to healthcare and social services that ought to be provided by local/national government (during the Covid-19 pandemic and the ongoing conflict in the Anglophone territories), these associations have become self-reliant development agents (cf. Fonchingong 2006; Fonchingong & Fonjong 2002) that continue to serve as the prime locus for the elaboration of moral citizenship.

Migration offers an alternative pathway to many young people who seek to position themselves as social adults – whether they belong to associations or not. I detail how certain migratory trajectories are not only seen as emancipatory (cf. Timera 2001) by young men and women but also how these mobilities are facilitated by the *faux dossier economy*. Without moralising the faux dossier economy, I frame it as a mediator of global processes of flows in which both government agents and marginalised citizens are implicated.

Young people in Old Town are moral beings as humans elsewhere. They have peculiar conceptions of what the good life constitutes – informed by the cultural universe in which they belong, but also informed by global trends and symbols. Having been positioned and perhaps banished by the state to *waithood* and "deferred citizenship" they are determined to re-position themselves as social adults by means of an ambiguous moral citizenship that nevertheless celebrates their individual and collective virtuosity. Such a focus on grassroots movements should inform and inspire further studies on what it takes to fight structural violence while seeking changes to everyday practices and meanings.

What I hope this ethnography has achieved is to have shown how young people who initially established their clubs as mere sites for "socialising" ended up facilitating our understanding of the microprocesses of how people reshape their identities and give meaning to their lives irrespective of the material conditions in which they find themselves.

References

Abbink, J. (2005). Being Young in Africa: The Politics of despair and renewal. In J. Abbink & I. van Kessel (Eds.), *Vanguard or Vandals: Youth, Politics and Conflict in Africa* (pp. 1-34). Leiden: Brill.

Abbink, J., & van Kessel, I. (Eds.). (2005). *Vanguard or Vandals: Youth, Politics and Conflict in Africa*. Leiden: Brill.

Adams, A. E. (1993). Dyke to Dyke: Ritual Reproduction at a U.S. Men's Military College. *Anthropology Today, 9*(5), 3-6.

Adebanwi, W. (2005). The carpenter's revolt: youth, violence and the reinvention of culture in Nigeria. *Journal of Modern African Studies, 43*(3), 339–365.

Adebanwi, W. (2022). Introduction: The Everyday State and Democracy in Africa. In W. Adebanwi (Ed.), *Everyday State and Democracy in Africa: Ethnographic Encounters* (pp. 1-46). Athens, OH: Ohio University Press.

African Union. (2006). *African Youth Charter*. Adopted by the Seventh Ordinary Session of the Assembly, Held in Banjul, The Gambia on 2nd July 2006

Aguilar, M. I. (1998). Gerontocratic, Aesthetic and Political Models of Age. In M. I. Aguilar (Ed.), *The Politics of Age and Gerontocracy in Africa: Ethnographies of the Past and Memories of the Present* (pp. 3-29). Trenton, NJ: Africa World Press.

Alpes, M. J. (2013). Imagining a future in 'bush': migration aspirations at times of crisis in Anglophone Cameroon. *Identities, 21*(3), 259-274. doi:10.1080/1070289X.2013.831350

Appadurai, A. (1996). *Modernity at Large - Cultural Dimensions of Globalization*. Minneapolis: Minnesota University Press.

Appadurai, A. (2008). Disjuncture and Difference in the Global Cultural Economy. In J. X. Inda & R. Rosaldo (Eds.), *The Anthropology of Globalization: A Reader* (pp. 47-65). Malden, MA: Blackwell.

Apter, A. (1999). IBB= 419: Nigerian Democracy and the Politics of Illusion. In J. L. Comaroff & J. Comaroff (Eds.), *Civil Society and the Political Imagination in Africa: Critical Perspectives*. Chicago: University of Chicago Press.

Ardener, E. (1996). *Kingdom on Mount Cameroon: Studies in the History of the Cameroon Coast, 1500-1970*. Providence and Oxford: Berghahn Books.

Ardener, E., Ardener, S., & Warmington, W. A. (1960). *Plantation and village in the Cameroons: Some economic and social studies.* Oxford: Oxford University Press.

Argenti, N. (2002). Youth in Africa: A Major Resource for Change. In A. de Waal & N. Argenti (Eds.), *Young Africa: Realising the Rights of Children and Youth.* Trenton, NJ: Africa World Press.

Argenti, N. (2005). Dancing in the Borderlands: The Forbidden Masquerades of Oku Youth and Women, Cameroon. In A. Honwana & F. de Boeck (Eds.), *Makers and Breakers: Children and Youth in Postcolonial Africa.* London: James Currey.

Argenti, N. (2007). *The Intestines of the State: Youth, Violence, and Belated Histories in the Cameroon Grassfields.* Chicago & London: The University of Chicago Press.

Ariès, P. (1962). *Centuries of Childhood: A social history of family life* (R. Baldick, Trans.). New York: Vintage Press.

Asad, T. (Ed.) (1990). *Anthropology and the Colonial Encounter.* New York: Humanities Press.

Atanga, M. L. (1994). *The Political Economy of West Cameroon: A Study in the Alienation of a Linguistic Minority.* (M. Sc. Thesis). Ahmadou Bello University, Zaria.

Aulette, J. R., & Wittner, J. (2015). *Gendered Worlds* (3rd ed.). New York & Oxford: Oxford University Press.

Awambeng, C. M. (1991). *Evolution and Growth of Urban Centres in the North-West Province (Cameroon): Case Studies (Bamenda, Kumbo, Mbengwi, Nkambe, Wum).* Berne: European Academic Publishers.

Bähre, E. (2007). Reluctant solidarity: Death, urban poverty and neighbourly assistance in South Africa. *Ethnography, 8*(1), 33-59.

Bangura, Y. (1997). Understanding the Political and Cultural Dynamics of the Sierra Leone War: A Critique of Paul Richard's Fighting for the Rain Forest. *Africa Development, 22*(3-4), 117-148.

Bank, A., & Bank, L. J. (Eds.). (2013). *Inside African Anthropology: Monica Wilson and Her Interpreters.* New York: Cambridge University Press.

Barkan, J. D., McNulty, M. L., & Ayeni, M. A. O. (1991). 'Hometown' Voluntary Associations, Local Development, and the Emergence of Civil Society in Western Nigeria. *The Journal of Modern African Studies, 29*(3), 457-480.

Bayart, J.-F., Ellis, S., & Hibou, B. (1999). *The Criminalization of the State in Africa.* Oxford: James Currey.

Bell, D. (1993). Introduction: The Context. In D. Bell, P. Caplan, & W. J. Karim (Eds.), *Gendered fields: Women, Men and Ethnography.* London: Routledge.

Berreman, G. D. (2007). Behind Many Masks: Ethnography and Impression Management. In A. C. G. M. Robben & J. A. Sluka (Eds.), *Ethnographic Fieldwork: An Anthropological Reader* (pp. 137-158). Malden, MA: Blackwell Publishing.

Bolten, C. E. (2020). *Serious Youth in Sierra Leone: An Ethnography of Performance and Global Connection.* Oxford & New York: Oxford University Press.

Brettell, C. B., & Sargent, C. F. (2006). Migration, Identity, and Citizenship: Anthropological Perspectives. *American Behavioral Scientist, 50*(1), 3-8.

Burgess, T. (2005). Introduction to Youth and Citizenship in East Africa. *Africa Today, 51*(3), vii-xxiv.

Butler, J. (1990). *Gender Trouble: Feminism and the Subversion of Identity.* London: Routledge.

Carrier, G. J. (1995). *Gifts and commodities: exchange and western capitalism since 1700.* London & New York: Routledge.

Carrithers, M. (2010). Person. In J. Spencer & A. Barnard (Eds.), *The Routledge Encyclopedia of Social and Cultural Anthropology* (2nd ed., pp. 532-535). London & New York: Routledge.

Carrithers, M., Collins, S., & Lukes, S. (Eds.). (1985). *The Category of the Person: Anthropology, Philosophy, History.* Oxford: Oxford University Press.

Ceuppens, B., & Geschiere, P. (2005). Autochthony: Local or Global? New Modes in the Struggle over Citizenship and Belonging in Africa and Europe. *Annual Review of Anthropology, 34*, 385-407.

Chiabi, E. (1997). *The Making of Modern Cameroon: A History of Substate Nationalism and Disparate Union, 1914-1961.* Lanham, MD: University Press of America.

Chilver, E. M. (1966). *Zintgraff's Exploration in Bamenda, Adamawa and the Benue Lands 1889-1892* (E. W. Ardener Ed.). Buea: Ministry of Primary Education and Social Welfare and West Cameroon Antiquities Commission.

Chilver, E. M., & Kaberry, P. (1967). *Traditional Bamenda: The Precolonial History and Ethnography of the Bamenda Grassfields.* Buea, Cameroon: Government Printer.

Chomsky, N. (2013). The Dewey Lectures 2013: What Kind of Creatures Are We? Lecture III: What Is the Common Good? *The Journal of Philosophy, 110*(12), 685-700.

Christiansen, C., Utas, M., & Vigh, H. E. (2006). Introduction: Navigating Youth, Generating Adulthood. In C. Christiansen, M. Utas, & H. E. Vigh (Eds.), *Navigating Youth, Generating Adulthood: Social Becoming in an African Context.* Uppsala: Nordic Africa Institute.

Cole, J. (2010). *Sex and Salvation: Imagining the Future in Madagascar.* Chicago:

The University of Chicago Press.

Comaroff, J., & Comaroff, J. L. (2000). Millenial Capitalism: First Thoughts on a Second Coming. *Public Culture, 12*(2), 291-343.

Comaroff, J., & Comaroff, J. L. (2001). Naturing the Nation: Aliens, Apocalypse and the Postcolonial State. *Journal of Southern African Studies, 27*(3), 627-651.

Comaroff, J., & Comaroff, J. L. (2005). Reflections on Youth, From the Past to the Postcolony. In F. de Boeck & A. Honwana (Eds.), *Makers and Breakers: Children and Youth in Postcolonial Africa* (pp. 267-281). London: James Currey.

Comaroff, J. L., & Comaroff, J. (2001). On Personhood: an Anthropological Perspective from Africa. *Social Identities, 7*(2), 267-283.

Connell, R. W. (1995). *Masculinities*. Oxford: Polity Press.

Cornwall, A. (1997). Men, Masculinity and 'gender in development'. *Gender & Development, 5*(2), 8-13.

Côté, J. E. (2000). *Arrested Adulthood: The Changing Nature of Identity and Maturity in the Late-Modern World*. New York: New York University Press.

Côté, J. E. (2002). The Role of Identity Capital in the Transition to Adulthood: The Individualization Thesis Examined. *Journal of Youth Studies, 5*(2), 117-134.

Cruise O'Brien, D. (1996). A Lost Generation? Youth Identity and State Decay in West Africa. In R. Werbner & T. Ranger (Eds.), *Postcolonial Identities in Africa* (pp. 55-74). London: Zed Books.

d'Almeida-Topor, H., & Goerg, O. (Eds.). (1989). *Le mouvement associatif des jeunes en Afrique noire francophone au XXe siècle*. Paris: L'Harmattan.

Dalsgaard, S. (2016). The Ethnographic Use of Facebook in Everyday Life. *Anthropological Forum, 26*(1), 96-114. doi:10.1080/00664677.2016.1148011

de Boeck, F., & Honwana, A. (2000). Enfant, Jeunes et politique. *Politique Africaine, 80*, 5-11.

DeLancey, M. W. (1977). Credit for the Common Man in Cameroon. *The Journal of Modern African Studies, 15*(2), 316-322.

DeLancey, M. W. (1987). Women's Cooperatives in Cameroon: The Cooperative Experiences of the Northwest and Southwest Provinces. *African Studies Review, 30*(1), 1-18.

DeWalt, K. M., & DeWalt, B. R. (2011). *Participant Observation: A Guide for Fieldworkers* (2nd ed.). Lanham & New York: Altamira Press.

Diouf, M. (1996). Urban Youth and Senegalese Politics: Dakar 1988-1994. *Public Culture, 2*(2), 225-250.

Diouf, M. (2003). Engaging postcolonial cultures: African youth and public space. *African Studies Review, 46*(1), 1-12.

Durham, D. (2004). Disappearing youth: Youth as a social shifter in Botswana. *American Ethnologist, 31*(4), 589 – 605.

E. Wanki, P., & Lietaert, I. (2019). 'Bushfalling': the ambiguities of role identities experienced by self-sponsored Cameroonian students in Flanders (Belgium). *Identities, 26*(6), 725-743.

Easterly, W. (2007). *The White Man's Burden: Why the West's Efforts to Aid the Rest Have Done So Much Ill and So Little Good.* New York: Penguin Books.

Escobar, A. (1992). Imagining a Post-Development Era? Critical Thought, Development and Social Movements. *Social Text*(31/32), 20-56.

Evans, K., & Furlong, A. (1997). Metaphors of youth transitions: niches, pathways, trajectories or navigations. In J. Bynner (Ed.), *Youth, Citizenship and Social Change in a European Context* (pp. 17-41). Aldershot: Ashgate.

Everatt, D. (2011). Xenophobia, State and Society in South Africa, 2008–2010. *Politikon, 38*(1), 7-36.

Fardon, R. (2006). *Lela in Bali: History through Ceremony in Cameroon.* Oxford: Berghahn Books.

Fetzer, J. S. (2000). Economic self-interest or cultural marginality? Anti-immigration sentiment and nativist political movements in France, Germany and the USA. *Journal of Ethnic and Migration Studies, 26*(1), 5-23. doi:10.1080/136918300115615

Fokwang, J. (1999). African Youth, Competing Cultures and the Future of Peace. *South-South Journal of Culture and Development, 1*(1), 46-65.

Fokwang, J. (2003). Ambiguous Transitions: Mediating Citizenship among Youth in Cameroon. *Africa Development, XXVIII*, 76-104.

Fokwang, J. (2006). Ambiguous Transitions: Mediating Citizenship among Youths in Cameroon. In B. Beckman & G. R. Adeoti (Eds.), *Intellectuals and African Development: Pretension and Resistance in African Politics* (pp. 69-92). London: Zed Books.

Fokwang, J. (2007). Youth Involvement in Civil Society in Cameroon since 1990. *Africa Insight, 37*(3), 308-326.

Fokwang, J. (2008). Themes and Legacies: Anthropology's Trajectories in Cameroon. In A. Boskovic (Ed.), *Other People's Anthropologies: Ethnographic Practice on the Margins* (pp. 125-141). Oxford: Berghahn Books.

Fokwang, J. (2009a). *Mediating Legitimacy: Chieftaincy and Democratisation in Two African Chiefdoms.* Bamenda: Langaa Research and Publishing.

Fokwang, J. (2009b). Southern Perspective on Sport-in-Development: A Case Study of Football in Bamenda, Cameroon. In R. Levermore & A. Beacom (Eds.), *Sport and International Development.* Houndsmills: Palgrave Macmillan.

Fokwang, J. (2009c). Student Activism, Violence and the Politics of Higher Education in Cameroon: A Case Study of the University of Buea (1993-2003). In D. Chimanikire (Ed.), *Youth and Higher Education in Africa: The Cases of*

Cameroon, South Africa, Eritrea and Zimbabwe (pp. 9-33). Dakar: CODES-RIA.

Fokwang, J. (2014). Anti-crisis. *Anthropology Southern Africa, 37*(3-4), 268-269.

Fokwang, J. (2015). Fabrics of Identity: Uniforms, Gender and Associations in the Cameroon Grassfields. *Africa,* 85(04), 677-696.

Fokwang, J. (2016). Politics at the Margins: Alternate Sites of Political Involvement among Young People in Cameroon. *Canadian Journal of African Studies / Revue Canadienne des Etudes Africaines, 50*(2), 211-228.

Fombe, L. F. (1983). *The Bamenda Urban Space: Evolution and Organisation.* (Postgraduate Diploma Dissertation). University of Yaounde, Yaounde.

Fonchingong, C. (2006). Expanding horizons: Women's voices in community-driven development in the Cameroon grasslands. *GeoJournal, 65,* 137–149.

Fonchingong, C., & Fonjong, L. (2002). The concept of self-reliance in community development initiatives in the Cameroon grassfields. *GeoJournal, 57*(1-2), 83-94.

Fowler, I., & Zeitlyn, D. (1996). Preface. In I. Fowler & D. Zeitlyn (Eds.), *African Crossroads: Intersections between History and Anthropology in Cameroon* (pp. xvii-xxvii). Providence & Oxford: Berghahn.

France, A. (2000). Towards a sociological understanding of youth and their risk-taking. *Journal of Youth Studies, 3*(3), 317-331.

Fuh, D. (2009). *Competing for attention: youth masculinities and prestige in Bamenda, Cameroon.* (PhD Dissertation). University of Basel, Basel, Switzerland.

Fuh, D. (2012). The Prestige Economy: Veteran Clubs and Youngmen's Competition in Bamenda, Cameroon. *Urban Forum, 23*(4), 501-526.

Fuh, D. (2020). Precarity, Fixers, and New Imaginative Subjectivities of Youth in Urban Cameroon. In S. Swartz, A. Cooper, C. M. Batan, & L. K. Causa (Eds.), *The Oxford Handbook of Global South Youth Studies.* Oxford: Oxford University Press.

Furlong, A. (2000). Introduction: Youth in a changing world. *International Social Science Journal, 164,* 129-134.

Geertz, C. (2005). Deep Play: Notes on the Balinese Cockfight. *Daedalus, 134*(4).

Gennep, A. v. (1960). *The rites of passage ; translated by Monika B. Vizedom and Gabrielle L. Caffee.* Chicago: University of Chicago Press.

Geschiere, P. (1993). Chiefs and Colonial Rule in Cameroon: Inventing Chieftaincy, French and British Style. *Africa, 63*(2), 151-175.

Geschiere, P. (2009). *The Perils of Belonging: Autochthony, Citizenship, and Exclusion in Africa and Europe.* Chicago: University of Chicago Press.

Geschiere, P., & Gugler, J. (1998). The politics of Primary patriotism (Special Issue). *Africa, 68*(3).

Geschiere, P., & Meyer, B. (1998). Globalization and Identity: Dialectics of Flow and Closure. Introduction. *Development and Change, 29*(4), 601-615. doi:10.1111/1467-7660.00092

Geschiere, P., & Nyamnjoh, F. B. (2000). Capitalism and Autochthony: The Seesaw of Mobility and Belonging. *Public Culture, 12*(2), 423-452.

Goheen, M. (1996). *Men Own the Fields, Women Own the Crops: Gender and Power in the Cameroon Grassfields*. Madison, Wisconsin: The University of Wisconsin Press.

Gordon, A. A., & Gordon, D. L. (Eds.). (2013). *Understanding Contemporary Africa*. Boulder: Lynne Rienner Publishers.

Gupta, A., & Ferguson, J. (1992). Beyond "Culture": Space, Identity, and the Politics of Difference. *Cultural Anthropology, 7*(1), 6-23.

Haenfler, R. (2004). Manhood in Contradiction: The Two faces of Straight Edge. *Men and Masculinities, 7*(1), 77-99.

Hall, T., & Montgomery, H. (2000). Home and away: 'Childhood', 'youth' and young people. *Anthropology Today, 16*(3), 13-15.

Hansen, K. T. (2005). Getting Stuck in the Compound: Some Odds against Social Adulthood in Lusaka, Zambia. *Africa Today, 51*(4), 3-16.

Henn, M., & Weinstein, M. (2006). Young people and political (in)activism: why don't young people vote? *Policy & Politics, 34*(3), 517-534.

Hoffman, D. (2003). Like beasts in the bush: synonyms of childhood and youth in Sierra Leone. *Postcolonial Studies, 6*(3), 295-308.

Holland, D., & Leander, K. (2004). Ethnographic Studies of Positioning and Subjectivity: An Introduction. *Ethos, 32*(2), 127-139.

Holston, J. (2009). *Insurgent Citizenship: Disjunctions of Democracy and Modernity in Brazil*. Princeton & Oxford: Princeton University Press.

Holston, J., & Appadurai, A. (1999). Introduction: Cities and Citizenship. In J. Holston (Ed.), *Cities and Citizenship* (pp. 1-20). Durham & London: Duke University Press.

Honwana, A. (2013). Youth, Waithood, and Protest Movements in Africa. *African Arguments*. Retrieved from https://africanarguments.org/2013/08/12/youth-waithood-and-protest-movements-in-africa-by-alcinda-honwana/

Honwana, A., & de Boeck, F. (Eds.). (2005). *Makers and Breakers: Children and Youth in Postcolonial Africa*. London: James Currey.

Hooker, J. R. (1966). Welfare associations and other instruments of accommodation in the Rhodesias between the world wars. *Comparative Studies in Society and History, 9*(1), 51-63.

IMF. (2006). Factsheet - Debt Relief Under the Heavily Indebted Poor Countries (HIPC) Initiative. Retrieved from http://www.imf.org/external/x10/

changecss/changestyle.aspx

International Crisis Group. (2019). *Cameroon's Anglophone Crisis: How to Get to Talks?*

International Labour Organization. (2016). *Youth Employment Social Outlook: Trends for Youth 2016.* Geneva: International Labour Organization

Jerrems, A. (2020). The politics of neighbouring: assembly politics, urban citizenship and regimes of visibility in post-crisis Madrid. *Citizenship Studies, 24*(8), 1047-1065.

Jindra, M. (2005). Christianity and the Proliferation of Ancestors: Changes in Hierarchy and Mortuary Ritual in the Cameroon Grassfields. *Africa, 75*(3), 356 -377.

Jindra, M. (2011). The Rise of "Death Celebration" in the Cameroon Grassfields. In M. Jindra & J. Noret (Eds.), *Funerals in Africa: Explorations of a Social Phenomenon.* New York & Oxford: Berghahn.

Johnson-Hanks, J. (2002). On the Limits of Life Stages in Ethnography: Toward a Theory of Vital Conjunctures. *American Anthropologist, 104*(3), 865-880.

Johnson-Hanks, J. (2005). When the Future Decides: Uncertainty and Intentional Action in Contemporary Cameroon. *Current Anthropology, 46*(3), 363-385.

Johnson-Hanks, J. (2006). *Uncertain Honor: Modern Motherhood in an African Crisis.* Chicago: The University of Chicago Press.

Jones, G., & Wallace, C. (1992). *Youth, Family and Citizenship.* Buckingham: Open University Press.

Jua, N. (2003). Differential Responses to Disappearing Transitional Pathways: Redefining Possibility among Cameroonian Youths. *African Studies Review, 46*, 13-36.

Kabeer, N. (2005). Gender equality and women's empowerment: A critical analysis of the third millennium development goal 1. *Gender & Development, 13*(1), 13-24.

Kerr, G. B. (1978). Voluntary associations in West Africa: "hidden" agents of social change. In *Social sciences and African development planning* (pp. 87-100): Crossroads Press.

Konings, P., & Nyamnjoh, F. B. (1997). The Anglophone problem in Cameroon. *Journal of Modern African Studies, 35*(2), 207-229.

Konings, P., & Nyamnjoh, F. B. (2003). *Negotiating an Anglophone Identity: A Study of the Politics of Recognition and Representation in Cameroon.* Leiden & Boston: Brill.

Konings, P., & Nyamnjoh, F. B. (2004). President Paul Biya and the "Anglophone Problem" in Cameroon. In J. M. Mbaku & J. Takougang (Eds.), *The Leadership Challenge in Africa: Cameroon Under Biya.* Trenton, NJ: Africa World

Press.

Lentz, C. (1995). 'Unity for Development' Youth Associations in North-Western Ghana. *Africa, 65*(3), 395-429.

Little, K. L. (1965). *West African urbanization: a study of voluntary associations in social change.* Cambridge: Cambridge University Press.

Little, K. L. (1972). Voluntary Associations and Social Mobility among West African Women. *Canadian Journal of African Studies, 6*(2), 275-288.

Little, K. L., & Southall, A. W. (1973). Urbanization and Regional Associations: Their Paradoxical Function. In A. W. Southall (Ed.), *Urban Anthropology: cross-cultural studies of urbanization* (pp. 407-423). Oxford: Oxford University Press.

Ly, B. (1988). The Present Situation of Youth in Africa. In J. Kuczynski, S. N. Eisenstadt, B. Ly, & L. Sarkar (Eds.), *Perspectives on Contemporary Youth.* Tokyo: United Nations University.

Maira, S., & Soep, E. (2004). Introduction. In S. Maira & E. Soep (Eds.), *Youthscapes: The Popular, the national, the global.* Philadelphia: University of Pennsylvania Press.

Malaquais, D. (2001). *Anatomie d'une arnaque: feymen et feymania au Cameroun.* No. 77: CERI.

Marcus, G. E. (1995). Ethnography in/of the World System: The Emergence of Multi-Sited Ethnography. *Annual Review of Anthropology, 24,* 95-117.

Marks, M. (2001). *Young Warriors : Youth Politics, Identity and Violence in South Africa.* Johannesburg: Witwatersrand University Press.

Mattingly, C. (2012). Moral Selves and Moral Scenes: Narrative Experiments in Everyday Life. *Ethnos,* 1-27.

Mbaku, J. M. (2002). Cameroon's Stalled Transition to Democratic Governance: Lessons for Africa's New Democrats. *African and Asian Studies, 1*(3), 125-163.

Mbaku, J. M. (2004). Economic Dependence in Cameroon: SAPs and the Bretton Woods Institutions. In J. M. Mbaku & J. Takougang (Eds.), *The Leadership Challenge in Africa: Cameroon Under Biya.* Trenton, NJ: Africa World Press.

Mbaku, J. M., & Awasom, N. F. (2004). Teen Life in Africa: Cameroon. In T. Falola (Ed.), *Teen Life in Africa* (pp. 29-54). Westport, CT: Greenwood Press.

Mbaku, J. M., & Takougang, J. (Eds.). (2004). *The leadership challenge in Africa : Cameroon under Paul Biya.* Trenton, N.J.: Africa World Press.

Mbembe, A. (1992). Provisional Notes on the Postcolony. *Africa, 62*(1), 3-37.

Mbembe, A. (2001). *On the Postcolony.* Berkeley and Los Angeles: University of Carlifornia Press.

Mbu, A. N. T. (1993). *Civil Disobedience in Cameroon.* Douala: Imprimerie Georges

Freres.

Mbunwe-Samba, P., Mzeka, P. N., Niba, M. L., & Wirmum, C. (Eds.). (1993). *Rites of Passage and Incorporation in the Western Grassfields of Cameroon Vol. 1*. Bamenda: Kaberry Research Centre.

Mercer, C., Page, B., & Evans, M. (2008). *Development and the African Diaspora*. London: Zed Books.

Merriam, S. B., Johnson-Bailey, J., Lee, M.-Y., Kee, Y., Ntseane, G., & Muhamad, M. (2001). Power and positionality: negotiating insider/outsider status within and across cultures. *International Journal of Lifelong Education, 20*(5), 405-416.

Meyer, B., & Geschiere, P. (Eds.). (1999). *Globalization and Identity: Dialectics of Flow and Closure*. Oxford: Blackwell Publishers.

Mills, M. B. (2002). *Thai Women in the Global Labor Force: Consuming Desires, Contested Selves*. New Brunswick: Rutgers University Press.

Monga, C. (1994). *Anthropologie de la Colère: Société civile et démocratie en Afrique Noire*. Paris: L'Harmattan.

Moyer, E. (2004). Popular Cartographies: youthful imaginings of the global in the streets of Dar es Salaam, Tanzania. *City & Society, 16*(2), 117–143.

Mukong, A. (Ed.) (1990). *The Case for the Southern Cameroons*. Enugu: Chuka Printing Company Ltd.

Murphy, W. (2003). Military Patrimonialism and Child Soldier Clientelism in the Liberian and Sierra Leonean Civil Wars. *African Studies Review, 46*, 61-87.

Narayan, K. (1993). How native is a "native" anthropologist? *American Anthropologist, 95*(3), 671-686.

Ndangam, G. (2014). *Cultural Encounters: Society, Culture and Language in Bali Nyonga From the 19th Century*. Collierville, TN: Instantpublisher.com.

Ndjio, B. (2006). *Feymania: New Wealth, Magic Money and Power in Contemporary Cameroon*. (PhD Thesis). University of Amsterdam, Amsterdam.

Nkwi, P. N., & Warnier, J.-P. (1982). *Elements for a History of the Western Grassfields*. Yaounde: Department of Sociology, University of Yaounde.

Northcote, J. (2006). Nightclubbing and the Search for Identity: Making the Transition from Childhood to Adulthood in an Urban Milieu. *Journal of Youth Studies, 9*(1), 1-16.

Nussbaum, M. C. (2000). *Women and human development: The capabilities approach*: Cambridge University Press.

Nyamnjoh, F. B. (1999). Cameroon: a country united by ethnic ambition and difference. *African Affairs, 98*(390), 101-118.

Nyamnjoh, F. B. (2002a). Cameroon: Over Twelves Years of Comestic Democracy. *Nordic Africa Institute Bulletin, 3*(02).

Nyamnjoh, F. B. (2002b). "A Child is One Person's Only in the Womb": Domestication, Agency and Subjectivity in the Cameroonian Grassfields. In R. Werbner (Ed.), *Postcolonial Subjectivities in Africa*. London: Zed Books.

Nyamnjoh, F. B. (2006). *Insiders & Outsiders: Citizenship and Xenophobia in Contemporary Southern Africa*. London: Zed Books.

Nyamnjoh, F. B. (2011). Cameroonian bushfalling: Negotiation of identity and belonging in fiction and ethnography. *American Ethnologist, 38*(4), 701–713.

Nyamnjoh, F. B. (2017). *Drinking from the Cosmic Gourd: How Amos Tutuola can Change Our Minds*. Mankon, Bamenda: Langaa Research & Publishing CIG

Nyamnjoh, F. B., & Page, B. (2002). Whiteman Kontri and the enduring allure of modernity among Cameroonian youth. *African Affairs, 101*(405), 607-634.

Nyamnjoh, H. (2021). Ambitions of Bushfalling through Further Education: Insights from Students in Cameroonian Universities. *Social Inclusion, 9*(1), 196-206.

O'neil, R. (1996). Imperialisms at the Century's End: Moghamo Relationships with Bali-Nyonga and Germany 1889-1908. In I. Fowler & D. Zeitlyn (Eds.), *African Crossroads: Intersections between History and Anthropology in Cameroon* (pp. 81-100). Providence and Oxford: Berghahn Books.

Ogden, J. A. (1996). 'Producing' Respect: The 'Proper Woman' in Postcolonial Kampala. In R. Werbner, T. Ranger, & P. Werbner (Eds.), *Postcolonial Identities in Africa* (pp. 165-191). London: Zed Books.

Orock, R. T. E. (2013). Manyu youths, belonging and the antinomies of patrimonial elite politics in contemporary Cameroon. *Cultural Dynamics, 25*(3), 269-290.

Orock, R. T. E. (2015). Elites, Culture, and Power: The Moral Politics of "Development" in Cameroon. *Anthropological Quarterly, 88*(2), 533-568.

Ottenberg, S. (1955). Improvement Associations Among the Afikpo Ibo. *Africa, 25*(1), 1-28.

Paret, M., & Gleeson, S. (2016). Precarity and agency through a migration lens. *Citizenship Studies, 20*(3-4), 277-294.

Pelican, M. (2011). Mbororo on the move: from pastoral mobility to international travel. *Journal of Contemporary African Studies, 29*(4), 427-440.

Pelican, M. (2012). International Migration: Virtue or Vice? Perspectives from Cameroon. *Journal of Ethnic and Migration Studies*, 1-21.

Pommerolle, M.-E., & Ngaméni, N. M. (2015). Fabrics of Loyalty: The Politics of International Women's Day Wax Print Cloth in Cameroon. *Africa, 85*(4), 656-676.

Postman, N. (1994). *The Disappearance of Childhood*. New York: Vintage Books.

Prokhovnik, R. (1998). Public and Private Citizenship: From Gender Invisibility to Feminist Inclusiveness. *Feminist Review, 60*, 84-104.

Regh, W. (2007). Solidarity and the Common Good: An Analytic Framework. *Journal of Social Philosophy, 38*(1), 7-21.

Roberts, K. (2007). Youth Transitions and Generations: A Response to Wyn and Woodman. *Journal of Youth Studies, 10*(2), 263-269.

Roitman, J. (2014). *Anti-crisis*. Durham: Duke University Press.

Röschenthaler, U. (2015). Introduction: United in Dress: Negotiating Gender and Hierarchy with Festival Uniforms. *Africa, 85*(4), 628-634.

Rowlands, M. (1994). The Material Culture of Success: Ideals and Life Cycles in Cameroon. In J. Friedman (Ed.), *Consumption and Identity* (pp. 116-135). London: Harwood Press.

Rowlands, M. (1996). The Consumption of an African Modernity. In M. J. Arnoldi, C. M. Geary, & K. L. Hardin (Eds.), *African Material Culture* (pp. 188-213). Bloomington & Indianapolis: Indiana University Press.

Sade-Beck, L. (2004). Internet Ethnography: Online and Offline. *International journal of Qualitative Methods, 3*(2), 45-51.

Samara, T. R. (2005). Youth, Crime and Urban Renewal in the Western Cape. *Journal of Southern African Studies, 31*(1), 209-227.

Schapera, I. (1970). *Tribal Innovators: Tswana Chiefs and Social Change 1795-1940*. London: Athlone Press.

Schmidt-Soltau, K. (1999). *Living on the edge of a volcano - The eruption of democracy and its enemies*. Douala, Cameroon: Telcam Press.

Seidler, V. J. (2006). *Young Men and Masculinities: Global Cultures and Intimate Lives*. London & New York: Zed Books.

Sen, A. (1999). *Development as Freedom*. New York: Anchor Books.

Sharp, L., A. (2002). *The Sacrificed Generation : Youth, History, and the Colonized Mind in Madagascar*. Berkeley, CA: University of Carlifornia Press.

Simone, A. (2001). Straddling the Divides: Remaking Associational Life in the Informal African City. *International Journal of Urban and Regional Research, 25*(1), 102-117.

Simone, A. (2014). Too Many Things to Do: Social Dimensions of City-Making in Africa. In M. Diouf & R. Fredericks (Eds.), *The Arts of Citizenship in African Cities: Infrastuctures and Spaces of Belonging* (pp. 25-47). New York: Palgrave Macmillan.

Skinner, E. P. (1978). Voluntary associations and ethnic competition in Ouagadougou. In *Ethnicity in modern Africa* (pp. 191-211): Boulder, Colorado: Westview Press, c1978.

Smith, D. J. (2010). Promiscuous Girls, Good Wives, and Cheating Husbands: Gender Inequality, Transitions to Marriage, and Infidelity in Southeastern Nigeria. *Anthropological Quarterly, 83*(1), 123-152.

Soares, C. (2000). Aspects of Youth, transitions, and the end of certainties. *International Social Science Journal, 164*, 209-217.

Soen, D., & Comarmond, P. d. (1971a). Modern co-operation and the male mutual help associations in the land of Bassa, south Cameroon. *Zeitschrift fur Ethnologie, 96*(2), 145-154.

Soen, D., & Comarmond, P. d. (1971b). Savings associations among the Bamileke: traditional and modern co-operation in south West-Cameroon. *Journal de la Societe des Africanistes, 41*(2), 189-201.

Soen, D., & Comarmond, P. d. (1972). Savings associations among the Bamileke: traditional and modern cooperation in southwest Cameroon. *American Anthropologist, 74*(5), 1170-1179.

Soh, P. B. (1983). *Abakpa-Mankon-Bamenda: Creation and evolution of an urban centre in a traditional milieu* (Vol. No 31). Yaounde: Institute of Human Sciences.

Takougang, J. (2003). Nationalism, Democratisation, and Political Opportunism in Cameroon. *Journal of Contemporary African Studies, 21*, 427-445.

Tazanu, M. P. (2012). *Being Available and Reachable: New Media and Cameroonian Transnational Sociality*. Mankon, Bamenda: Langaa Research and Publishing CIG.

Timera, M. (2001). Les migrations des jeunes Sahéliens: affirmation de soi et émancipation. *Autrepart, 18*, 37-49.

Tostensen, A., Tvedten, I., & Vaa, M. (Eds.). (2001). *Associational Life in African Cities: Popular Responses to the Urban Crises*. Uppsala: The Nordic Africa Institute.

Trager, L. (1998). Home-town Linkages and Local Development in South-Western Nigeria. Whose Agenda? Whose Impact? *Africa, 68*(3), 360-382.

Turner, B. (1993). Contemporary Problems in the Theory of Citizenship. In B. Turner (Ed.), *Citizenship and Social Theory* (pp. 1-18). London: Sage Publications.

Turner, V. W. (1969). *The ritual process : structure and anti-structure*. Ithaca, NY: Cornell University Press.

Turner, V. W. (Ed.) (1967a). *Betwixt and Between: The Liminal Period in Rites de Passage*. Ithaca & London: Cornell University Press.

United Nations. (2005). *World Youth Report 2005: Young people today, and in 2015*. New York: United Nations Publication

United Nations. (2007). *Young People's Transition to Adulthood: Progress and Challenges*. New York: United Nations Publication

United Nations. (2015). Youth Empowerment.

Vale, P. (2002). Migration, xenophobia and security-making in post-apartheid south africa. *Politikon, 29*(1), 7-30.

Vigh, H. E. (2006). Social Death and Violent Life Chances. In C. Christiansen, M. Utas, & H. E. Vigh (Eds.), *Navigating Youth Generating Adulthood: Social Becoming in an African Context*. Uppsala: Nordic Africa Institute.

Wallace, C., & Helve, H. (Eds.). (2001). *Youth, Citizenship and Empowerment*. Burlington, VT: Ashgate Publishing Company.

Waller, R. (2006). Rebellious Youth in Colonial Africa. *Journal of African History, 47*, 77-92.

Wallerstein, I. (1964). Voluntary associations. In J. Coleman & C. G. Rosberg (Eds.), *Political Parties and National Integration in Tropical Africa* (pp. 318—339). Berkeley, California: University of California Press.

Warnier, J.-P. (1993). *L'esprit de l'entreprise au Cameroun*. Paris: Karthala.

Warnier, J.-P. (1996). Rebellion, Defection and the Position of Male Cadets: A Neglected Category. In I. Fowler & D. Zeitlyn (Eds.), *African Crossroads: Intersections between History and Ethnography in Cameroon* (pp. 115-124). Providence & Oxford: Berghahn Books.

Warnier, J.-P. (2012). *Cameroon Grassfields Civilization*. Bamenda: Langaa Research and Publishing CIG.

Werbner, P. (1998). Exoticising Citizenship: Anthropology and the new Citizenship Debate. *Canberra Anthropology, 21*, 1-27.

Werbner, P. (1999). Political motherhood and the feminisation of citizenship: Women's activisms and the transformation of the public sphere. In N. Yuval-Davis & P. Werbner (Eds.), *Women, Citizenship and Difference*. London: Zed Books.

Werbner, R. (2002). Introduction: The Personal, the Political and the Moral. In R. Werbner (Ed.), *Postcolonial Subjectivities in Africa*. London: Zed Books.

Westberg, A. (2004). Forever Young? Young People's Conception of Adulthood: The Swedish Case. *Journal of Youth Studies, 7*(1), 35-53.

Williamson, H. (1997). Youth work and citizenship. In J. Bynner, L. Chisholm, & A. Furlong (Eds.), *Youth, Citizenship and Social Change in a European Context* (pp. 196-213). Aldershot: Ashgate.

Willis, R., McAulay, J., Ndeunyema, N., & Angove, J. (2019). *Human Rights Abuses in the Cameroon Anglophone Crisis: A Submission of Evidence to UK Parliament*. Retrieved from Oxford:

Wilson, S. M., & Leighton, C. P. (2002). The Anthropology of Online Communities. *Annual Review of Anthropology, 31*, 449-467.

World Bank. (2012). *Cameroon Economic Update* (Issue No. 3 ed.). Yaounde: World Bank.

Wyn, J., & Woodman, D. (2006). Generation, Youth and Social Change in Australia.

Journal of Youth Studies, 9(5), 495 - 514.

Yuval-Davis, N. (1997). Women, Citizenship and Difference. *Feminist Review, 57*, 4-27.

Zintgraff, E. (1895). *Nord-Kamerun*. Berlin: Paetel.

Index

www.ingramcontent.com/pod-product-compliance
Lightning Source LLC
Chambersburg PA
CBHW021541260326
41914CB00001B/114